Teach Yourself VISUALLY™

Samsung® Galaxy S®6

by Guy Hart-Davis

Visual

A Wiley Brand

Teach Yourself VISUALLY™ Samsung® Galaxy S®6

Published by
John Wiley & Sons, Inc.
10475 Crosspoint Boulevard
Indianapolis, IN 46256

www.wiley.com

Published simultaneously in Canada

Wiley publishes in a variety of print and electronic formats and by print-on-demand. Some material included with standard print versions of this book may not be included in e-books or in print-on-demand. If this book refers to media such as a CD or DVD that is not included in the version you purchased, you may download this material at http://booksupport.wiley.com. For more information about Wiley products, visit www.wiley.com.

Library of Congress Control Number: 2015945793

ISBN: 978-1-119-11349-2

Manufactured in the United States of America

10 9 8 7 6 5 4 3 2 1

Trademark Acknowledgments

Contact Us

For general information on our other products and services please contact our Customer Care Department within the U.S. at 877-762-2974, outside the U.S. at 317-572-3993 or fax 317-572-4002.

For technical support please visit www.wiley.com/techsupport.

Sales | Contact Wiley at (877) 762-2974 or fax (317) 572-4002.

Credits

Acquisitions Editor
Aaron Black

Project Editor
Lynn Northrup

Technical Editor
Andrew Moore

Copy Editor
Lynn Northrup

Production Editor
Barath Kumar Rajasekaran

Manager, Content Development & Assembly
Mary Beth Wakefield

Vice President, Professional Technology Strategy
Barry Pruett

About the Author

Guy Hart-Davis is the author of various computer books, including *Teach Yourself VISUALLY Android Phones and Tablets, 2nd Edition; Teach Yourself VISUALLY Apple Watch; Teach Yourself VISUALLY iPhone; Teach Yourself VISUALLY iPad; Teach Yourself VISUALLY MacBook Pro, 2nd Edition; Teach Yourself VISUALLY MacBook Air; Teach Yourself VISUALLY iMac, 3rd Edition;* and *iWork Portable Genius*.

Author's Acknowledgments

My thanks go to the many people who turned my manuscript into the highly graphical book you are holding. In particular, I thank Aaron Black for asking me to write the book; Lynn Northrup for keeping me on track and skillfully editing the text; Andrew Moore for reviewing the book for technical accuracy and contributing helpful suggestions; and SPi Global for laying out the book.

How to Use This Book

Who This Book Is For

This book is for the reader who has never used this particular technology or software application. It is also for readers who want to expand their knowledge.

The Conventions in This Book

① Steps

This book uses a step-by-step format to guide you easily through each task. **Numbered steps** are actions you must do; **bulleted steps** clarify a point, step, or optional feature; and **indented steps** give you the result.

② Notes

Notes give additional information — special conditions that may occur during an operation, a situation that you want to avoid, or a cross reference to a related area of the book.

③ Icons and Buttons

Icons and buttons show you exactly what you need to click to perform a step.

④ Tips

Tips offer additional information, including warnings and shortcuts.

⑤ Bold

Bold type shows command names, options, and text or numbers you must type.

⑥ Italics

Italic type introduces and defines a new term.

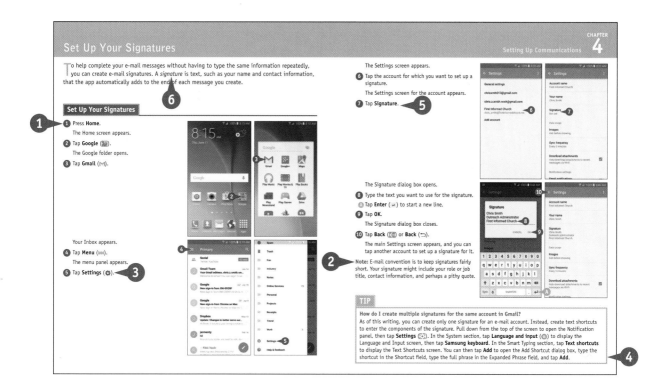

Table of Contents

Chapter 1 Getting Started with Your Galaxy S6

Meet the Galaxy S6's Hardware and Controls.................. 4

Perform the Initial Setup Routine............................ 6

Connect to a Wireless Network 14

Explore the User Interface and Launch Apps 16

Using Multi Window 18

Navigate with Gestures 22

Using the Notification Panel.................................. 24

Download and Install Samsung Smart Switch 26

Copy Files from Your Computer............................... 28

Using the Galaxy S6 Edge...................................... 30

Chapter 2 Customizing Your Galaxy S6

Find the Settings That You Need 34

Customize the Quick Settings................................. 36

Choose Which Notifications to Receive..................... 38

Configure Do Not Disturb 42

Choose Volume and Sound Settings 44

Set Screen Brightness and Wallpaper....................... 46

Choose Location Access Settings 48

Secure Your Galaxy S6 with Smart Lock.................... 50

Encrypt Your Galaxy S6 54

Choose Language and Input Settings 56

Customize the Home Screens 58

Customize the Lock Screen 62

Set Up Sleep and Daydream 64

Chapter 3　Working with Text and Voice

Using the On-Screen Keyboard and
Continuous Input 68

Work with Different Keyboards 72

Edit Text and Use Cut, Copy, and Paste 74

Using Voice Input and Voice Recorder 76

Using S Voice 78

Set Up Accessibility Features 80

Using Galaxy TalkBack 84

Chapter 4　Setting Up Communications

Set Up Your E-Mail Accounts in the Gmail App 88

Choose Settings in Gmail 94

Remove an E-Mail Account 98

Set Up Your Signatures 100

Set Up and Use Priority Inbox 102

Choose Which Contacts to Display 104

Import Your Contacts into the Contacts App 106

Choose S Planner Notifications and Reminders 108

Choose Week and Time Zone Settings 110

Table of Contents

| Chapter 5 | Networking and Communicating |

Control Wi-Fi, Bluetooth, and Cellular Access 114
Connect Bluetooth Devices......................................116
Control Data Roaming and Cellular Usage 118
Connect to a Wi-Fi Direct Device 120
Using USB Tethering 122
Using Mobile Hotspot..124
Manage Your Wireless Networks..............................128
Log In to Wi-Fi Hotspots.......................................130
Transfer Data Using Android Beam..........................132
Make Payments with Tap and Pay 134

| Chapter 6 | Phoning, Messaging, and Social Networking |

Make Phone Calls 138
Make a Conference Call 140
Call Using Call Logs and Frequently Contacted 142
Send and Receive Instant Messages 144
Manage Your Instant Messages 146
Set Up Google+ 148
Navigate Google+ 150
Using Facebook and Twitter...................................152

Chapter 7   Working with Apps

Switch Quickly from One App to Another 156

Pin a Window to the Screen 158

Find and Download Apps from Google Play 160

Update Your Apps 162

Remove an App 164

Choose Which Apps to Update Automatically 166

Install an App Manually 168

Understanding the Galaxy Apps 170

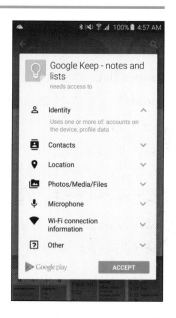

Chapter 8   Browsing the Web and E-Mailing

Browse the Web 174

Create Bookmarks for Web Pages 176

Using Bookmarks, Saved Pages, and History 178

Search for Information 180

Fill in Forms Using Auto Fill 182

Tighten Up Your Browsing Privacy Settings 184

Read Your E-Mail Messages with Gmail 186

Reply to or Forward a Message with Gmail 188

Write and Send E-Mail Messages with Gmail 190

Send and Receive Files with Gmail 192

Label and Archive Your Messages with Gmail 194

Browse by Label and Search with Gmail 196

Table of Contents

Chapter 9   Taking and Using Photos and Videos

Take Photos with the Camera App.............................200

Using Zoom, Manual Focus, and
    Tracking Auto-Focus 202

Using Selective Focus 204

Using the Flash and HDR Mode 206

Using Pro Mode 208

Take Panoramic Photos 210

Choose Settings for Taking Photos..........................212

Edit Your Photos..214

Capture Video..218

View Your Photos and Videos..................................220

Share Your Photos and Videos................................222

Chapter 10   Navigating, Working, and Productivity

Find Your Location and Display Different Layers.........226

Get Directions 228

Rotate, Zoom, and Tilt the Map..............................230

Make a Map Available Offline 232

Explore with Street View 234

Explore the Clock App...236

Explore Other Included Apps..................................238

Set Up Private Mode 240

Using Private Mode 242

Connect to a Work Network via VPN 246

Connect to Exchange Server...................................248

Install Credentials..252

Chapter 11   Playing Music and Videos

Play Music with the Music App.................................256

Adjust the Sound with the SoundAlive Equalizer........258

Create a Playlist...260

Customize the Audio Settings for Your Headset.........262

Play Music Through Other Devices 264

Watch Videos 266

Using the Pop-Up Video Player...............................268

Chapter 12   Troubleshooting Your Galaxy S6

Close an App That Has Stopped Responding 272

Update Your Galaxy S6's Software 274

Extend the Runtime on the Battery..........................276

Using Ultra Power Saving Mode..............................278

Reset Your App Preferences 280

Check Free Space and Clear Extra Space...................282

Back Up and Restore Online...................................284

Back Up Your Data with Smart Switch 286

Restore Your Data with Smart Switch 288

Reset Your Galaxy S6 to Factory Settings 290

Troubleshoot Wireless Network Connections.............292

Locate or Wipe Your Missing Galaxy S6....................294

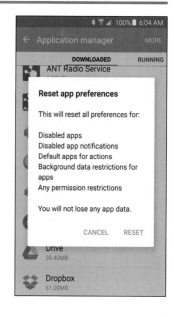

Index.. 296

CHAPTER 1

Getting Started with Your Galaxy S6

In this chapter, you will set up your Galaxy S6, meet its hardware controls, and learn to navigate the TouchWiz interface. You will also learn to transfer files to your Galaxy S6 from your PC or Mac.

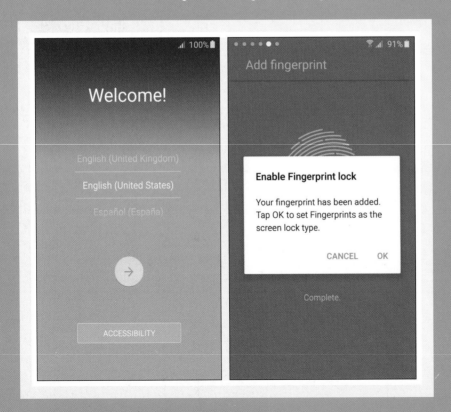

Meet the Galaxy S6's Hardware and Controls 4

Perform the Initial Setup Routine 6

Connect to a Wireless Network 14

Explore the User Interface and Launch Apps 16

Using Multi Window 18

Navigate with Gestures 22

Using the Notification Panel 24

Download and Install Samsung Smart Switch 26

Copy Files from Your Computer 28

Using the Galaxy S6 Edge 30

Meet the Galaxy S6's Hardware and Controls

After getting your Galaxy S6 and unboxing it, you should plug it in to charge if the battery level is low. If your carrier has not installed a SIM card, you should install one. You can then start the Galaxy S6 and meet its hardware and controls. The Galaxy S6 has three physical buttons: Power, Volume, and Home. The phone also has two soft buttons, the Recents button (⬒) to the left of the Home button, and the Back button (⤺) to the right.

Meet the Galaxy S6's Hardware and Controls

A If necessary, insert a SIM card. Insert the SIM-removal tool into the hole and push to open the SIM tray. Insert a nano-SIM card and replace the SIM tray.

1 Press and hold the Power button for a couple of seconds.

The Galaxy S6 vibrates to indicate that it is starting.

At the top of the screen are the following:

B The earpiece for making phone calls.

C The front camera.

D The proximity/gesture sensor.

E The light sensor.

F The notification light.

G As the Galaxy S6 starts, its name and model number appear on-screen, followed by the Samsung logo.

H The Home button, which incorporates the fingerprint sensor, is at the bottom of the screen.

On the left side of the Galaxy S6 are the volume buttons.

I You press the upper button to increase the volume.

J You press the lower button to decrease the volume.

On the back of the Galaxy S6 are the following:

K The main camera lens.

L The flash for the main camera, and the fingerprint sensor, built into a single unit.

At the top of the Galaxy S6 are the following:

M The microphone for the speakerphone.

N The infrared LED.

When the Galaxy S6 finishes startup, you can perform the initial setup routine, as explained in the next section, "Perform the Initial Setup Routine."

TIP

What is on the bottom of my Galaxy S6?
On the bottom of your Galaxy S6 are the multipurpose jack, the headphone port, and another microphone. You use the multipurpose jack to connect your Galaxy S6 to your computer or other devices, such as an HDTV you are using to display photos. You use the headphone port to connect headphones or speakers. The microphone at the bottom of the Galaxy S6 is the one that picks up your voice when you are making a phone call and holding the phone to your face.

Perform the Initial Setup Routine

The first time you turn on your Galaxy S6, it displays the Welcome screen, on which you choose which language to use. You then perform the initial setup routine, a one-time procedure in which you select essential settings and connect the phone to a wireless network.

During setup, you can use the Tap & Go feature to transfer settings and data from another Android device to your Galaxy S6.

Perform the Initial Setup Routine

1 Turn on your Galaxy S6 by pressing and holding the Power button on the right side for a couple of seconds.

The Welcome screen appears.

2 Tap the language you want to use.

Ⓐ You can tap **Accessibility** if you need to use accessibility features during setup.

3 Tap **Start** (⊙).

Note: If the Smart Network Switch dialog box opens, tap **Cancel** to close it. See the first tip for more information.

The Wi-Fi screen appears.

4 Tap the Wi-Fi network to which you want to connect.

The dialog box for connecting to the network opens.

5 Type the password for the network.

Ⓑ You can tap **Show password** (☐ changes to ✓) to display the password.

6 Tap **Connect**.

Your Galaxy S6 connects to the network.

Ⓒ The *Connected to Wi-Fi network* readout appears briefly.

7 Tap **Next**.

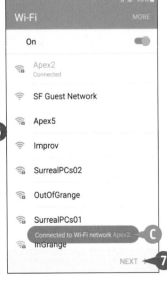

The Terms and Conditions screen appears.

8 Under Diagnostic Data, tap **Consent to Provide Diagnostic and Usage Data** (☑ changes to ☐) if you do not want your Galaxy S6 to provide diagnostic data and usage data to Samsung.

9 Tap **Next**.

The Terms and Conditions dialog box opens.

10 Tap **Agree** if you want to proceed.

Your Galaxy S6 checks for software updates.

The Tap & Go screen then appears.

You can now set up your device using Tap & Go, as explained in the next subsection, or manually, as explained in the subsection "Set Up Your Galaxy S6 Manually."

Set Up Your Galaxy S6 Using Tap & Go

1 With the Tap & Go screen displayed on your Galaxy S6, turn on and unlock your other Android device.

2 Bring the two devices back to back.

A tone plays when the Near Field Communication chips — NFC chips for short — connect.

Note: You may need to move the devices around to line up the NFC chips.

D Your Galaxy S6 displays the *Check your other device* message once the devices have established the NFC connection.

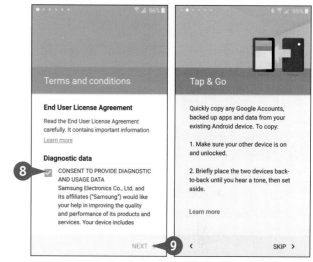

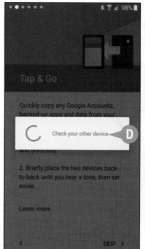

The Tap & Go dialog box appears on your other device.

3 Tap **Lock & Verify**.

TIPS

What is Smart Network Switch?
Smart Network Switch is a feature that enables your Galaxy S6 to switch automatically from a Wi-Fi network to the cellular network to maintain its Internet connection. Turning Smart Network Switch on may cause your Galaxy S6 to use the cellular connection when you want to use Wi-Fi, so it is best to leave Smart Network Switch off during initial setup.

Should I create a Google account if I do not have one?
If you do not already have a Google account, you should create one at this point. Having a Google account enables you to get the most out of your Galaxy S6.

continued ▶

During the initial setup routine, you can choose whether to back up the data from your Galaxy S6 to your Google account. You can also decide whether to allow apps to determine your location and send anonymous location data to Google's servers, and whether to allow Google's location service to scan for Wi-Fi networks even when Wi-Fi is turned off. Google uses the data provided to improve location accuracy.

Perform the Initial Setup Routine (continued)

Your other device locks, and the Restore Accounts screen appears, prompting you for your unlock method to verify your identity.

④ Provide the unlock method. For example, type your PIN and tap **Next**.

Another Tap & Go dialog box appears, prompting you to copy accounts and data to the Galaxy S6.

⑤ Tap **OK**.

Ⓔ The Tap & Go screen displays its progress as it adds your accounts to the Galaxy S6.

The Google Services screen appears. Go to the subsection "Finish the Setup Routine."

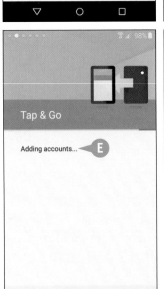

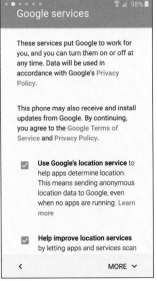

Set Up Your Galaxy S6 Manually

1 On the Tap & Go screen, tap **Skip**.

The Add Your Account screen appears.

2 Tap **Enter your email** and type your e-mail address.

Note: You can tap **Or create a new account** to create a new account.

3 Tap **Next**.

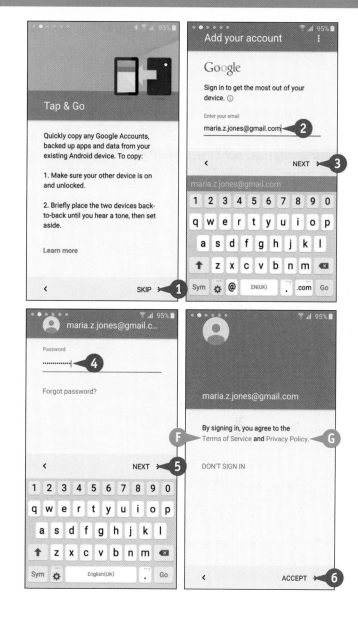

The Password screen appears.

4 Type your password.

5 Tap **Next**.

The Terms of Service and Privacy Policy screen appears.

F You can tap **Terms of Service** to view the Terms of Service.

G You can tap **Privacy Policy** to view the Privacy Policy.

6 Tap **Accept**.

The Google Services screen appears, and you can proceed as explained in the next subsection.

TIP

Should I back up my Galaxy S6 to my Google account?

Backing up your Galaxy S6 to your Google account is a good idea unless you prefer not to store sensitive data online, no matter how securely. Backing up to your Google account enables you to restore your data if your Galaxy S6 suffers a failure.

continued ▶

During the initial setup routine, you can set your Galaxy S6 to use a Samsung account. This is a free account that enables you to store data on Samsung's servers, share it among your devices, and restore it if your device suffers a failure. If you do not have a Samsung account yet, you can create one during setup.

You can set a wake-up command that you speak to wake your Galaxy S6 with your voice. You can then give commands with your voice.

Perform the Initial Setup Routine (continued)

Finish the Setup Routine

1 On the Google Services screen, tap **Back up your phone's apps, app data, settings, and Wi-Fi password** (☑ changes to ☐) if you do not want to back up these items.

2 Tap **Use Google's location service** (☑ changes to ☐) if you want to turn off location services.

3 Tap **More**.

The lower part of the Google Services screen appears.

4 Tap **Help improve location services** (☑ changes to ☐) if you do not want to send anonymous data to Google.

5 Tap **Help improve your Android experience** (☑ changes to ☐) if you do not want to send diagnostic and usage data to Google.

6 Tap **Next**.

The Samsung Account screen appears.

Ⓗ You can tap **Sign Up with Google ID** or **Create Account** to create a new Samsung account.

Ⓘ You can tap **Sign In** to sign in to your existing Samsung account.

7 Tap **Skip**.

The first Set Wake-Up Command screen appears.

8 Tap **Set**.

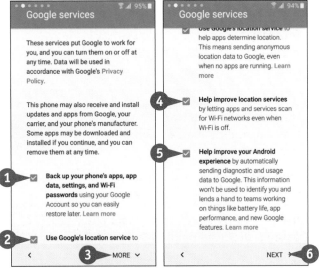

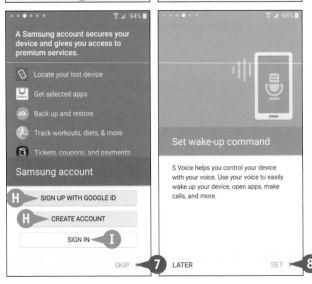

The second Set Wake-Up Command screen appears.

Note: Samsung states that your wake-up command should be three to five syllables long, but gives the two-syllable example "Hi there." Choose a distinctive command that you will not say in normal conversation.

9 Tap **Start**.

The third Set Wake-Up Command screen appears.

10 Following the on-screen prompts, say your wake-up command four times.

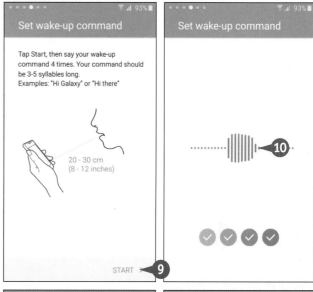

The fourth Set Wake-Up Command screen appears, showing example voice commands.

J You can tap **Expand** (⌄) to see more examples.

K You can tap **Try Again** to re-record your wake-up command.

11 Tap **Done**.

The Add Fingerprint screen appears.

L You can tap **Later** to skip adding your fingerprint.

12 Tap **Add**.

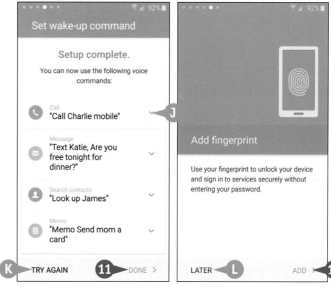

TIP

Should I create a Samsung account?

If you want to get the most out of your Galaxy S6, you will need to have a Samsung account. Several compelling features — such as locating your Galaxy S6 if it goes missing, backing up and restoring data, and tracking your activities and your diet in the S Health app — require a Samsung account.

A Samsung account is free and takes only seconds to set up. The only disadvantage is that you are entrusting Samsung with your data.

continued ▶

Your Galaxy S6 includes a fingerprint-recognition feature that helps you to keep your valuable data and personal items secure against intruders. After registering your fingerprint, you can unlock your Galaxy S6 quickly and easily by placing your finger on the Home button. You must also set a password in case fingerprint recognition fails.

You set up fingerprint recognition by scanning your finger or thumb in various positions. Register multiple fingers in case you abrade the skin on your fingertip or injure your finger.

Perform the Initial Setup Routine (continued)

The Disclaimer dialog box opens, warning you that your fingerprint will be registered and stored with your device.

13 Tap **Confirm**.

The Disclaimer dialog box closes.

14 Tap **Continue.**

The Add Fingerprint screen for registering your fingerprint appears.

15 Place your finger or thumb on the Home button repeatedly, following the prompts.

M The indicator shows your progress.

The Complete screen appears briefly.

The Add Fingerprint screen prompts you to enter a backup password.

16 Type the backup password you will use.

Note: For security, use at least 8 characters in your password; 12 characters or more is better. Do not use a word in any language; you could use random characters, or create a memorable password by using the first letters of a memorable phrase or sentence, such as a line from a song. Include uppercase, lowercase, numbers, and symbols.

17 Tap **Continue**.

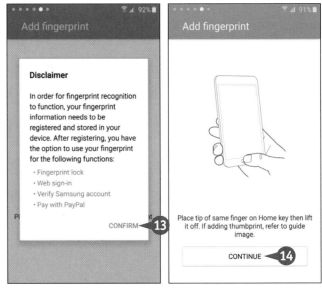

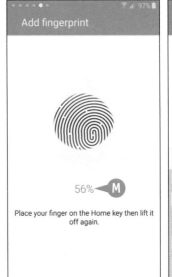

The Add Fingerprint screen prompts you to confirm your backup password.

18 Type the password again.

19 Tap **OK**.

The Enable Fingerprint Lock dialog box opens.

20 Tap **OK** if you want to use Fingerprints as the method of unlocking your Galaxy S6. This is usually the most convenient.

The Setup Complete screen appears.

N You can set the **Easy mode** switch to On (⬤ changes to ⬤) if you want to use Easy Mode. See the second tip for more information.

21 Tap **Finish**.

The Home screen appears, and you can start using your Galaxy S6.

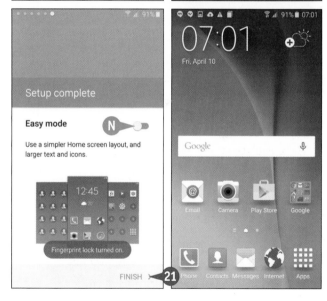

TIPS

How can I add other fingerprints?
Press **Home**, tap **Apps** (⧉), and then tap **Settings** (⚙). In the Personal section, tap **Lock screen and security** (🔒), and then tap **Fingerprints** in the Security section on the Lock Screen and Security screen. On the Fingerprints screen, tap **Add Fingerprint** to start adding another fingerprint.

What is Easy Mode?
Easy Mode simplifies the Home screen by displaying fewer icons and showing them at a larger size. Easy Mode has three Home screen panels: The first panel provides quick access to selected contacts, and the other two panels give you access to apps.

Connect to a Wireless Network

To get the most use out of your Galaxy S6, you likely will need to connect it to several wireless networks in different locations. Many wireless networks broadcast the network name, and often you need to provide only the password to make a connection. To connect to a wireless network that does not broadcast its name, you need to type the name to identify the network and then provide the password. For some networks, you may need to specify an IP address or proxy server details.

Connect to a Wireless Network

Display the Wi-Fi Screen

1 Pull down from the top of the screen.

The Notification panel opens.

2 Tap and hold **Wi-Fi** (📶).

The Wi-Fi screen appears.

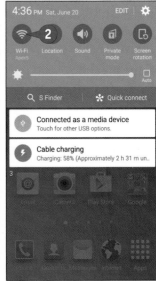

Connect to a Wireless Network That Broadcasts Its Name

A If the **Wi-Fi** switch is set to Off (⬤), set it to On (⬤).

1 Tap the network to which you want to connect.

A dialog box opens for connecting to the network.

2 Type the password.

B You can tap **Show password** (☐ changes to ☑) to display the characters.

3 Tap **Connect**.

Your Galaxy S6 connects to the wireless network.

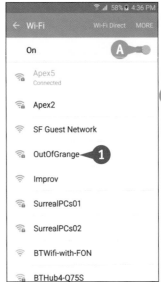

Connect to a Wireless Network That Does Not Broadcast Its Name

1 On the Wi-Fi screen, tap **More**.

The menu opens.

2 Tap **Add network**.

The Add Network dialog box opens.

3 Type the network name.

4 Tap **Security** and then tap the security type, such as **WPA/WPA2/FT PSK**.

5 Tap **Password** and type the password.

6 Tap **Connect**.

Your Galaxy S6 connects to the network.

Connect to a Network and Specify Settings

1 Tap the network.

The network's dialog box opens.

2 Type the password.

3 Tap **Show advanced options** (☐ changes to ☑).

4 To set IP address information, tap **IP settings**, tap **Static**, and then choose the settings.

Note: To set proxy server information, tap **Proxy**, tap **Manual**, and then choose the settings.

5 Tap **Connect**.

Your Galaxy S6 connects to the network.

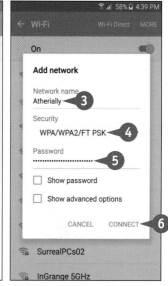

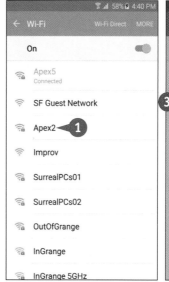

TIPS

How do I stop using a particular wireless network?

On the Wi-Fi screen, tap the network's name. In the dialog box that opens, tap **Forget network**.

Is there an easier way to set up a wireless network?

Yes, if the wireless network has Wi-Fi Protected Setup (WPS) and you have physical access to the wireless router. If so, display the Wi-Fi screen, tap **More**, and then tap **WPS push button**. On your router, press the WPS button to set up the network connection automatically.

Explore the User Interface and Launch Apps

When you press Power or Home to wake your Galaxy S6 from sleep, Android displays the lock screen. You then unlock your phone to reach the Home screen, which contains a Favorites tray of icons for running frequently used apps, shortcuts to apps, and the Apps icon for accessing the full list of apps installed.

You can add other icons to the Home screen as needed. When you launch an app, its screen appears. From the app, you can return to the Home screen by pressing Home. You can then launch another app.

Explore the User Interface and Launch Apps

1 Press **Home**.

The phone's screen lights up and displays the lock screen.

Note: You can use various means of unlocking the lock screen. The default is the swipe explained here.

2 Swipe up.

The Home screen appears.

Note: If your Galaxy S6 displays an app instead of the Home screen, press **Home**.

3 Tap **Apps** (⊞).

The Apps screen appears.

4 Tap the app you want to use, such as **Calculator** (⊞).

The app opens.

5 Use the app as needed. For example, tap the buttons to perform a calculation.

A In the Calculator app, the result appears here.

6 Press **Home**.

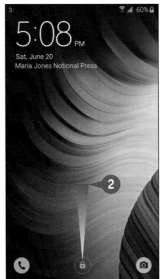

The Home screen appears.

7 Tap **Apps** (▦).

The Apps screen appears.

8 If the screen is full of apps, swipe your finger from right to left across the screen.

Note: If the Apps screen is not full, most likely there is no second screen of apps to display.

The next screen of apps appears.

9 Tap the app you want to launch.

The app opens, and you can start working in it.

TIP

Is there just one Home screen, or are there several Home screens?
The TouchWiz user interface on your Galaxy S6 provides two Home panels by default, plus the Briefing information screen. You create new Home screen panels as needed. To navigate from one Home screen panel to another, either swipe right or left or tap the appropriate dot on the row of dots above the Favorites tray.

Using Multi Window

The Multi Window feature enables you to view two or more apps at the same time. Multi Window can be useful for both work and play, but it works with only some of the apps on your Galaxy S6.

Multi Window has a split-screen view and a pop-up view. In split-screen view, you can view two apps at once. In pop-up view, you can open multiple apps and position them where you want on the screen.

Using Multi Window

Access Multi Window from the Recents Screen

1 Open the apps you want to use, as explained in the previous section, "Explore the User Interface and Launch Apps."

2 Tap and hold **Recents** (▭).

The Recents screen appears, showing the open apps and tabs.

A The Multi Window icon (☰) appears on each app or tab that supports Multi Window.

3 Tap **Multi Window** (☰) on the app or tab you want to display in the upper half of the screen.

The app or tab appears in the upper half of the screen.

The lower half of the screen displays the other open apps and tabs that support Multi Window.

4 Tap the app or tab you want to display in the lower half of the screen.

The app or tab appears in the lower half of the screen.

B The Multi Window control appears in the middle of the divider bar between the two windows.

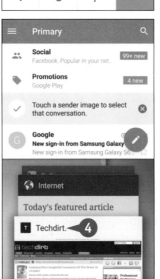

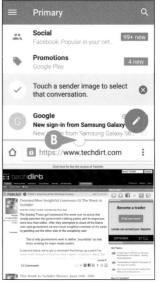

Access Multi Window from Within an App

1 Tap and hold **Recents** (▭).

Note: If the active app does not support Multi Window, or if you start from the Home screen, the upper half of the screen displays the message *The current screen does not support split screen view*.

The Multi Window panel appears, showing the apps that support Multi Window.

C You can tap **Recents** (▭) to display recently used apps that support Multi Window.

D You can swipe left to display other apps that support Multi Window.

2 Tap the app you want to display in the lower half of the screen.

The app appears.

Resize the Windows

1 Tap the **Multi Window control** (◯) and drag it up or down.

The Galaxy S6 resizes the windows to fit the new position of the divider bar.

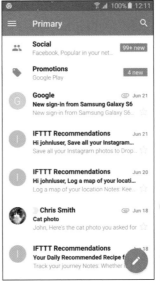

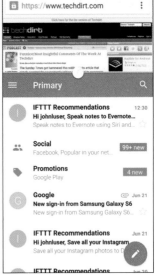

TIP

How does Multi Window work in landscape mode?

In landscape mode, Multi Window places the first window in the left half of the screen and the second window in the right half. You can drag the Multi Window control (◯) left or right to make one window larger and the other smaller.

continued ▶

Using Multi Window (continued)

Multi Window enables you to switch the apps in the upper window and the lower window easily, minimize a window, or close a window. You can also copy text from the app in one window to the app in the other window, or insert a screenshot of one window's contents in the other window.

The pop-up feature lets you shrink a window down to a small icon that you can position as needed on the screen. When you need that window, you can display its contents.

Using Multi Window (continued)

Switch the Positions of Apps in Multi Window

1 Tap the **Multi Window control** ( ).

The Multi Window toolbar appears.

2 Tap **Switch Windows** ( ).

The windows switch positions.

Minimize or Close an App

1 Tap the window you want to minimize or close.

2 Tap the **Multi Window control** ( ).

The Multi Window toolbar appears.

E You can tap **Close** (✕) to close the window.

F You can tap **Full Screen** ( ) to switch the app to full screen.

3 Tap **Minimize** ( ).

G The window shrinks down to a round icon.

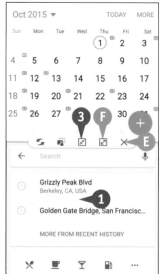

Work with Pop-Up Windows

1 With an app open, swipe down diagonally from the upper-left corner of the screen.

The app switches to a pop-up window.

The previous app appears behind the pop-up window.

2 Tap the **Multi Window control** ( ) and drag the window to where you want it.

The window appears in its new position.

H You can tap the blue border and drag to resize the pop-up window.

3 Tap the **Multi Window control** ( ).

The Multi Window toolbar appears, and you can use the buttons as explained earlier in this section.

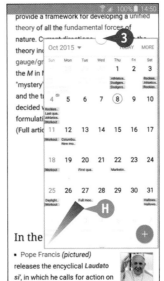

TIP

How do I use the Copy feature?

First, display the source app and the destination app in Multi Window. Then, in the source app, select the text or display the picture or map you want to copy. Tap the **Multi Window control** ( ) to display the Multi Window toolbar. Tap **Copy** ( ) and drag the selected text, picture, or map to the destination app.

Navigate with Gestures

To navigate the TouchWiz user interface smoothly and swiftly, you can use seven main gestures. To trigger the default action for an item, you tap it and then raise your finger off the screen. To access extra functionality, you tap and hold until you get a response. To select text or zoom in on content, you double-tap. To scroll from one screen to another, you swipe right, left, up, or down. To move a shorter distance, you drag a finger across the screen. To zoom in or out, you place two fingers on the screen and pinch outward or inward.

Navigate with Gestures

1 Press **Home**.

The Home screen appears.

2 Tap **Google** ().

The Google folder opens.

3 Tap **Maps** ().

Note: This section uses the Maps app as an example, but you can use these gestures in most apps.

The Maps app opens and displays the area around your current location.

4 Swipe left by moving your finger rapidly from the right side of the screen to the left side.

The map scrolls freely, following the direction you swiped.

5 With one finger, double-tap an item of interest on the screen.

Note: The double-tap gesture is also called *double-touch*.

The map zooms in on the area.

Note: In Maps, double-tapping zooms in by increments. You can zoom out by the same increments by double-tapping with two fingers.

6 Place your thumb and finger together on the screen and pinch outward.

The map zooms in on that point.

7 Tap and hold a road on the screen for a moment.

Note: The tap-and-hold gesture is also called a *long press*.

A pin appears on the map and the location bar appears at the bottom of the screen.

8 Tap the location bar.

The info panel opens.

9 Tap **Street View** on the information panel.

The Street view of the location appears, showing photos of the road.

10 Tap the screen and drag to the right.

The view moves to the left.

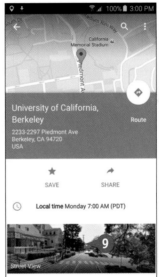

TIPS

What is the difference between swiping and dragging?
Swiping is a more expansive gesture than dragging and does not involve a specific object on the screen. You swipe to move from one screen to another, whereas you drag to move an object within a screen.

What other gestures can I use with my Galaxy S6?
Your Galaxy S6 supports several gestures other than those explained in this section. You learn about these other gestures in Chapter 2.

Using the Notification Panel

Your Galaxy S6 integrates a wide range of different types of alerts into the Notification panel, a panel you can pull down from the top of the screen over whichever app or screen is currently displayed. You can quickly open the Notification panel from the Home screen or almost any other screen. With the Notification panel open, you can go to the app that raised a particular alert, dismiss an alert, dismiss all alerts, or simply close the panel.

Using the Notification Panel

Open the Notification Panel

1 Press **Home**.

The Home screen appears.

Note: You can open the Notification panel from the Home screen or from almost any Android app. A few apps, such as the Camera app, are exceptions.

2 Tap the status bar at the top of the screen and drag downward.

The Notification panel opens.

Open the App That Raised an Alert

1 In the Notification panel, tap the alert.

The app opens and displays the source of the alert.

You can now work in that app.

2 Drag or swipe open the Notification panel when you want to work with other alerts.

Dismiss One or More Alerts

1 To dismiss an alert, swipe the alert to the left or right.

The alert disappears from the list.

2 To dismiss all alerts, tap **Clear** (⛶).

Android dismisses all the alerts that do not require your attention.

The Notification panel closes.

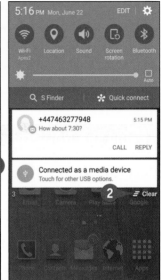

Close the Notification Panel Manually

1 If you do not dismiss all alerts, as explained in the preceding subsection, tap the bottom of the Notification panel and drag it upward to close the panel.

Note: You can also swipe up from the bottom of the screen to close the Notification panel.

The Notification panel closes, and Android displays the Home screen or the app that was last open.

TIPS

To open the Notification panel, do I drag down or do I swipe down?

You can either drag or swipe. Dragging the status bar down enables you to peek at the contents of the Notification panel without opening it fully. Swiping opens the Notification panel fully so that you can see its contents.

What other actions can I take in the Notification panel?

When you miss a phone call, you can tap **Call back** in the notification to return the call or tap **Message** to send a text message instead. When you receive a notification for new e-mail messages, drag your finger down the notification to expand the list of messages so that you can decide how to handle them.

Download and Install Samsung Smart Switch

Samsung provides the Smart Switch app for managing the Galaxy S6 and other recent phones and tablets. You can use Smart Switch to back up your Galaxy S6 to your PC or Mac and restore files from backup; see Chapter 12 for details.

To use Smart Switch, you must download it and install it on your computer. If you do not intend to use Smart Switch to manage your Galaxy S6, skip this section.

Download Smart Switch

To get Smart Switch, open your web browser, such as Microsoft Edge or Internet Explorer in Windows or Safari on the Mac. Enter www.samsung.com in the address box and press **Enter** or **Return** to go to the Samsung website, which automatically redirects you to the website for your country or region. Type **Smart Switch** in the Search box and press **Enter** or **Return** to search for Smart Switch, and then click the appropriate search result to go to the Smart Switch page. Click **Download for Windows** or **Download for Mac OS** to download the version of Smart Switch for your operating system. If your browser prompts you to choose between saving the downloaded file and running it, select the option for saving it.

Install Smart Switch in Windows

After downloading the Smart Switch setup file for Windows, run the file, either by clicking the **Run** button when your browser prompts you or by double-clicking the file in a File Explorer window. If the User Account Control dialog box opens, confirm that the verified publisher is Samsung Electronics and click **Yes**. The installation routine then runs, displaying information screens as it does so.

When the Installation Complete dialog box appears, click **Create Shortcut on Desktop** (☑ changes to ☐) if you do not want to create a Smart Switch shortcut on the desktop. Click **Run Smart Switch** (☐ changes to ☑) if you want to run Smart Switch immediately, as you probably do. Then click **Finish**.

Install Smart Switch on the Mac

When your Smart Switch download finishes on the Mac, OS X may automatically open a Finder window showing the contents of the disk image file. If not, click **Downloads** on the Dock to open a Finder window showing your Downloads folder, and then double-click the Smart Switch disk image file to open it.

Save any unsaved work in your open apps before running the installer, because the installation requires restarting OS X. Then, in the Finder window called *SmartSwitchMac,* double-click the **SmartSwitchMac.pkg** file to start the installer. Follow through the screens of the installer, accepting the Smart Switch end user license agreement and choosing either to accept the default install location — usually the best choice — or to specify a different location. When the installer warns that you must restart your computer after the software finishes installing, click **Continue Installation**. On the screen that announces, *The installation was successful*, click **Restart**.

Launch Smart Switch

After installing Smart Switch, you can launch it using the normal technique for your computer's operating system.

In Windows 10, move the mouse pointer to the lower-left corner of the desktop, click **Start** to display the Start menu, and click **Smart Switch** (⑤). If you have just installed Smart Switch, you can find it in the Recently Added section of the Start menu.

On OS X, click **Launchpad** (🚀) on the Dock to display the Launchpad screen and then click **Smart Switch** (⑤).

Smart Switch opens and prompts you to connect your device. You can then sync files as explained in the following section, "Copy Files from Your Computer."

Copy Files from Your Computer

You can load files on your Galaxy S6 by connecting it to your PC or Mac via a USB cable and transferring files. On a PC, you can use File Explorer or Windows Explorer, the file-management programs that come built in to different versions of Windows. The storage space on your phone or tablet appears as a drive.

On a Mac, your Galaxy S6 does not appear in the Finder, but you can use the free Android File Transfer app to copy files to or from the device.

Copy Files from Your Computer

1 Connect your Galaxy S6 to your PC via the USB cable.

Note: Unlock the Galaxy S6 to allow your computer to access it.

2 Click **File Explorer** (▣) on the taskbar.

A File Explorer window opens.

3 Click **This PC**.

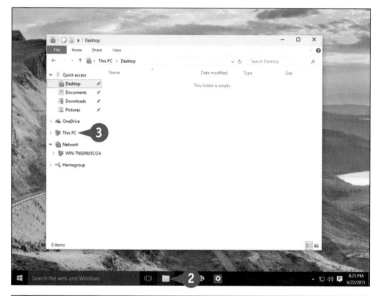

The This PC list expands.

4 Click **Galaxy S6**.

The Galaxy S6 list expands.

5 Click **Phone**.

The contents of the Phone storage appear in the main part of the window.

6 Double-click the appropriate folder. For example, if you want to copy music to your device, double-click **Music**.

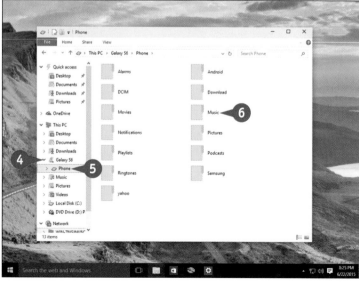

The Music folder opens.

7 Open the folder or library that contains the files you want to copy. For example, right-click **Music** and click **Open in new window** on the contextual menu.

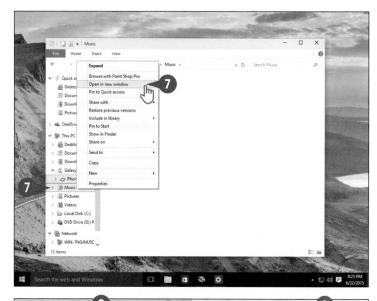

The folder or library you clicked opens.

8 Rearrange the two windows so you can see them both. For example, drag one window to the left side of the screen until the Snap feature docks it, and then click the other window to dock it to the right side of the screen.

9 Click the first item you want to copy.

10 Hold down Shift and click the last item you want to copy.

Windows selects the range of items.

11 Drag the items to the destination folder on your device.

Windows copies the files.

12 When Windows finishes copying the files, disconnect your Galaxy S6 from your computer.

TIP

How do I copy files to my Galaxy S6 using a Mac?

After installing the Android File Transfer app on your Mac, connect your Galaxy S6 to the Mac via USB. Android File Transfer opens automatically and displays the phone's contents. You can then open a Finder window, select the files you want to copy to the Galaxy S6, and then drag them to the appropriate folder in the Android File Transfer window.

Using the Galaxy S6 Edge

Samsung makes multiple models of Galaxy S6 smartphones with different features. The main model is simply called Galaxy S6; this is the model shown on the cover of this book and the model that this book covers fully. The Galaxy S6 Edge is a premium model with curved edges and several enhancements, whose main features this section explains briefly. The Galaxy S6 Active is a toughened model that is water resistant and shockproof; it has a larger battery and a dedicated hardware button for launching an app of your choosing. As of this writing, the Galaxy S6 Active is available only through AT&T.

Understanding the Differences in the Galaxy S6 Edge

Whereas the screen on the Galaxy S6 is flat, like the screens of most smartphones, the screen on the Galaxy S6 Edge is curved to wrap around the sides of the device. The curved sections at the sides of the device provide the space for the Galaxy S6 Edge's to display extra information.

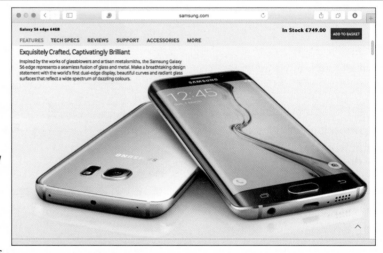

If your local retailers do not stock the Galaxy S6 Edge, go to Samsung's website, www.samsung.com, to view pictures of the device and understand its features. You can also order the Galaxy S6 Edge online if necessary.

Display the Edge Screen Screen in Settings

To configure the Edge features, you work on a screen called the Edge Screen in the Settings app. Follow these steps to access the Edge Screen screen:

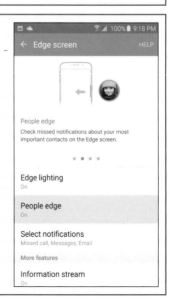

1 Press **Home**.

2 Tap **Apps** (▦).

3 Tap **Settings** (⚙).

4 Tap **Edge Screen**.

Choose Which Side to Display the Edge

You can display the edge on either the left side or the right side of the Galaxy S6 Edge. To choose which side to use, tap **Edge screen position** on the Edge Screen screen, and then tap **Right side** (○ changes to ◉) or **Left side** (○ changes to ◉) on the Edge Screen Position screen.

Enable Edge Lighting

The edge screen can display color-coded lights for the five contacts you assign to the edge. The Edge Lighting feature makes the edge display a lighted bar in the color assigned to the contact who is contacting you, enabling you to see who is calling or messaging without looking at the screen — for example, when your Galaxy S6 Edge is lying facedown.

To enable Edge Lighting, tap **Edge lighting** on the Edge Screen screen, and then set the **Edge lighting** switch to On (⬤ changes to ⬤).

Using People Edge

The People Edge feature enables you to connect quickly to five of your most important contacts.

To configure People Edge, tap **People edge** on the Edge Screen screen. On the People Edge screen, set the **People edge** switch to On (⬤ changes to ⬤), tap **My people**, and then use the resulting Edit screen to choose the five contacts you want to use on People Edge.

Choose Which Notifications to Receive

You can control which apps can notify you using the edge screen. To do so, tap **Select notifications** on the Edge Screen screen. On the Select Notifications screen, set the **Missed call** switch, the **Messages** switch, and the **Email** switch to On (⬤ changes to ⬤) or Off (⬤ changes to ⬤), as needed.

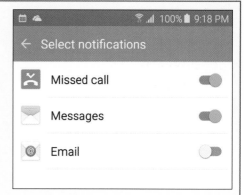

CHAPTER 2

Customizing Your Galaxy S6

To make your Galaxy S6 work the way you prefer, you can configure its many settings. In this chapter, you will learn how to access the most important settings and use them to personalize your Galaxy S6. You will discover how to control notifications, audio preferences, screen brightness, and other key aspects of your phone's behavior.

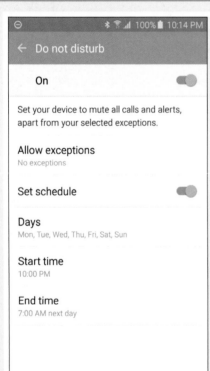

Find the Settings That You Need 34

Customize the Quick Settings. 36

Choose Which Notifications to Receive 38

Configure Do Not Disturb. 42

Choose Volume and Sound Settings 44

Set Screen Brightness and Wallpaper 46

Choose Location Access Settings 48

Secure Your Galaxy S6 with Smart Lock 50

Encrypt Your Galaxy S6. 54

Choose Language and Input Settings 56

Customize the Home Screens 58

Customize the Lock Screen 62

Set Up Sleep and Daydream. 64

Find the Settings That You Need

To make your Galaxy S6 work the way you prefer, you configure its settings. You can access key settings via the Quick Settings buttons in the Notification panel, but to reach most settings, you open the Settings app and then select the appropriate category.

Some apps provide access to settings through the apps themselves instead of through the Settings app. If you cannot find the settings for an app in the Settings app, look within the app itself.

Find the Settings That You Need

Use the Quick Settings Buttons and Quick Settings Panel

1 Pull down from the top of the screen.

The Notification panel opens.

A You can tap one of the Quick Settings buttons to turn that feature on or off.

B You can tap and hold one of the Quick Settings buttons to display the screen of associated settings.

2 Tap the Quick Settings buttons and scroll left.

C The remaining Quick Settings buttons appear.

3 Tap **Settings** (⚙).

The Settings app appears.

D The Quick Settings panel appears at the top of the Settings screen. If necessary, scroll up to locate it.

E You can tap a button on the Quick Settings panel to display that screen of settings.

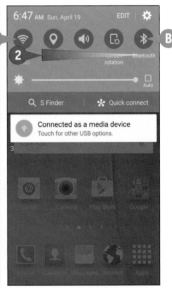
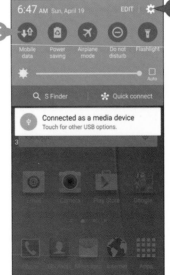
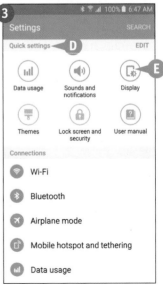

Navigate the Settings App

1 Press **Home**.

The Home screen appears.

2 Tap **Apps** (▦).

The Apps screen appears.

3 Tap **Settings** (⊙).

Note: You can also open the Settings app by pulling down from the top of the screen and then tapping **Settings** (⚙) in the Notification panel.

The Settings app opens.

F The Settings app divides the settings into five categories: Quick Settings, Connections, Device, Personal, and System. Scroll down to explore the categories.

G You can tap **Search** and search for a setting by keyword.

4 Tap the button for the appropriate settings screen.

The screen appears.

5 Tap **Back** (◁) or **Back** (↰) to return to the previous screen.

Note: In many apps, you can go back by tapping **Back** (the left-arrow icon, such as ◁) in the upper-left corner of the screen, as well as by tapping the **Back** soft button (↰) below the screen.

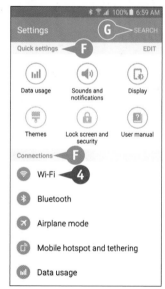

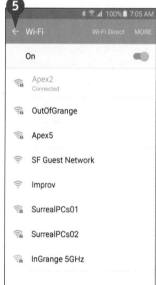

TIP

How do I choose settings within an app?

Open the app by tapping its button on the Home screen or the Apps screen. Tap **Menu** (such as ⋮ or ≡) to display the menu and then tap **Settings**. The Settings screen opens, and you can tap its buttons and options to choose settings. Tap **Back** (↰) or tap **Back** (such as ◁) in the upper-left corner of the screen when you are ready to return to the app.

Customize the Quick Settings

The Quick Settings buttons at the top of the Notification panel give you instant access to key individual settings and related screens. The Quick Settings panel at the top of the Settings screen gives you direct access to the settings screens you use most often. You can customize both the Quick Settings buttons and the Quick Settings panel. You can have up to ten Quick Settings buttons and up to nine icons in the Quick Settings panel.

Customize the Quick Settings

1 Pull down from the top of the screen.

The Notification panel opens.

2 Tap **Edit**.

Note: The Quick Settings buttons area can contain a minimum of five buttons and a maximum of ten buttons.

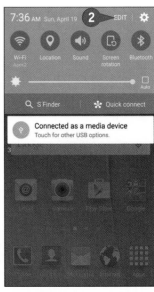

The screen for editing the Quick Settings buttons appears.

A The highlighted area shows the current Quick Settings buttons.

3 Drag an icon you do not use from the highlighted area to the lower area.

Note: If the highlighted area contains ten icons, dragging another icon to the area moves the last icon out of the highlighted area.

4 Drag an icon you wish to use from the lower area to the highlighted area.

Note: You can drag the icons in the highlighted area into your preferred order.

5 Tap **Done**.

The Notification panel appears again.

The Quick Settings buttons appear in your custom configuration.

6 Tap **Settings** (⚙).

The Settings app opens.

Note: If the Quick Settings area is not visible, scroll up to the top of the Settings screen.

7 Tap **Edit**.

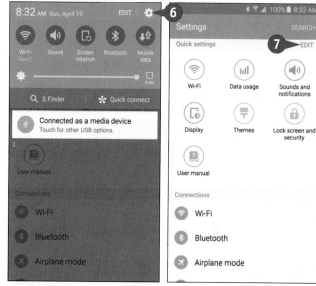

The Edit Quick Settings screen appears.

8 Tap each item you want to display (☐ changes to ☑).

Ⓑ The readout shows how many icons the Quick Settings panel contains out of the nine it can hold.

9 Tap **Back** (◀) or **Back** (↩).

The Quick Settings panel shows your choice of icons.

How can I restore the original set of Quick Settings buttons?

As of this writing, there is no easy way to restore the original group of buttons. You can tap **Edit** to open the buttons for editing, drag them into their original order — Wi-Fi, Location, Sound, Screen Rotation, Bluetooth, Mobile Data, Power Saving, Airplane Mode, and Flashlight — and then tap **Done**. Beyond that, resetting your Galaxy S6 restores the buttons to their original order, but this is a drastic move to effect such a small change.

Choose Which Notifications to Receive

Some apps can display notifications to alert you to events such as calendar items, incoming e-mail messages, and software updates becoming available. Notifications enable you to keep track of important information, but you likely want to receive only some notifications rather than all notifications. You can control which apps can give you notifications. You can also choose whether to have the blue LED blink to alert you to notifications you have missed while the screen was turned off.

Choose Which Notifications to Receive

1 Pull down from the top of the screen.

The Notification panel opens.

2 Tap **Settings** (⚙).

The Settings screen appears.

3 In the Device section, tap **Applications** (⊞).

The Applications screen appears.

4 Tap **Application manager** (▦).

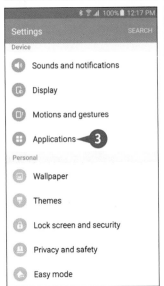

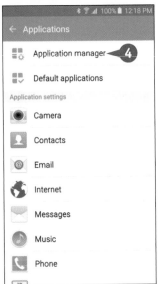

The Application Manager screen appears.

Note: If the app you want to configure does not appear on the Downloaded list, swipe left twice to display the All list.

5 Tap the app for which you want to configure notifications.

The App Info screen appears.

6 Tap **Show notifications** (☐ changes to ✓) if you want to receive notifications for this app.

7 Tap **Back** (⬅) or **Back** (↩).

The Application Manager screen appears.

8 Repeat steps **5** to **7** to choose settings for other apps as needed.

9 Tap **Back** (⬅) or **Back** (↩).

The Applications screen appears.

10 Tap **Back** (⬅) or **Back** (↩).

The Settings screen appears.

11 Tap **Sounds and notifications** (◀).

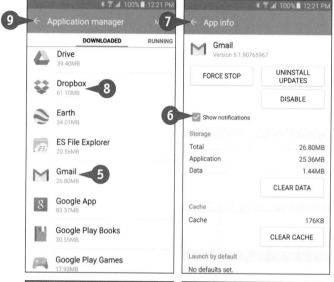

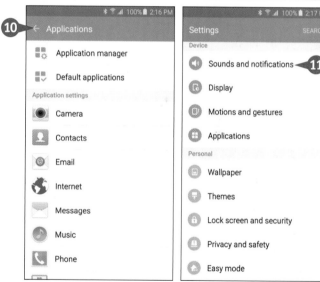

TIP

What other actions can I take on the App Info screen for an app?
You can take several other actions on the App Info screen:

• Tap **Force stop** to force the app to stop if it has ceased to respond to your taps.

• Tap **Uninstall** to begin the process of uninstalling the app. For a system app, you can tap **Uninstall Updates**.

• Tap **Clear data** to delete the app's data files, including account details you have entered and settings you have chosen.

• Tap **Clear cache** to clear any data the app has stored in its cache for future use.

continued ▶

The lock screen can display notifications so that you can view the latest information without unlocking your phone. For security, Android offers you three options: You can choose to display notifications and their content on the lock screen, show that apps have raised notifications but hide notification content that may be sensitive, or simply not display any notifications on the lock screen.

Choose Which Notifications to Receive (continued)

The Sounds and Notifications screen appears.

12 Tap **Ringtones and sounds**.

The Ringtones and Sounds screen appears.

13 Tap **Default notification sound**, tap the sound you want (○ changes to ◉), and then tap **Back** (◁) or **Back** (⤺).

14 Tap **Back** (◁) or **Back** (⤺).

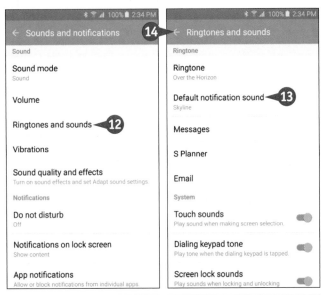

The Sounds and Notifications screen appears.

15 Tap **Notifications on lock screen**.

A pop-up panel appears.

16 Tap **Show content**, **Hide content**, or **Do not show notifications**, as needed.

17 Set the **LED indicator** switch to On (⬤ changes to ⬤) if you want the LED indicator to light up when you have notifications.

18 Tap **App notifications** to display the App Notifications screen, which shows the available apps.

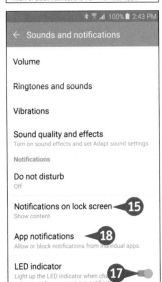

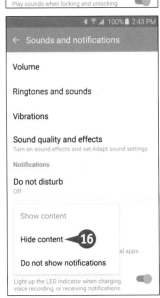

19 Tap the app you want to affect.

The App Notifications screen for the app appears.

A You can set the **Block notifications** switch to On (⬤ changes to ⬤) to prevent Android from showing notifications from this app.

B You can set the **Set as priority** switch to On (⬤ changes to ⬤) to give this app's notifications priority. See the tip for details on priority.

C You can set the **Hide content on lock screen** switch to On (⬤ changes to ⬤) to hide content in this app's notifications.

20 If Settings (✿) appears, tap **Settings** (✿).

A screen with notification settings for the app appears.

21 Set the **Notifications** switch to On (⬤ changes to ⬤) to receive notifications from this app.

22 Tap **Notification sound** and choose a different sound to distinguish this app's notifications.

23 Set the **Vibrate** switch to On (⬤ changes to ⬤) to receive vibrations for this app's notifications.

24 Tap **Back** (⬅) or **Back** (↩).

The App Notifications screen appears.

25 Tap **Back** (⬅) or **Back** (↩) three times.

The Settings screen appears.

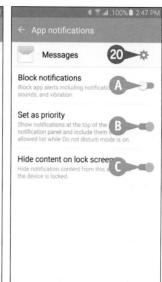

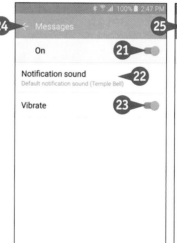

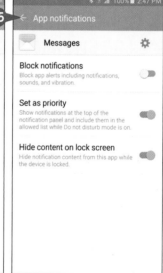

TIP

How does Android treat priority notifications?

Android treats priority notifications in two ways. First, it displays priority notifications at the top of the list on the Notification panel, and at the top of the list on the lock screen if you display notifications there. Second, Android includes all priority notifications when you set your device to display only priority notifications.

Configure Do Not Disturb

Your Galaxy S6 includes a Do Not Disturb feature that enables you to set the phone to disturb you only with the notifications you want and at suitable times. You can choose which apps and which contacts can disturb you while Do Not Disturb is on.

You can configure the Do Not Disturb feature to block off hours when you want to receive no notifications, such as at night. You can also turn Do Not Disturb on and off as needed.

Configure Do Not Disturb

1 Pull down from the top of the screen.

The Notification panel opens.

2 Tap and hold **Sound** (◀), **Vibrate** (☒), or **Mute** (☒).

Note: Sound (◀), Vibrate (☒), and Mute (☒) are three sound-mode icons that share the same icon position in the Quick Settings buttons.

The Sounds and Notifications screen appears.

3 Tap **Do not disturb**.

The Do Not Disturb screen appears.

A You can set the **Do not disturb** switch to On (◯ changes to ●) to turn on Do Not Disturb immediately.

4 Set the **Set schedule** switch to On (◯ changes to ●).

5 Tap **Days** and choose the days on the Days screen, and then tap **Back** (◀) or **Back** (↩).

6 Tap **Start time** and choose the start time.

7 Tap **End time** and choose the end time.

8 Tap **Allow exceptions**.

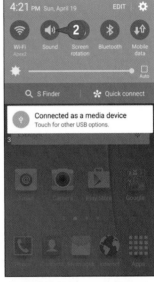

The Allow Exceptions screen appears.

9 Set the **Allow exceptions** switch to On (changes to).

10 Set the **Alarms** switch, **Calls** switch, **Messages** switch, and **Events and reminders** switch to On (changes to) or Off (changes to), as needed.

11 Tap **Calls and/or messages from**.

A pop-up menu opens.

12 Tap **All**, **Favorite contacts only**, or **Contacts only**, as needed.

13 Tap **App notifications**.

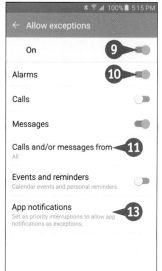

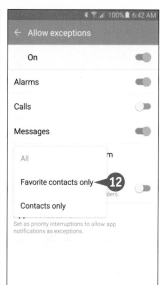

The App Notifications screen appears, showing the list of apps.

14 Tap the app you want to affect.

The App Notifications screen for the app appears.

15 Set the **Set as priority** switch to On (changes to) to make the app a priority, enabling it to display notifications when Do Not Disturb is on.

16 Tap **Back** ( ) or **Back** ( ) five times.

The Settings screen appears.

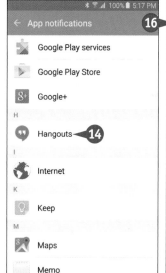

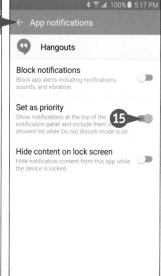

TIPS

Is there a quick way to turn Do Not Disturb on or off?
Yes: Open the Notification panel and tap **Do not disturb** (changes to or changes to).

Why would I hide notification content on the lock screen for a priority app?
You might need to know that you have received important notifications, such as instant messages, but ensure that anybody else who can see your phone's lock screen cannot learn their content.

Choose Volume and Sound Settings

Your Galaxy S6 enables you to control the playback volume of sounds and music by pressing the physical Volume buttons on the left side of the phone and by using on-screen controls.

You can control which audio feedback your phone gives by choosing settings on the Sound screen. You can set the ringtone and vibration, specify the default notification sound, and choose whether to play sounds to give feedback when you take actions such as locking the screen.

Choose Volume and Sound Settings

1 Pull down from the top of the screen.

The Notification panel opens.

2 Tap and hold **Sound** (🔊), **Vibrate** (📳), or **Mute** (🔇).

Note: Sound (🔊), Vibrate (📳), and Mute (🔇) are three sound-mode icons that share the same icon position in the Quick Settings buttons.

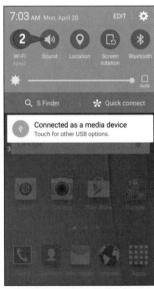

The Sounds and Notifications screen appears.

3 Tap **Volume**.

The Volume screen appears.

4 Drag the **Ringtone** slider (🔵) to set the ringtone volume.

5 Drag the **Media** slider (🔵) to set the media volume.

6 Drag the **Notifications** slider (🔵) to set the notifications volume.

7 Drag the **System** slider (🔵) to set the volume for system sounds, such as for screen taps.

8 Tap **Back** (⬅) or **Back** (↩).

The Sounds and Notifications screen appears.

9 Tap **Vibrations**.

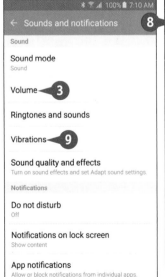

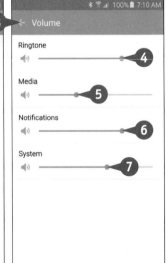

The Vibrations screen appears.

10 Tap **Vibration intensity**.

The Vibration Intensity screen appears.

11 Drag the **Incoming call** slider (●), the **Notifications** slider (●), and the **Vibration feedback** slider (●) to set vibration intensity.

12 Tap **Back** (⬅) or **Back** (↩).

The Vibrations screen appears.

13 Set the **Vibrate when ringing** switch, **Vibration feedback** switch, and **Keyboard vibration** switch to On (➧ changes to ➧) or Off (➧ changes to ➧), as needed.

14 Tap **Back** (⬅) or **Back** (↩).

The Sounds and Notifications screen appears.

15 Tap **Ringtones and sounds**.

The Ringtones and Sounds screen appears.

16 Tap **Ringtone** and select the ringtone to use as the default.

17 Set the **Touch sounds** switch, the **Dialing keypad tone** switch, the **Screen lock sounds** switch, and the **Keyboard sound** switch to On (➧ changes to ➧) or Off (➧ changes to ➧), as needed.

18 Tap **Back** (⬅) or **Back** (↩) twice.

The Home screen appears.

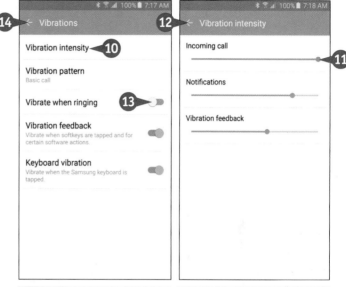

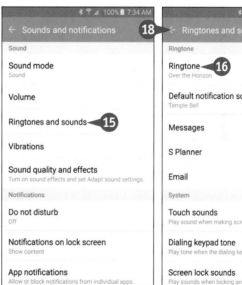

TIPS

What does the Sound Mode button do?
The Sound Mode button enables you to switch among having your Galaxy S6 play sounds, having it vibrate, and having it be mute and still. Tap **Sound mode** and then tap **Sound**, **Vibrate**, or **Mute**, as needed. Alternatively, open the Notification panel and tap **Sound** (◀), **Vibrate** (▨), or **Mute** (◣) until the appropriate icon appears.

How do I set a distinctive ringtone for someone important?
Tap **Contacts** (▣) on the Home screen or the Apps screen, tap the contact, tap **Edit**, and then tap **Ringtone**.

Set Screen Brightness and Wallpaper

You can set the brightness of your Galaxy S6's display manually or use the Automatic Brightness feature to automatically adjust the display brightness to suit the ambient brightness.

You can customize the Home screen or the lock screen by changing the wallpaper that appears in the background. You can choose a picture of your own, select a built-in static wallpaper, or pick a live wallpaper that shows changing patterns.

Set Screen Brightness and Wallpaper

Adjust the Screen Brightness

1 Pull down from the top of the screen.

The Notification panel opens.

2 Drag the **Brightness** slider ( ) to set the brightness.

3 Tap **Auto** (changes to ✓) if you want to turn on Automatic Brightness.

Note: You can also control the brightness on the Display screen in the Settings app.

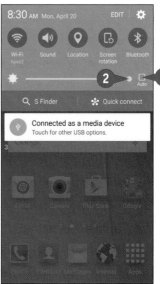

Set the Wallpaper

1 Press **Home**.

2 Tap and hold open space.

The controls for customizing the Home screen appear.

3 Tap **Wallpapers**.

Note: You can also set wallpaper in the Settings app. Press **Home**, tap **Apps** (▦), tap **Settings** (⚙), and then tap **Wallpaper** (▨) to display the Wallpaper screen.

The Wallpaper screen appears.

4 Tap the pop-up menu button ().

The pop-up menu opens.

5 Tap **Home screen**, **Lock screen**, or **Home and lock screens**, depending on which screen you want to affect.

Note: This example uses the Home and lock screens.

6 Scroll the thumbnails left to explore the available wallpapers.

7 Tap the thumbnail for the wallpaper you want to view.

The wallpaper preview appears.

8 Tap **Set As Wallpaper**.

Settings applies the wallpaper.

9 Press **Home**.

The wallpaper appears, and you can judge how well it works with your desktop items.

TIP

How do I use one of my photos as wallpaper?

Press **Home** to display the Home screen, tap and hold open space until the customization controls appear, and then tap **Wallpapers** (). Tap the pop-up menu button () and then tap **Home screen**, **Lock screen**, or **Home and lock screens**, as needed. Tap **From Gallery** to display the photos in the Gallery app, and then tap the photo you want to use. When the photo opens, you can pinch apart to expand it if necessary; you can then drag the photo so that the appropriate part appears in the preview area. Tap **Done** to use the photo.

Choose Location Access Settings

Your Galaxy S6 can determine your location using three sources: satellites in the Global Positioning System (GPS), known wireless networks, and cellular phone towers. Android and your apps can use your location data to tag your photos, customize your searches, and provide local information where appropriate. Android enables you to choose whether to allow location access and which means of determining your location to allow. You control location access separately for Google apps and for other apps.

Choose Location Access Settings

1 Press **Home**.

The Home screen appears.

2 Tap **Apps** (⊞).

The Apps screen appears.

3 Tap **Settings** (⚙).

Note: If the Location icon appears in the Quick Settings buttons on your phone, you can go straight to the Location screen by opening the Notification panel and then tapping and holding **Location** (⚲).

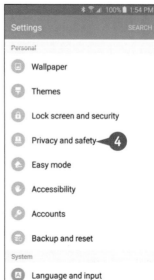

The Settings screen appears.

4 Tap **Privacy and safety** (🔒).

The Privacy and Safety screen appears.

Note: The Send SOS Messages feature on the Privacy and Safety screen enables you to send an emergency message, optionally with photos and an audio recording attached, to predefined contacts by pressing the Power button three times in quick succession.

5 Tap **Location**.

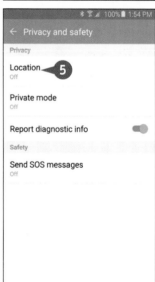

The Location screen appears.

6 Set the **Location** switch to On (changes to).

The Improve Location Accuracy? dialog box opens, requesting your permission for Google's location service to run and collect anonymous data.

Ⓐ You can tap **Don't show again** (changes to) to suppress the Improve Location Accuracy? dialog box in the future.

7 Tap **Agree** or **Disagree**.

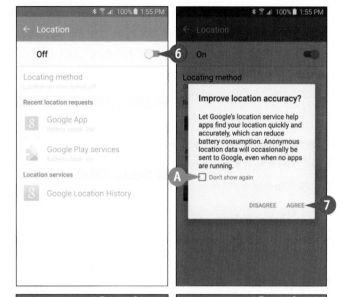

The controls on the Location screen become enabled.

Ⓑ You can see which apps and services have requested your location recently.

8 Tap **Locating method**.

The Locating Method screen appears.

9 Tap **GPS, Wi-Fi, and mobile networks**, **Wi-Fi and mobile networks**, or **GPS only** (changes to).

The Location screen appears again.

10 Tap **Back** ( ) or **Back** ( ) twice.

The Settings screen appears.

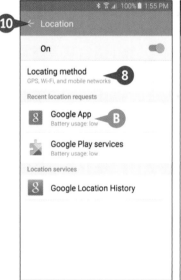
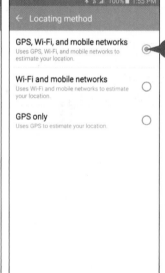

 TIP

Should I grant location access when apps request it?
That is entirely up to you. Each time an app requests location access, verify that it has a good reason for using location data and is not just snooping on your movements. Granting location access to apps can help you to get more out of your Galaxy S6, but it also raises privacy concerns. For example, allowing social media apps to access your location enables your friends to keep up with your movements, but it can also enable people to stalk you. Similarly, adding location information to your photos enables you to sort them by location, which is helpful. But if you post photos containing location information online, other people can tell exactly where you took the photos.

Secure Your Galaxy S6 with Smart Lock

For security, you should apply a screen lock with a Personal Identification Number (PIN), password, or fingerprint to your Galaxy S6. To unlock the phone, you must provide the PIN, password, or fingerprint. You can turn on the Smart Lock feature to disable locking in trusted situations. You can also encrypt your phone, as explained in the following section, "Encrypt Your Galaxy S6"; to encrypt, you must use a PIN, or a password of six characters or longer.

Secure Your Galaxy S6 with Smart Lock

1 Press **Home**.

The Home screen appears.

2 Tap **Apps** (▦).

The Apps screen appears.

3 Tap **Settings** (⚙).

The Settings app opens.

4 Tap **Lock screen and security** (🔒).

The Lock Screen and Security screen appears.

5 Tap **Screen lock type**.

Note: If your Galaxy S6 currently has a screen lock other than Swipe applied, you must unlock it before you can proceed. For example, if you have applied a fingerprint, you must scan your finger or enter your backup PIN.

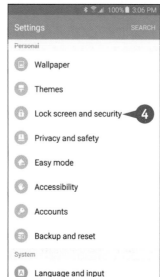

The Screen Lock Type screen appears.

6 Tap **PIN**.

The Set PIN screen appears.

7 Type a PIN of four digits or more.

8 Tap **Continue**.

A second Set PIN screen appears, prompting you to confirm your PIN.

9 Type the same PIN.

10 Tap **OK**.

Note: If the Notifications on Lock Screen screen appears, tap **Show content**, **Hide content**, or **Do not show notifications** (○ changes to ◉), as appropriate, and then tap **Done**.

The Lock Screen and Security screen appears.

11 Tap **Secure lock settings**.

The Secure Lock Settings screen appears.

12 Tap **Lock automatically** and then tap a short interval, such as **Immediately** or **5 seconds** (○ changes to ◉).

13 Set the **Lock instantly with power key** switch to On (changes to).

14 Tap **Smart Lock**.

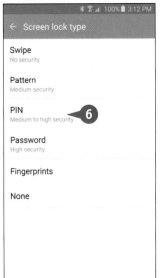

TIP

Instead of a PIN, how else can I secure my Galaxy S6?

On the Select Screen Lock screen, you can choose four other methods of unlocking the screen. **Swipe**, the default method in which you swipe your finger across the screen, provides no security. **Pattern** requires you to draw a pattern on a grid of nine dots and provides medium security. **Fingerprint** requires you to place one of your registered fingers on the scanner built into the Home button; this method provides good security but requires a PIN as a backup. **Password** requires you to type a password and provides high security. Alternatively, choose **None** to disable locking altogether.

continued ▶

After securing your Galaxy S6 with a PIN, password, or fingerprint, you can turn on Smart Lock. Smart Lock can automatically disable the screen lock when your Galaxy S6 is near a trusted device, is in a trusted place, or can detect a trusted face. For example, a trusted device might be your Android Wear watch, a trusted place could be your workplace or your home, and a trusted face would normally be your own.

Secure Your Galaxy S6 with Smart Lock (continued)

Your Galaxy S6 prompts you to verify your identity.

15 Verify your identity. For example, place your fingertip on the Home button so that the scanner can scan it.

The Smart Lock screen appears.

16 Tap **Trusted devices**, **Trusted places**, or **Trusted voice**, and then work as explained in the rest of this section.

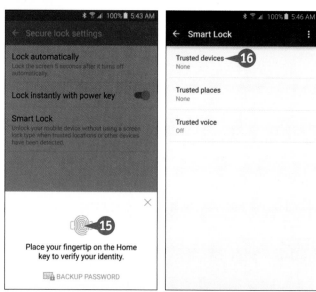

Set Up a Trusted Device

1 Tap **Trusted devices** on the Smart Lock screen.

The Trusted Devices screen appears.

2 Tap **Add Trusted Device**.

The Choose Device Type screen appears.

3 Tap **Bluetooth** or **NFC**, as appropriate. This example uses Bluetooth.

Note: If you tap **NFC** on the Choose Device Type screen, Android prompts you to tap your Galaxy S6 to an NFC tag or device. When you do so, Android establishes the pairing.

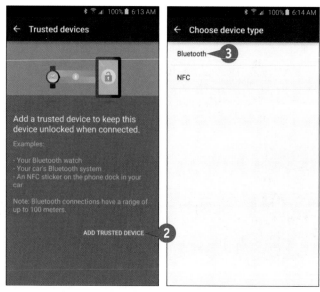

The Choose Device screen appears, showing available Bluetooth devices.

④ Tap the device you want to use.

The Add Trusted Device button appears.

⑤ Tap **Add trusted device**.

Android sets up the device as a trusted device.

Set Up a Trusted Place

① Tap **Trusted places** on the Smart Lock screen.

The Trusted Places screen appears.

Ⓐ You can tap an existing place, such as Home.

② Tap **Add trusted place**.

The Pick a Place screen in Maps appears.

③ Navigate to the appropriate location, such as your workplace.

④ Tap **Select this location**.

A dialog box appears.

⑤ At the top of the dialog box, type the name you want to give the location, such as **Work**.

⑥ Tap **OK**.

Android sets up the place as a trusted place.

TIPS

How do I set up a trusted voice?
Tap **Trusted voice** on the Smart Lock screen to display the Settings screen, then set the **From the Google app** switch to On (changes to).

Can I use another smartphone or a tablet as a trusted device?
Yes, you can use a smartphone or a tablet as a trusted device via Bluetooth. As of this writing, you cannot use a smartphone or a tablet as a trusted device via NFC. The Galaxy S6 detects the other device's NFC chip but displays a message saying that the device is not supported.

Encrypt Your Galaxy S6

After securing your Galaxy S6, you can protect your data further by encrypting it. Encryption encodes the data using a digital key, helping ensure that the data can be read only by someone authorized.

Before encrypting your Galaxy S6, you must charge its battery fully. During encryption, the phone must be connected to a power source. Android requires two sources of power to ensure that encryption can finish successfully because encryption failing may cause data loss.

Encrypt Your Galaxy S6

1 Connect your Galaxy S6 to a power source and charge the battery fully.

2 With the Galaxy S6 still connected to the power source, press **Home**.

The Home screen appears.

3 Tap **Apps** (▦).

The Apps screen appears.

4 Tap **Settings** (⚙).

The Settings app opens.

5 In the Personal section, tap **Lock screen and security** (🔒).

The Lock Screen and Security screen appears.

6 Tap **Other security settings** at the bottom of the screen.

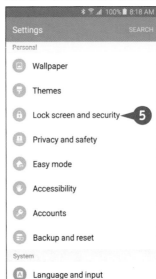
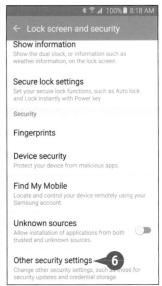

The Other Security Settings screen appears.

7 Tap **Encrypt device**.

Note: If your Galaxy S6 has no password applied or if the password is shorter than six characters, you are prompted to set an unlock password. Tap **Set screen lock type** and follow the prompts.

The Encrypt Device screen appears.

Note: If your Galaxy S6 is not plugged into a power source, the Encrypt Device button is dimmed to indicate that it is unavailable.

8 Tap **Encrypt Device**.

The Confirm Backup Password screen appears.

9 Type your password.

10 Tap **Continue**.

The Confirm Encryption screen appears.

A You can tap **Fast encryption** (☐ changes to ✓) to encrypt only used memory space.

11 Tap **Encrypt Device**.

Android encrypts your device.

The Enter Your PIN or Password to Use the Encrypted Device Memory screen appears.

12 Type your password.

13 Tap **Done**.

The lock screen appears, and you can unlock your Galaxy S6 as usual.

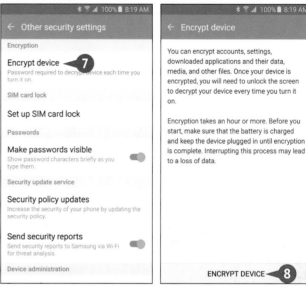

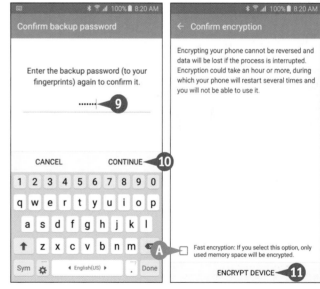

TIPS

Do I need to encrypt my Galaxy S6?
You need to encrypt it only if you store highly sensitive or valuable personal or business data on it. If you use your phone mostly for enjoying media and browsing the web, a fingerprint, PIN, or password probably offers adequate protection.

How do I remove encryption from my Galaxy S6?
The only way to remove encryption is to perform a factory data reset, which wipes all data from your Galaxy S6 and restores it to the factory settings. You can then set up the phone again from scratch. See Chapter 12 for instructions on performing a factory data reset.

Choose Language and Input Settings

Android enables you to choose which language to use for its user interface. Android supports many languages, and you can switch quickly among them as needed. Android also provides various ways of entering text, ranging from assorted keyboard layouts to using speech to input text with the Google Voice feature. You use the Language and Input screen in Settings to configure your UI language and input methods.

Choose Language and Input Settings

① Pull down from the top of the screen.

The Notification panel opens.

② Tap **Settings** (⚙).

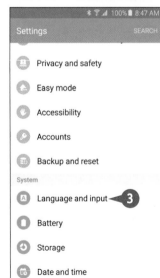

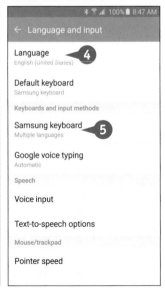

The Settings app opens.

③ In the System section, tap **Language and input** (Ⓐ).

The Language and Input screen appears.

④ To change the language, tap **Language**, tap the desired language on the Language screen, and then tap **Back** (◁) or **Back** (⊃).

⑤ Tap **Samsung keyboard**.

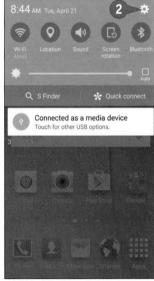

The Samsung Keyboard screen appears.

6 Tap **Select input languages**.

Note: If the Input Languages dialog box opens, tap **OK** to update the language list.

The Select Input Languages screen appears.

7 Set the switch to On (changes to) for each input language you will use.

Ⓐ You can tap **Update** to update a language's data.

Ⓑ You can tap a language to download it.

8 Tap **Back** ( ) or **Back** ( ).

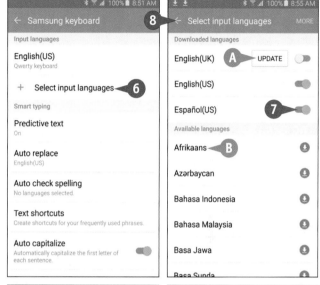

The Samsung Keyboard screen appears again.

9 Choose options in the Smart Typing section. See the tip for details.

10 Further down the screen, set the **Sound** switch to On (changes to) to hear tap sounds.

11 Set the **Vibration** switch to On (changes to) to receive vibration feedback.

12 Set the **Character preview** switch to On (changes to) to see the character bubble when you tap a key.

Ⓒ You can tap **Reset settings** to reset the keyboard settings to their defaults.

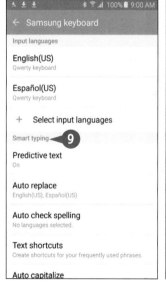

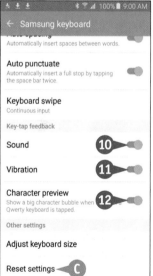

TIP

What do the options in the Smart Typing section do?

Tap **Predictive text** to display the Predictive Text screen. For best results, set the **Predictive text** switch, the **Live word update** switch, and the **Personalized data** switch to On (changes to). Tap **Back** ( ) or **Back** ( ).

Tap **Auto replace** to display the Auto Replace screen. Set the **Auto replace** switch to On, and set the switch for each language to On (changes to). Tap **Back** ( ) or **Back** ( ).

Tap **Auto check spelling** to display the Auto Check Spelling screen, on which you can choose which languages to check. Tap **Text shortcuts** to display the Text Shortcuts screen, on which you can create shortcuts for phrases you type often.

Customize the Home Screens

Android enables you to customize the Home screens on your Galaxy S6. You can add the apps and widgets that you find the most useful and remove any apps or widgets that you do not need. You can reposition the apps and widgets on each Home screen to suit your preferences, and you can customize the Favorites tray at the bottom of the Home screen with apps that you use frequently. You can also resize the widgets to their optimum sizes.

Customize the Home Screens

Place an App on a Home Screen

1 Press **Home**.

The Home screen appears.

2 Swipe left or right to display the Home screen on which you want to place the app.

A You can also navigate by tapping the dots that represent the Home screens.

3 Tap **Apps** (###).

The Apps screen appears.

4 Tap and hold the app you want to add to the Home screen.

The Home screen appears with the app on it.

5 Drag the app to where you want it to appear and then release the app.

Note: You can drag the app to another Home screen at this point if necessary.

The app's button appears on the screen.

Customize the Favorites Tray

1 Press **Home**.

The Home screen appears.

2 Swipe left or right to display the Home screen that contains the button that you want to put in the Favorites tray.

Note: The Favorites tray can contain up to four icons plus the Apps icon.

3 Tap and hold the icon that you want to remove from the Favorites tray.

The icon becomes movable.

4 Drag the icon out of the Favorites tray, and then drop it.

5 Tap and hold the icon you want to put in the Favorites tray.

The icon becomes movable.

6 Drag the icon to the appropriate position in the Favorites tray, and then drop it.

TIP

What are widgets?

Widgets are miniature apps that display useful information or give you quick access to frequently used apps. For example, the Dual Clock widget enables you to see the time in two locations at once. The Gmail widget displays the contents of an e-mail folder, and you can tap a message to open it in the Gmail app. Your Galaxy S6 comes with a wide range of built-in widgets, but you can also download other widgets from the Play Store and other online sources.

continued ▶

If you put many apps on your Home screens, you may want to create folders to organize the apps into convenient categories. After creating and naming a folder, you drag icons to the folder to add apps to it.

You can create folders both on the main part of the Home screen and in the Favorites tray. After creating a folder, you can populate it with as many apps as needed. You can quickly open an app from within the folder, and you can remove an app from the folder if necessary.

Customize the Home Screens (continued)

Place a Widget on the Home Screen

1 Press **Home**.

The Home screen appears.

2 Tap a dot or swipe left or right to display the Home screen on which you want to place the widget.

3 Tap and hold an empty space on the Home screen.

The customization options appear.

4 Tap **Widgets** (▦).

The Widgets screen appears.

5 Tap and hold the widget you want to add.

The Home screen appears with the widget on it.

6 Drag the widget to where you want it and then release it.

Note: After you add the widget, you may need to choose options for it. For example, the Gmail widget displays the Choose Folder dialog box so that you can select the folder to display.

Note: To resize a widget, tap and hold it, and then drag the blue handles that appear.

Create a Folder

1 Press **Home**.

The Home screen appears.

2 Tap a dot or swipe left or right to display the Home screen that contains the apps you want to put into a new folder.

3 Tap and hold one of the apps.

The app becomes movable.

4 Drag the app to the other app.

Android creates the folder and displays its contents.

5 Tap **Enter folder name**.

The keyboard appears.

6 Type the folder name.

7 Tap **Done**.

8 Tap outside the folder.

The folder closes.

You can add other apps to the folder by dragging them to it.

Note: To launch an app from the folder, tap the folder so that the folder's contents appear, and then tap the app.

TIPS

How do I remove an app or a widget from the Home screen?

Tap and hold the app or widget until the Remove button appears at the top of the screen. Drag the app or widget to the Remove button and then drop it.

How do I remove an app from a folder?

Tap the folder to open it, tap and hold the app's button, and then drag the app's button out of the folder and drop it in open space on the Home screen. When only one app remains in the folder, Android removes the folder automatically.

Customize the Lock Screen

Android enables you to customize the lock screen, the screen that appears when you turn on your Galaxy S6 or wake it from sleep. You can add the dual clock feature to the lock screen, showing the time in your home city and — when you are roaming — in your current location. You can also display the date, your owner information, and weather and pedometer information.

In order to be able to take photos quickly, you can also can add the Camera shortcut to the lock screen.

Customize the Lock Screen

1 Pull down from the top of the screen.

The Notification panel opens.

2 Tap **Settings** (⚙️).

Note: If you set the screen lock method to None, the lock screen does not appear, and you cannot set options for it.

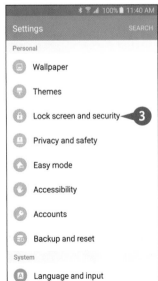

The Settings app opens.

3 In the Personal section, tap **Lock screen and security** (🔒).

The Lock Screen and Security screen appears.

4 Tap **Show information**.

The Show Information screen appears.

5 Tap **Dual clock**.

The Dual Clock screen appears.

6 Set the **Dual clock** switch to On (changes to).

7 Tap **Set home city**, tap the appropriate time zone on the Set Home City screen, and then tap **Back** ( ) or **Back** ( ).

8 Tap **Back** ( ) or **Back** ( ).

The Show Information screen appears.

9 Tap **Weather**, choose the location for the weather, and then tap **Back** ( ) or **Back** ( ).

10 Tap **Owner information**.

11 Type your information.

12 Tap **OK**.

13 Tap **Back** ( ) or **Back** ( ).

The Lock Screen and Security screen appears.

14 Tap **Back** ( ) or **Back** ( ) again.

The Settings screen appears.

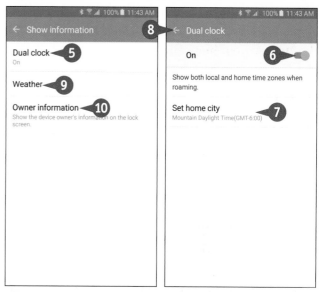

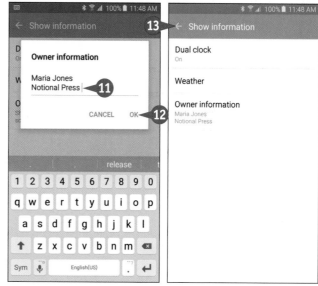

What screen lock method should I choose for security?
Use the Fingerprint screen lock if you are content with medium security; use the Password screen lock if you need top security. To secure your Galaxy S6 effectively, tap **Lock automatically** on the Secure Lock Settings screen and then tap **Immediately** (changes to). You should also set the **Lock instantly with power key** switch to On (changes to) so that you can lock your Galaxy S6 at a moment's notice by pressing the Power button.

Set Up Sleep and Daydream

To conserve battery power, your Galaxy S6 automatically goes to sleep after a period of inactivity. You can control how long this period is.

Android includes Daydream, a feature similar to screen savers on computers. By turning on Daydream and choosing settings, you can make your Galaxy S6 display animations, photos, or information in the Flipboard app on-screen while it sleeps or charges.

Set Up Sleep and Daydream

1 Pull down from the top of the screen.

The Notification panel opens.

2 Tap **Settings** (⚙️).

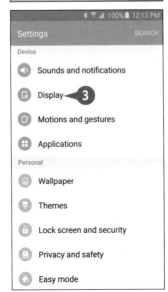

The Settings app opens.

3 In the Device section, tap **Display** (🔲).

The Display screen appears.

4 Tap **Screen timeout**.

The Screen Timeout dialog box opens.

5 Tap the period of inactivity to allow before your Galaxy S6 goes to sleep, such as **15 seconds**.

6 Tap **Daydream**.

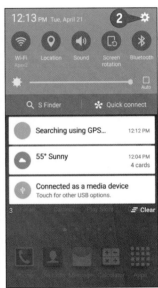

The Daydream screen appears.

7 Set the **Daydream** switch to On (changes to).

8 Tap **Colors**, **Google Photos**, **Photo Frame**, or **Photo Table** (○ changes to ◉).

9 Tap **Settings** (✿), if it appears.

The settings screen for the theme appears.

10 Tap the options that you want to use (☐ changes to ☑).

A You can tap **Select All** to select all the options.

11 Tap **Back** (↩).

The Daydream screen appears.

12 Tap **More**.

The menu opens.

13 Tap **Select when to daydream**.

The Select When to Daydream dialog box opens.

14 Tap **While docked**, **While charging**, or **Both** (○ changes to ◉).

15 Tap **More**.

The menu opens.

16 Tap **Preview**.

The Daydream theme appears, and you can preview it.

17 Press **Home**.

The lock screen appears, and you can unlock it using your usual method.

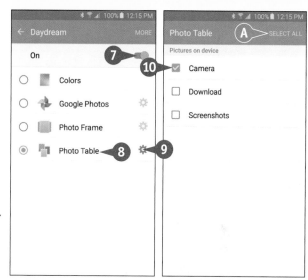

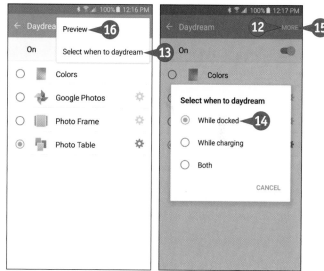

TIP

What is the difference between the Photo Frame theme and the Photo Table theme?
The Photo Frame theme shows one photo at a time and is good for enjoying your photos. Generally speaking, Photo Frame works better on Android tablets than on Android phones, simply because it is easier to view photos on the larger screens of tablets than on the smaller screens of phones. The Photo Table theme gradually arranges miniature versions of your photos onto a table-like surface and is more of a decorative effect.

CHAPTER 3

Working with Text and Voice

You can input text into your Galaxy S6 using the on-screen keyboard, the continuous input feature, and voice input. You can also control your Galaxy S6 with your voice by using features such as voice search, and you can use accessibility features including Galaxy TalkBack.

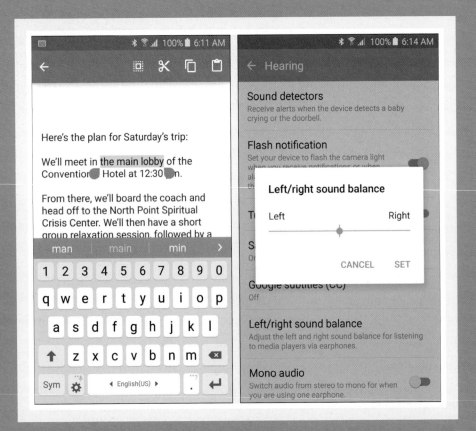

Using the On-Screen Keyboard and Continuous Input . . . 68

Work with Different Keyboards 72

Edit Text and Use Cut, Copy, and Paste 74

Using Voice Input and Voice Recorder. 76

Using S Voice 78

Set Up Accessibility Features 80

Using Galaxy TalkBack 84

Using the On-Screen Keyboard and Continuous Input

You can enter text easily by tapping the keys on the on-screen keyboard that Android automatically displays when you tap an input field. The keyboard appears at the bottom of the screen by default, but you can move it elsewhere if you prefer.

The continuous input feature enables you to enter a word by tapping its first letter, keeping your finger on the screen, and then sliding your finger to each of the other letters in turn.

Using the On-Screen Keyboard and Continuous Input

Open an App That Accepts Text Input

1 Press **Home**.

The Home screen appears.

Note: This example uses the Gmail app. You can use a different app, such as Memo. For example, tap **Apps** (⚏), tap **Tools** (🔧), and then tap **Memo** (⬜).

2 Tap **Google** (🔳).

The Google folder opens.

3 Tap **Gmail** (M).

4 Tap **Compose** (✏️).

A new message opens.

Ⓐ The on-screen keyboard opens automatically.

Note: Android automatically turns Shift on (⬆ changes to ⬆) at the beginning of a paragraph or sentence. After you type the first letter of a sentence or paragraph, Android turns Shift off (⬆ changes to ⬆), so the keyboard types lowercase letters unless you tap **Shift** (⬆). You can turn on Caps Lock by double-tapping **Shift** (⬆ changes to ⬆).

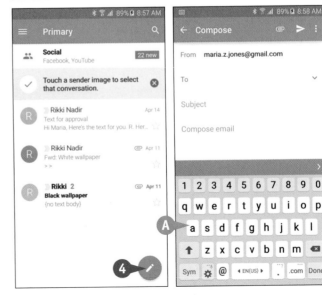

Type on the On-Screen Keyboard

1 Tap **Compose email**.

B Android turns on Shift (↑ changes to ↑) at the beginning of the paragraph.

2 Start typing.

C As you type, the Suggestions bar shows words you may be typing.

3 If a suggestion is correct, tap it. Otherwise, keep typing.

D The word appears in the document.

4 Tap **More** (▶).

The Suggestions panel opens.

5 Tap the word you want to insert.

Note: If none of the words in the Suggestions panel is correct, tap **Less** (◀) to close the Suggestions panel.

TIP

Why does continuous input not work on my Galaxy S6?
Continuous input may be turned off. Follow these steps to turn it on:

1 Pull down from the top of the screen.

2 Tap **Settings** (⚙) to open the Settings app.

3 Tap **Language and input** to display the Language and Input screen.

4 Tap **Samsung keyboard** to display the Samsung Keyboard screen.

5 In the Smart Typing area, tap **Keyboard swipe** to display the Keyboard Swipe screen.

6 Tap **Continuous input** (○ changes to ◉).

continued ▶

To help you enter text quickly, the Samsung keyboard provides a feature called Continuous Input. You place your finger on the first letter of a word and then slide your finger to each of the other letters in turn. When you stop, Android automatically inserts the most likely matching word. You can even slide your finger over the spacebar to indicate the end of a word, and continue sliding your finger to the letters of the next word.

Using the On-Screen Keyboard and Continuous Input (continued)

Ⓔ The word appears in the document.

6 Tap **Sym**.

The first section of the symbols keyboard appears, and you can type widely used symbols.

7 Tap **1/2**.

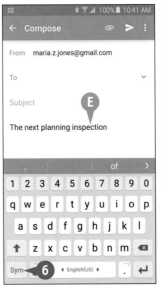

The second section of the symbols keyboard appears, and you can type other symbols.

8 Tap **ABC**.

The letter keyboard appears again.

9 If you need to enter an alternative character or related character, tap and hold the base character. In this example, tap and hold the **a** key.

The pop-up panel appears.

10 Tap the character you want to insert.

Ⓕ The character with the blue background is the default. You can enter it by lifting your finger from the base character after the pop-up panel appears.

11 Tap and hold the period (**.**) key on the letter keyboard.

The punctuation pop-up panel appears.

Note: You can lift your finger once the punctuation pop-up panel appears.

12 Tap the character you want to enter.

The character appears in the document.

13 Tap **Enter** (↵) when you want to create a new paragraph.

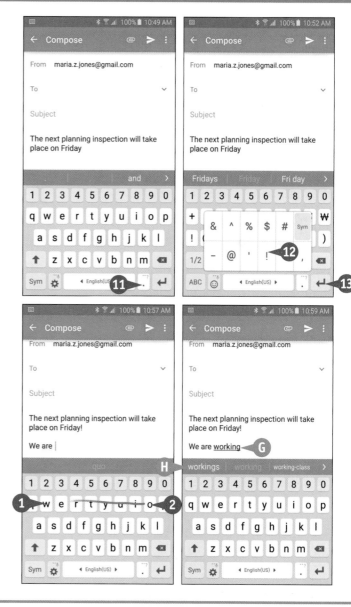

Use Continuous Input

1 Place your finger on the first letter of the word.

2 Without raising your finger, slide to each successive letter in turn.

G The word appears in the document.

H You can tap a word on the Suggestions bar to enter that word instead.

Note: You can also slide your finger over the spacebar to indicate the end of a word, and then continue sliding your finger on the keyboard to start the next word.

TIP

Can I enter a period by tapping the spacebar twice?

Yes, but you may have to turn this feature on. On the keyboard, tap and hold the key to the left of the spacebar, and then tap **Settings** (⚙) on the pop-up panel to display the Samsung Keyboard screen in the Settings app. Set the **Auto punctuate** switch to On (⬤ changes to ⬤).

While on the Samsung Keyboard screen, make sure the **Auto spacing** switch is set to On (⬤) if you want Android to insert spaces automatically between words. Set the **Auto capitalize** switch to On (⬤) if you want Android to capitalize the first letter of each sentence or paragraph or to Off (⬤) if you do not.

Work with Different Keyboards

Your Galaxy S6 provides several different keyboards to enable you to enter text and other items quickly in your documents. For example, you can type on a standard keyboard or a floating keyboard, insert *emoticons* — smiley characters and similar graphics — in your documents, or enter text by handwriting with your finger on the screen. To access these features, you tap and hold the button to the left of the spacebar, and then tap the appropriate icon on the pop-up panel that appears.

Work with Different Keyboards

Open an App That Accepts Text Input

1 Press **Home**.

The Home screen appears.

Note: This example uses the Gmail app. You can use a different app, such as Memo. For example, tap **Apps** (⊞), tap **Tools** (🔧), and then tap **Memo** (▭).

2 Tap **Google** (▦).

The Google folder opens.

3 Tap **Gmail** (Ⓜ).

4 Tap **Compose** (✎).

A new message opens.

Explore the Available Keyboards

1 Tap **Compose email**.

Ⓐ The keyboard appears.

2 Tap and hold the key to the left of the spacebar. This key shows the last-used keyboard item, such as Settings (⚙), emoticon (☺), or voice input (🎤).

Note: You can tap that button to switch straight to the last keyboard item that you used.

The keyboard panel appears.

3 Tap **Voice Input** (🎤).

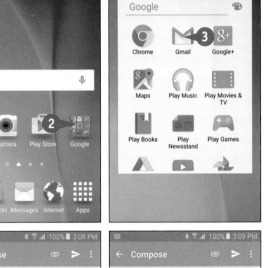

The voice input keyboard appears.

4 Speak the text you want to enter.

B You can tap **Tap to pause** to turn off the microphone.

Note: The microphone automatically turns off after several seconds of inactivity.

C You can tap **Tap to speak** to turn on the microphone again.

5 Tap **Keyboard** (⌨).

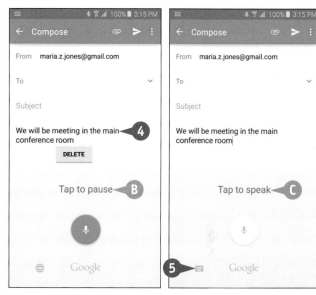

The keyboard appears.

6 Tap and hold the key to the left of the spacebar. In this case, the key is **Voice input** (🎤); at other times, different keys appear in this position.

The keyboard panel appears.

7 Tap **Emoticon** (☺).

The Emoticon keyboard appears.

D You can tap a tab to display another set of emoticons.

8 Tap the emoticon that you want to insert.

The emoticon appears in the document.

9 Tap **ABC**.

The regular keyboard appears.

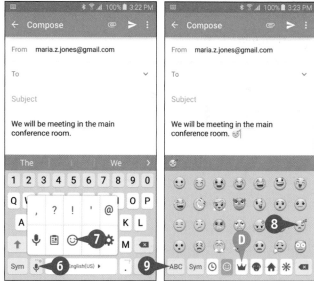

TIPS

How do I display the floating keyboard?
Tap **Floating Keyboard** (⌨) on the keyboard pop-up panel to switch to the floating keyboard, which you can reposition by dragging the handle at the top. To return to the normal keyboard, tap **Keyboard** (⌨).

What do the other icons on the keyboard pop-up panel do?
Tap one of the five punctuation symbols on the top row — Comma, Question Mark, Exclamation Point, Quote, or At Sign — to display that symbol on the key to the left of the spacebar so that you can type that character easily. Tap **Clipboard** (📋) to display the clipboard, explained in the next section.

Edit Text and Use Cut, Copy, and Paste

Your Galaxy S6 enables you to edit existing text in documents and to select part or all of the text. You can cut selected text or copy it to the clipboard and then paste it elsewhere in the same app or another app. Cutting text removes the selection from the document, whereas copying text leaves the selection in the document. The clipboard can contain multiple items, and you can paste each item as many times as you need.

Edit Text and Use Cut, Copy, and Paste

Edit Text

1. Open the document you want to edit.
2. Tap where you want to position the insertion point.

   The arrow for moving the insertion point (⬤) appears.
3. If necessary, drag the arrow (⬤) to move the insertion point.
4. Edit the text as needed.

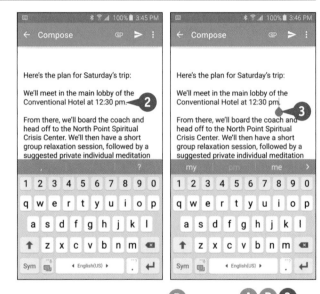

Select Text and Use Cut, Copy, and Paste

1. Tap and hold a word.

   The word becomes highlighted.

   Selection handles (◖ and ◗) appear.
2. Drag the **start handle** (◖) or the **end handle** (◗) to change the selection as needed.
   - Ⓐ You can tap **Select All** (▦) to select all the text.
3. Tap **Copy** (🗐) to copy the text.
   - Ⓑ You can tap **Cut** (✂) to cut the text to the clipboard.
   - Ⓒ You can tap **Delete** (⌫) to delete the text.
   - Ⓓ You can tap **Back** (◁) or **Back** (↰) to turn off selection mode.

④ Tap where you want to paste the copied text.

Note: If you want the text you paste to replace existing text, select that text and then tap **Paste** ( ).

⑤ Tap the arrow ( ).

The Paste button appears.

⑥ Tap **Paste**.

The copied text appears in the document.

Paste Multiple Items

① Tap and hold the key to the left of the spacebar.

The keyboard panel appears.

② Tap **Clipboard** ( ).

The Clipboard pane appears.

③ Tap the item that you want to paste.

Ⓔ The item appears in your document.

④ Tap another item that you want to paste.

Ⓕ You can tap **Delete All** to clear the contents of the clipboard.

⑤ Tap **Close** ( ).

The Clipboard pane closes, and the previous keyboard appears.

TIP

Can I transfer the contents of the clipboard to my computer?
You cannot access the clipboard directly from your computer, but you can easily transfer the contents of the clipboard using workarounds. For example, begin a new e-mail message in the Gmail app and address it to an e-mail account that your computer can access. You can then paste items from the clipboard and send the message.

Using Voice Input and Voice Recorder

The Voice Input feature on your Galaxy S6 enables you to enter text by speaking. This feature can be great for creating documents quickly. You access Voice Input directly from the on-screen keyboard in any app that accepts it.

When you need to create an audio note, you can use the Voice Recorder app. You can either simply record audio or create a voice memo, a memo that contains both your recorded audio and an automatic transcription of the text.

Using Voice Input and Voice Recorder

Use Voice Input

1. Open a new document by following steps 1 to 4 in the section "Work with Different Keyboards," earlier in the chapter.

2. Tap where you want to input text.

3. Tap and hold the key to the left of the spacebar.

   The keyboard pop-up panel opens.

4. Tap **Voice Input** (🎤).

   The Voice Input pane appears.

5. Speak the text.

   The text appears in your document.

Ⓐ You can tap **Tap to pause** to turn off the microphone.

Ⓑ You may need to edit incorrectly transcribed words and phrases.

Ⓒ You can tap **Delete** to delete your latest entry.

Ⓓ You can tap an underlined word or phrase to display a menu of possible corrections.

   The keyboard appears.

6. Tap the key to the left of the spacebar. In this case, this key is **Voice input** (🎤).

   The Voice Input screen appears, and you can dictate more text.

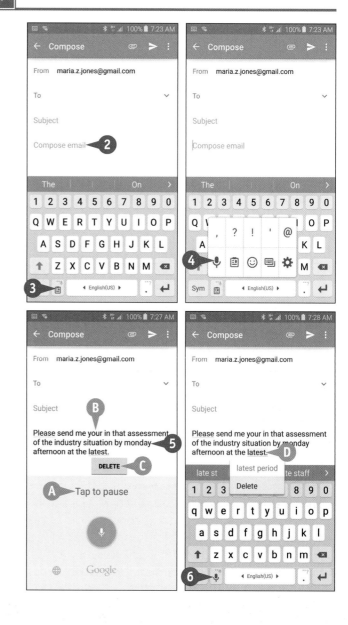

Use Voice Recorder

1 Press **Home**.

The Home screen appears.

2 Tap **Apps** (▦).

The Apps screen appears.

3 Tap **Tools**.

The Tools folder opens.

4 Tap **Voice Recorder** (▣).

Voice Recorder opens.

5 If you need to change the recording type, tap the pop-up menu, and then tap **Standard**, **Interview**, or **Voice memo**, as needed. See the first tip for details on the recording types.

6 Tap **Record** (⬤).

Voice Recorder starts recording.

E The readout shows the time.

F The waveform indicates the audio signal.

G You can tap **Bookmark** (★) to place a bookmark for navigation.

H You can tap **Pause** (❙❙) to pause recording.

7 Tap **Stop** (◼) when you finish the memo.

Voice Recorder stops recording.

The Recordings screen appears.

8 Tap the memo you want to hear.

I You can tap **Record** (⬤) to record another memo.

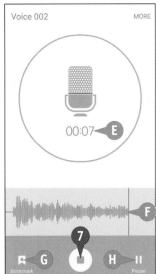

TIPS

Which Voice Recorder mode should I use?
Use Standard mode for regular recordings of your voice using the main microphone. Use Interview mode for recording two-person or group interviews using both the device's microphones. Use Voice Memo mode when you need words transcribed as well as recorded, but be warned that this mode's maximum recording length is 5 minutes.

Can I use Voice Recorder for recording music?
Yes, but it is better to use a third-party app designed for recording music. Voice Recorder is optimized for recording spoken words without taking up much storage space, so the audio quality is lower than that normally needed for music to sound good.

Using S Voice

S Voice enables you to take actions by speaking instructions to your Galaxy S6. S Voice requires an Internet connection because the speech recognition runs on Samsung's servers.

You can use S Voice either with the built-in microphone or with the microphone on a compatible headset. Unless you are in a quiet environment or you hold your Galaxy S6 close to your face, a headset microphone normally gives better results than the built-in microphone.

Using S Voice

Turn Voice Wake-Up On or Off

1 Press **Home**.

The Home screen appears.

2 Tap **Apps** (▦).

The Apps screen appears.

3 Tap **S Voice** (◉).

A The S Voice bar appears across the bottom of the screen.

B S Voice listens for a command.

4 Tap **Settings** (⚙).

The S Voice Settings screen appears.

5 Tap **Voice wake-up**.

The Voice Wake-Up screen appears.

6 Set the **Voice wake-up** switch to On (◯ changes to ●).

7 Tap **Set wake-up command**.

The Set Wake-Up Command screen appears.

8 Follow the prompts to set your wake-up command, such as "Hi, Galaxy!" or "Hey, wake up!"

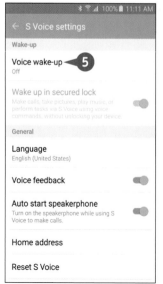

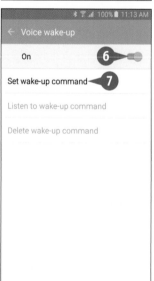

Wake S Voice and Give a Command

1 Say, "Hi, Galaxy!"

C The S Voice bar appears across the bottom of the screen.

2 Speak your command.

Note: For example, you can say, "Memo buy dog food on the way home."

D S Voice displays its interpretation of what you said.

Note: Depending on the command, S Voice may prompt you for further instructions. If so, give any commands needed.

E S Voice acts on your command, such as saving a memo.

F You can say, "Hi, Galaxy!" or tap the microphone to make the microphone active again.

TIP

What actions can I take with S Voice?

You can take many other actions, including these:

- **Open an app.** Say, "Open Gmail."
- **Dial a call.** Say, "Call Alice Smith mobile."
- **Send a text.** Say, "Text Sam message where are the car keys."
- **Schedule an event.** Say, "New event breakfast with Tiffany 8 a.m. October 1st at El Torito."
- **Create a task.** Say, "New task mend the broken window."

Set Up Accessibility Features

Android provides a range of accessibility features that enable you to make your Galaxy S6 easier and more convenient to use. These features range from general accessibility features, such as enabling or disabling automatic rotation of the screen, to features for helping with vision, hearing, or mobility problems. You can configure these features by opening the Settings app and working on the Accessibility screen.

Set Up Accessibility Features

Display the Accessibility Screen and Choose Vision Accessibility Features

1 Press **Home**.

The Home screen appears.

2 Tap **Apps** (⊞).

The Apps screen appears.

3 Tap **Settings** (○).

The Settings app opens.

4 In the Personal section, tap **Accessibility** (○).

The Accessibility screen appears.

5 Tap **Vision**.

The Vision screen appears.

6 Tap **Font size**.

The Font Size screen appears.

7 Drag the **Font Size** slider (●) along the Tiny–Huge scale.

A The *Main text will look like this* readout shows you the current size.

8 Tap **Done**.

The Vision screen appears again.

9 Tap **Magnification gestures**.

The Magnification Gestures screen appears.

10 Set the **Magnification gestures** switch to On (⬤ changes to ●).

11 Tap **Back** (◀) or **Back** (↰).

The Vision screen appears.

B You can tap **Magnifier window** to set up the Magnifier Window feature, which shows part of the screen enlarged.

C You can set the **Grayscale** switch to On (⬤ changes to ●) to view the screen in grayscale.

D You can set the **Negative colors** switch to On (⬤ changes to ●) to invert the screen colors.

E You can tap **Text-to-speech options** to configure the Text-to-Speech feature.

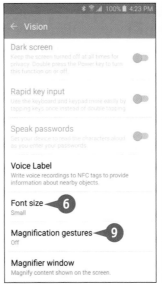

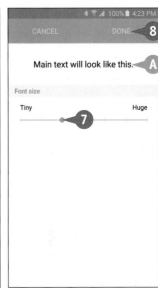

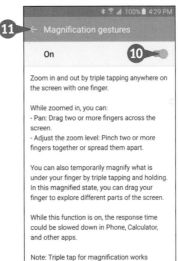

TIP

How do I use the Magnification Gestures feature?

After setting the **Magnification gestures** switch to On (●), triple-tap the screen to zoom in or out. After zooming in, drag two or more fingers across the screen to pan around. Pinch inward or outward with two fingers to adjust the zoom level. You can also triple-tap and hold to magnify an item temporarily; while holding, move your finger around the screen to pan to different areas.

continued ▶

Set Up Accessibility Features (continued)

To improve readability and visibility, you can increase the font size, turn on magnification gestures, or invert the screen colors or use grayscale. You can also configure how the Text-to-Speech feature reads on-screen content.

Android also provides helpful hearing-related accessibility features. You can adjust the sound balance, use mono audio for a single earphone, or turn off all sounds. You can also make the camera light flash to alert you to notifications.

Set Up Accessibility Features (continued)

Choose Hearing Accessibility Features

1. On the Accessibility screen, tap **Hearing**.

   The Hearing screen appears.

   F You can tap **Sound detectors** to display the Sound Detectors screen, on which you can turn on the Baby Crying Detector or the Doorbell Detector.

2. Set the **Flash notification** switch to On (○ changes to ●) to make the Camera light flash when notifications arrive.

3. Set the **Turn off all sounds** switch to On (○ changes to ●) to turn off all sounds temporarily.

   G You can tap **Samsung subtitles (CC)** to configure subtitles on Samsung services.

   H You can tap **Google subtitles (CC)** to configure subtitles on Google services.

4. Set the **Mono audio** switch to On (○ changes to ●) to play mono audio.

Note: Mono audio is useful when you use an earphone.

5. Tap **Left/right sound balance**.

6. Drag the slider (●) toward the Left end or the Right end, as needed.

7. Tap **Set**.

8. Tap **Back** (◁) or **Back** (↰).

   The Accessibility screen appears.

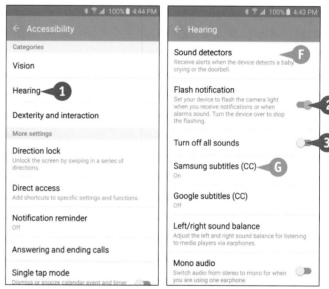

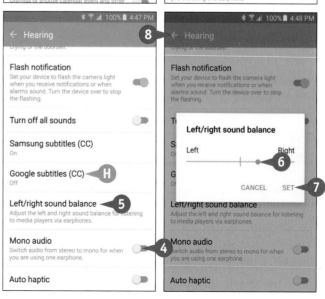

82

Choose Direct Access Settings

1 On the Accessibility screen, tap **Direct access**.

The Direct Access screen appears.

2 Set the **Direct access** switch to On (changes to).

3 In the Accessibility Settings area, set the switch to On (changes to) for each item — **Accessibility**, **Galaxy TalkBack**, **Universal switch**, **Magnifier window**, **Negative colors**, **Grayscale**, and **Color Adjustment** — that you want to appear in the Direct Access dialog box.

4 Tap **Back** ( ) or **Back** ( ).

The Accessibility screen appears.

Choose Settings for Answering/Ending Calls

1 On the Accessibility screen, tap **Answering and ending calls**.

2 Set the **Pressing the Home key** switch to On (changes to) to answer calls by pressing Home.

3 Set the **Using voice commands** switch to On (changes to) to answer calls by saying "Answer" or reject calls by saying "Reject."

4 Set the **Pressing the Power key** switch to On (changes to) to end calls by pressing Power.

5 Tap **Back** ( ) or **Back** ( ).

The Accessibility screen appears.

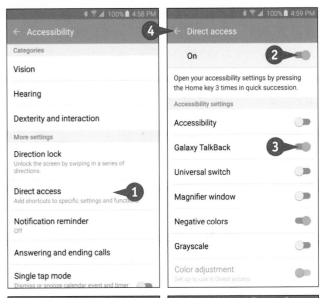

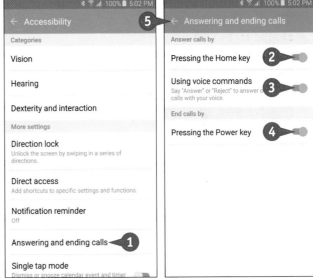

TIP

How can I transfer my accessibility settings to another device?
On the Accessibility screen, tap **Manage accessibility** to display the Manage Accessibility screen. There, you can transfer your accessibility settings in two ways:

- Tap **Import/Export** to display the Import/Export dialog box, which enables you to import a file to or export a file from My Files.
- Tap **Share via** to copy the accessibility settings to a specific location from which you can then share them.

Using Galaxy TalkBack

The Galaxy TalkBack feature can read the items on the screen for you. Galaxy TalkBack can be a big help when you find it hard to see what your screen is displaying. Galaxy TalkBack says the name of the current screen or dialog box and announces the items that you tap on the screen, enabling you to navigate by listening.

Using Galaxy TalkBack

1 Press **Home**.

The Home screen appears.

2 Tap **Apps** (▦).

The Apps screen appears.

3 Tap **Settings** (○).

Note: Android cannot use Galaxy TalkBack at the same time as some other features, such as Smart Screen and Multi Window. If these features are enabled when you turn on Galaxy TalkBack, Android disables them.

The Settings app opens.

4 In the Personal section, tap **Accessibility** (●).

The Accessibility screen appears.

5 Tap **Vision**.

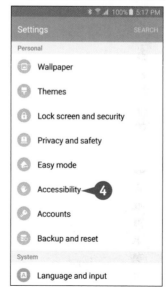
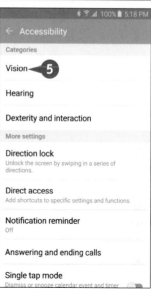

The Vision screen appears.

6 Tap **Galaxy TalkBack**.

The Galaxy TalkBack screen appears.

Note: The first time you turn on Galaxy TalkBack, a tutorial runs. Follow through it, tapping once to select a button and tapping again to press it.

7 Set the Galaxy **TalkBack** switch to On (◯ changes to ●).

The Use Galaxy TalkBack? dialog box opens.

8 Tap **Turn on**.

9 Tap **Settings**.

The Settings screen appears.

10 Tap **Speech volume** and choose the volume to use.

11 Tap **Speech rate** and choose the rate to use.

12 Set the **Pitch changes** switch to On (◯ changes to ●) to use a lower-pitched voice for keyboard feedback.

13 Set the **Use proximity sensor** switch to On (◯ changes to ●) to stop TalkBack when you bring your phone to your face.

14 Set the **Vibration feedback** switch to On (◯ changes to ●) to receive feedback via vibration.

15 Set the **Sound feedback** switch to On (◯ changes to ●) to receive feedback via sound.

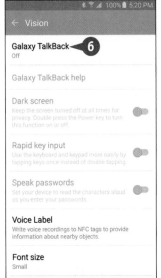

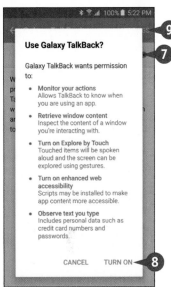

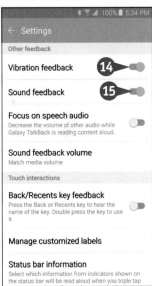

TIP

What other settings can I choose for TalkBack?

Tap **Keyboard feedback** and then tap **Always read keyboard feedback aloud**, **Only for virtual keyboard**, or **Never read keyboard input aloud** (◯ changes to ●) in the Keyboard Feedback dialog box. Set the **Focus on speech audio** switch to On (◯ changes to ●) to make your Galaxy S6 decrease the volume of any other audio it is playing while Galaxy TalkBack is speaking. Set the **Back/Recents key feedback** switch to On (◯ changes to ●) to hear the key's name spoken when you tap it once; you must double-tap to give the key's command.

CHAPTER 4

Setting Up Communications

To unleash the communications power of your Galaxy S6, you can set up your e-mail accounts in the Gmail app, import your contacts, and configure the S Planner calendaring app.

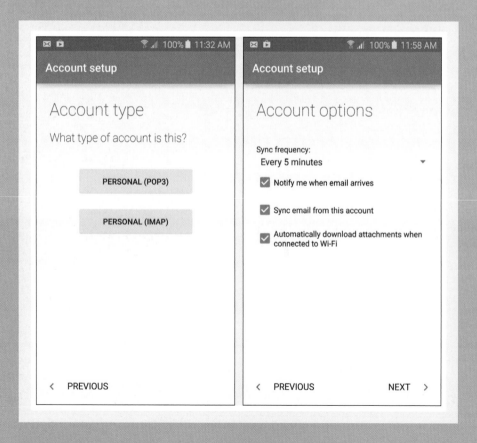

Set Up Your E-Mail Accounts in the Gmail App 88

Choose Settings in Gmail 94

Remove an E-Mail Account 98

Set Up Your Signatures 100

Set Up and Use Priority Inbox 102

Choose Which Contacts to Display 104

Import Your Contacts into the Contacts App 106

Choose S Planner Notifications and Reminders 108

Choose Week and Time Zone Settings 110

Set Up Your E-Mail Accounts in the Gmail App

The Gmail app included with your Galaxy S6 enables you to access e-mail accounts on both Google's Gmail service and most other personal e-mail services. Android walks you through setting up your primary Gmail account when you first set up your phone. You can subsequently add your other e-mail accounts manually.

To access e-mail accounts the Gmail app cannot access, such as Microsoft Exchange accounts, you use the Email app. See the section "Connect to Exchange Server" in Chapter 10 for details.

Set Up Your E-Mail Accounts in the Gmail App

Open the Gmail App and Display the Add Account Dialog Box

1 Press **Home**.

The Home screen appears.

2 Tap **Google** (▨).

The Google folder opens.

3 Tap **Gmail** (M).

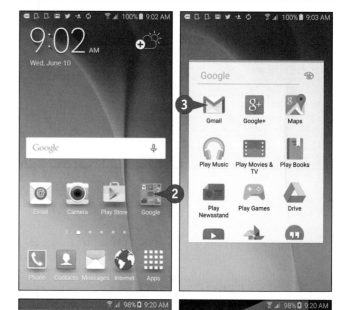

The Gmail app opens.

4 Tap **Menu** (≡).

The menu panel opens.

5 Tap the account name.

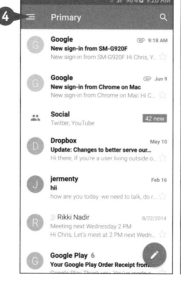
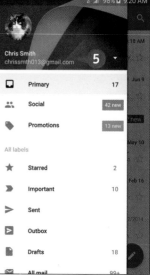

The account-management panel opens.

6 Tap **Add account** (+).

The Add Account dialog box opens.

7 Tap **Google** or **Personal (IMAP/ POP)** (○ changes to ◉), as needed, and then follow the instructions in the appropriate subsection.

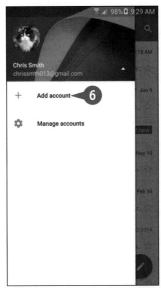

Add a Google Account

1 In the Add Account dialog box, tap **Google** (○ changes to ◉).

Note: Use the Google account type for both Gmail accounts and Google Apps accounts.

2 Tap **OK**.

The Add Account dialog box closes.

The Add Your Account screen appears.

3 Tap the **Enter your email** prompt and type your e-mail address.

4 Tap **Next**.

TIP

Which items should I sync with my Gmail account?
To get the most out of your Galaxy S6, it is usually helpful to sync most, if not all, of the items that appear on the Account Sign-in Successful screen. If you want to sync only essential items and not entertainment items, sync App Data, Calendar, Contacts, and Gmail with your account.

continued ▶

When setting up a POP3 account or an IMAP account, you may need to provide the hostnames of the incoming mail server and the outgoing mail server. You may also need to select the correct security type, the port number for the incoming server and outgoing server, and whether your e-mail app needs to sign in to the outgoing server. It is a good idea to ask your e-mail provider for this information before trying to set up your account.

Set Up Your E-Mail Accounts in the Gmail App (continued)

The Password screen appears.

5 Tap **Password** and type your password.

6 Tap **Next**.

The Terms of Service and Privacy Policy appear.

7 Tap **Accept** if you want to proceed.

The account-management panel appears, showing the new account.

Your Gmail account is now set up.

8 Tap the account in the accounts list.

A You can also tap the account's icon in the upper part of the menu panel.

The inbox for the account appears, and you can start working with messages.

Add an IMAP or POP Account

1 In the Add Account dialog box, tap **Personal (IMAP/POP)** (◯ changes to ◉).

2 Tap **OK**.

The Add Account dialog box closes.

The Email Account screen appears.

3 Tap **Email address** and type your e-mail address.

Ⓑ You can enter other widely used domain suffixes — such as .net or .edu — by tapping and holding the **.com** key and then tapping the appropriate domain suffix on the pop-up panel.

4 Tap **Next**.

The Account Type screen appears.

5 Tap **Personal (POP3)** for a POP3 account, or tap **Personal (IMAP)** for an IMAP account.

Note: See the tip for information about POP3 and IMAP.

The Sign In screen appears.

6 Tap **Password** and type your password.

7 Tap **Next**.

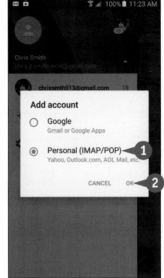

TIP

Should I choose Personal (POP3) or Personal (IMAP) for my e-mail account?

Ask your e-mail provider whether your account uses POP3 or IMAP. POP3 and IMAP are different technologies for incoming mail servers: POP3 is the Post Office Protocol, and IMAP is Internet Mail Access Protocol.

Some e-mail providers let you use either POP3 or IMAP for e-mail accounts. If your provider gives you this choice, it is best to use IMAP for an account that you access from multiple computers and devices.

continued ▶

The Gmail app can set up some accounts automatically after you provide the e-mail address and password: Gmail detects or looks up the servers for the address and applies suitable settings. If Gmail is unable to find the server names, it prompts you to provide them. Automatic setup is usually helpful, but for some accounts you may need to specify the servers manually. In such cases, you can tap the Manual Setup button instead of the Next button on the Email Account screen.

Set Up Your E-Mail Accounts in the Gmail App (continued)

The Incoming Server Settings screen appears.

8 If necessary, tap **Server** and edit the server name.

9 Tap **Security Type** and then tap the required security type.

10 Verify that the port number is correct. If not, change it.

Note: Select the security type before you change the port number, because Gmail automatically applies the default port for the security type you select.

11 Tap **Next**.

The Outgoing Server Settings screen appears.

12 If necessary, tap **SMTP server** and edit the name.

13 Tap **Security Type** and then tap the required security type.

14 Verify that the port number is correct. If not, change it.

15 Tap **Require signin** (☐ changes to ☑) if your e-mail provider requires you to sign in to the outgoing server.

16 Edit your username and password if necessary.

17 Tap **Next**.

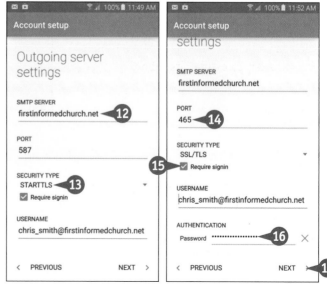

The Account Options screen appears.

Note: The options on the Account Options screen vary depending on the account type.

18 Tap **Sync frequency** and then tap the frequency, such as **Every 5 minutes**.

19 Tap **Notify me when email arrives** (☐ changes to ☑) to receive notifications.

20 Tap **Sync email from this account** (☐ changes to ☑) to sync this account.

21 Tap **Automatically download attachments when connected to Wi-Fi** (☐ changes to ☑) to download attachments via Wi-Fi.

22 Tap **Next**.

The Your Account Is Set Up and Email Is on Its Way! screen appears.

23 Type the descriptive name you want to see for this account.

24 Type your name as you want it to appear on messages you send.

25 Tap **Next**.

The account-management panel appears.

ⓒ You can tap the icon for the new account to display its inbox.

ⓓ Alternatively, you can tap the listing for the new account to display its inbox.

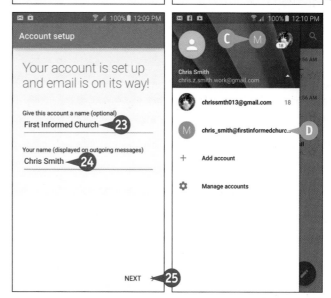

TIPS

Is there a disadvantage to choosing Automatic for the Inbox checking frequency?
The Automatic setting causes the Gmail app to use a technology called Push, in which the server notifies your device whenever new mail is available. Using Push, you receive your messages more quickly, but your device uses more battery power.

Is it a good idea to automatically download attachments when connected to Wi-Fi?
Yes. Downloading automatically when your device has a Wi-Fi connection helps you avoid downloading attachments over a cellular connection, which can quickly consume your data plan.

Choose Essential Settings for Gmail

The Gmail app provides a wide variety of settings that enable you to control your e-mail account closely. To get the most out of Gmail on your Galaxy S6, spend a few minutes exploring the settings that you can change and configuring them to suit your needs.

When customizing Gmail, start with the General settings category, which contains settings that apply to all your Gmail accounts. After that, move on to choose account-specific settings for each Gmail account.

Choose Essential Settings for Gmail

Display the Settings Screen

1 Press **Home**.

The Home screen appears.

2 Tap **Google** (⬚).

The Google folder opens.

3 Tap **Gmail** (M).

Your Inbox appears.

4 Tap **Menu** (≡).

The menu opens.

5 Tap **Settings** (⚙).

The Settings screen appears.

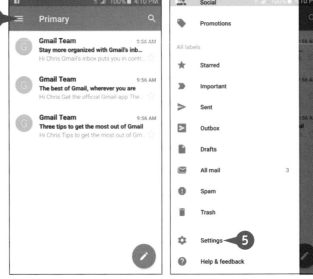

Choose General Settings

1 On the Settings screen, tap **General settings**.

The General Settings screen appears.

2 Tap **Conversation view** (☐ changes to ☑) to have the Gmail app group messages in the same conversation. This applies only to IMAP and POP3 accounts, not to Google accounts.

3 Tap **Swipe actions** (☐ changes to ☑) to enable swipe actions in the conversation list.

4 Tap **Sender image** (☐ changes to ☑) to display sender images in mailboxes.

5 Tap **Reply all** (☐ changes to ☑) if you want to use the Reply All action by default.

6 Tap **Gmail default action**.

The Default Action dialog box opens.

7 Tap **Archive** or **Delete** (◯ changes to ◉), as needed.

The Default Action dialog box closes.

8 Tap **Auto-fit messages** (☐ changes to ☑) to have Gmail shrink messages so that they fit on the screen. This is usually helpful.

9 Tap **Auto-advance**.

TIP

Should I turn on the Reply All option on the General Settings screen?

Not unless your company or organization mandates it. Turning on this option makes Gmail use Reply All as the default action for any message on which you were not the only recipient. The result is that you are much more likely to send a reply to all recipients when you intended to send it only to the message's sender.

continued ▶

Choose Settings in Gmail (continued)

You can choose to have the Gmail app confirm any or all of three actions: deleting messages, archiving messages, and sending messages. These confirmations are useful if you use your device anywhere you may get bumped or jostled, such as on public transit, or if your touch is unsure. The settings you can configure for an individual e-mail account depend on the account type, but most account types enable you to choose whether to receive notifications, download attachments via Wi-Fi, and show all images in messages.

Choose Settings in Gmail (continued)

The Advance To dialog box opens.

10 Tap **Newer**, **Older**, or **Conversation list** (○ changes to ◉), as needed.

The Advance To dialog box closes.

11 Tap **Confirm before deleting** (☐ changes to ☑) for confirmation before deleting messages.

12 Tap **Confirm before archiving** (☐ changes to ☑) for confirmation before archiving.

13 Tap **Confirm before sending** (☐ changes to ☑) for confirmation before sending.

14 Tap **Back** (⬅) or **Back** (↩).

The Settings screen appears.

Choose Account-Specific Settings

1 Tap the account you want to configure.

The account's settings screen opens.

Note: The settings available depend on the account type. This section shows the settings for a Gmail account.

2 Tap **Inbox type**.

The Inbox Type dialog box opens.

3 Tap **Default Inbox** (○ changes to ◉).

Note: Gmail offers two inbox types: Default Inbox and Priority Inbox. See the section "Set Up and Use Priority Inbox" later in this chapter for coverage of Priority Inbox.

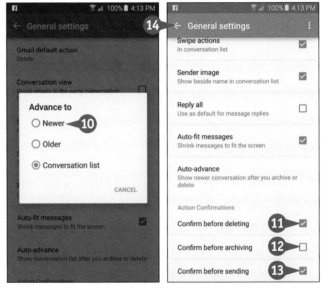

4 Tap **Notifications** (☐ changes to ✓) to receive notifications from this account in the status bar.

A You can tap **Signature** to create a signature for outgoing messages.

5 Tap **Inbox categories**.

The Inbox Categories screen appears.

6 Tap each category (☐ changes to ✓) you want to use in a Gmail account.

7 In the Starred Messages area, tap **Include in Primary** (☐ changes to ✓) to include starred messages in the Primary category.

8 Tap **Back** (◀) or **Back** (↰).

The account's settings screen appears.

B You can tap **Inbox sound & vibrate** and then choose sync, notification, and vibration settings on the Sync & Notify screen.

9 Tap **Download attachment**s (☐ changes to ✓) to download attachments automatically via Wi-Fi.

10 Tap **Images**.

The Images dialog box opens.

11 Tap **Always show** or **Ask before showing** (○ changes to ◉), as needed.

12 Tap **Back** (◀) or **Back** (↰).

The Settings screen appears.

13 Tap **Back** (◀) or **Back** (↰).

Your Inbox appears.

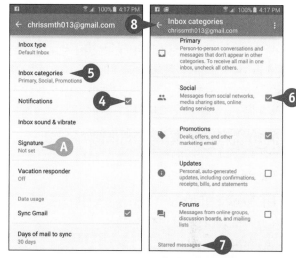

Remove an E-Mail Account

Sometimes you may need to remove an e-mail account from your Galaxy S6 — for example, because you no longer use the account. You can remove an account easily by using the Settings app. You can also start the process of removing the account directly from the account-management panel in the Gmail app. But because this approach also takes you to the Settings app, it is usually easier to go directly to the Settings app.

Remove an E-Mail Account

1 Press **Home**.

The Home screen appears.

2 Tap **Apps** (▦).

The Apps screen appears.

3 Tap **Settings** (⊙).

Note: If Settings (⊙) is not on the Apps screen that appears first, scroll left or right until you find Settings (⊙).

The Settings app opens.

4 In the Personal section, tap **Accounts** (⊙).

The Accounts screen appears.

5 Tap the account type you want to remove.

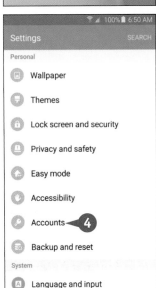

The account's screen appears.

6 Tap the account name.

The Sync Settings screen appears, showing the account's sync settings.

7 Tap **More**.

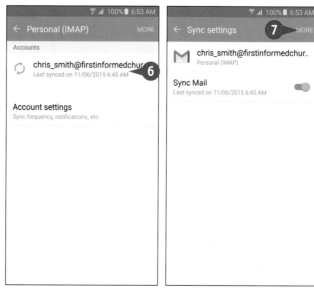

The menu opens.

8 Tap **Remove account**.

The Remove Account dialog box opens.

9 Tap **Remove Account**.

The Settings app removes the account.

The Settings screen appears.

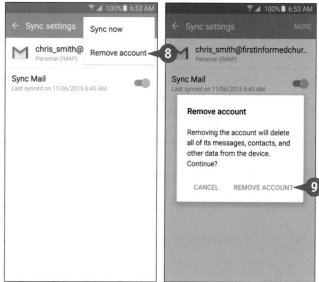

TIP

How can I stop an account from syncing without removing it from my device?

Press **Home** to display the Home screen, then tap **Apps** (▦) to display the Apps screen. Tap **Settings** (◯) to display the Settings screen, tap **Accounts** to display the Accounts screen, and then tap the account you want to affect. Tap the account's name to display the Sync Settings screen, and then set the switch for each item, such as the **Sync Mail** switch or the **Sync Contacts** switch, to Off (⬤ changes to ◯).

Set Up Your Signatures

To help complete your e-mail messages without having to type the same information repeatedly, you can create e-mail signatures. A *signature* is text, such as your name and contact information, that the app automatically adds to the end of each message you create.

Set Up Your Signatures

1 Press **Home**.

The Home screen appears.

2 Tap **Google** (▦).

The Google folder opens.

3 Tap **Gmail** (M).

Your Inbox appears.

4 Tap **Menu** (☰).

The menu panel appears.

5 Tap **Settings** (⚙).

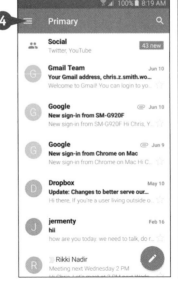

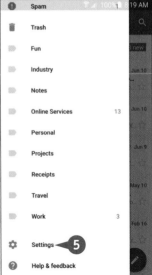

The Settings screen appears.

6 Tap the account for which you want to set up a signature.

The Settings screen for the account appears.

7 Tap **Signature**.

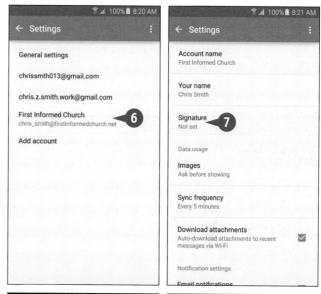

The Signature dialog box opens.

8 Type the text you want to use for the signature.

A Tap **Enter** (↵) to start a new line.

9 Tap **OK**.

The Signature dialog box closes.

10 Tap **Back** (◄) or **Back** (⊃).

The main Settings screen appears, and you can tap another account to set up a signature for it.

Note: E-mail convention is to keep signatures fairly short. Your signature might include your role or job title, contact information, and perhaps a pithy quote.

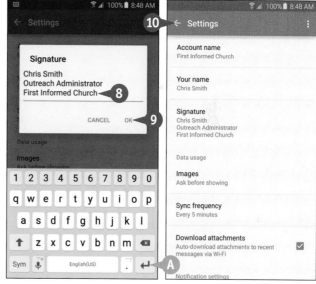

TIP

How do I create multiple signatures for the same account in Gmail?

As of this writing, you can create only one signature for an e-mail account. Instead, create text shortcuts to enter the components of the signature. Pull down from the top of the screen to open the Notification panel, then tap **Settings** (⊡). In the System section, tap **Language and input** (Ⓐ) to display the Language and Input screen, then tap **Samsung keyboard**. In the Smart Typing section, tap **Text shortcuts** to display the Text Shortcuts screen. You can then tap **Add** to open the Add Shortcut dialog box, type the shortcut in the Shortcut field, type the full phrase in the Expanded Phrase field, and tap **Add**.

Set Up and Use Priority Inbox

The Gmail app includes a feature called *Priority Inbox* that helps you to identify the messages that need your attention urgently. Priority Inbox is especially useful if you receive many e-mail messages. Priority Inbox works only for Google accounts.

Priority Inbox attempts to identify your important messages so that it can present them to you separately from your less important messages. To use Priority Inbox, you turn on the feature in Gmail's settings. You can then display Priority Inbox in Gmail and work through its contents.

Set Up and Use Priority Inbox

1. Press **Home**.

   The Home screen appears.

2. Tap **Google** (▦).

   The Google folder opens.

3. Tap **Gmail** (M).

   Your Inbox appears.

4. Tap **Menu** (≡).

   The menu panel opens.

5. Tap **Settings** (⚙).

   The Settings screen appears.

6. Tap the account for which you want to set up Priority Inbox.

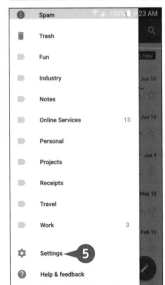

The settings screen for the account appears.

7 Tap **Inbox type**.

The Inbox Type dialog box opens.

8 Tap **Priority Inbox** (○ changes to ◉).

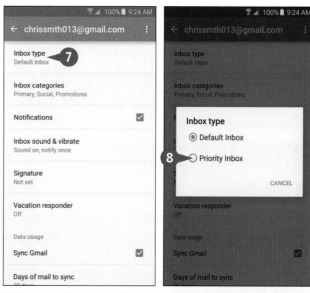

Options for configuring Priority Inbox appear.

9 Tap **Priority inbox sound & vibrate**.

The Label Settings screen appears.

10 Tap **Sound**, tap the sound in the Ringtones dialog box (○ changes to ◉), and then tap **OK**.

11 Tap **Vibrate** (☐ changes to ☑) to receive vibrations.

12 Tap **Notify for every message** (☐ changes to ☑) if you want notifications for each message.

13 Tap **Back** (←) or **Back** (↰) three times to return to your Inbox.

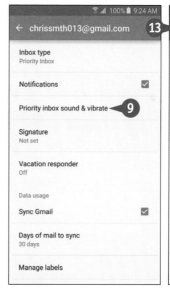

TIPS

How do I use Priority Inbox?

In Gmail, tap **Menu** (☰) and then tap **Priority Inbox**. If necessary, switch to another Google account by tapping the icons at the top of the menu panel.

How does Priority Inbox work?

Priority Inbox collects any messages in conversations you and Gmail have labeled as important. You can mark a message as important by tapping **Menu** (⋮) and then tapping **Mark important**. Gmail automatically labels messages as important for various reasons, such as messages from people you contact frequently. Even if Priority Inbox seems to be catching all your important messages, check your other messages in case any vital ones have ended up with your less-important messages.

Choose Which Contacts to Display

Your Galaxy S6's Contacts app enables you to manage your contacts, syncing contact data automatically from your Google account or other e-mail accounts. If you have many contacts, you may want to display only one group of them — for example, only your Facebook contacts or only your Corporate contacts. You can do this easily, but you can also create a custom display group that contains exactly the contacts you want to see.

Choose Which Contacts to Display

1 Press **Home.**

The Home screen appears.

2 Tap **Contacts** (👤).

A If Contacts (👤) does not appear on the Home screen, tap **Apps** (▦) and then tap **Contacts** (👤).

The Contacts app opens.

3 Tap **More.**

The menu opens.

4 Tap **Settings.**

The Contacts Settings screen appears.

5 Tap **Contacts to display.**

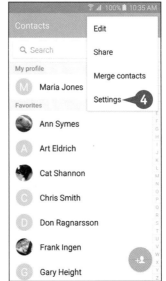

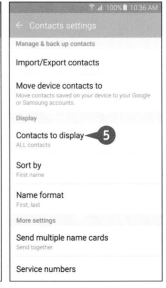

B To display an existing group, tap it (○ changes to ◉) and skip the remaining steps in this section.

6 To create a custom group of contacts, tap **Settings** (⚙).

7 Tap the heading of an account whose listing is collapsed (∨ changes to ∧).

The groups within the account appear.

8 Tap each group that you want to include (☐ changes to ☑).

9 Tap **Done**.

The Contacts Settings screen appears again.

10 Tap **Back** (◀) or **Back** (↰).

The Contacts screen appears, showing the contacts in the group that you chose.

C The Contacts in Custom View heading or Contacts in *Account* heading indicates which contacts are displayed.

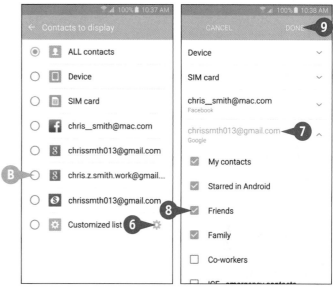

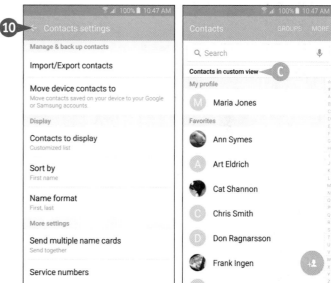

TIP

How do I display all my contacts again?

1 Follow steps **1** through **5** in the main text to show the Contacts to Display screen.

2 Tap **ALL contacts** (○ changes to ◉).

3 Tap **Back** (◀) or **Back** (↰) twice.

Import Your Contacts into the Contacts App

Your Galaxy S6 can sync contacts with your Google account or with other e-mail accounts that you set up, such as Exchange Server. But if you have contact data stored elsewhere, you will need to import it into the Contacts app. You can import contact information from vCard files, a widely used format. If you have the contacts stored on a SIM card that fits into your Galaxy S6, you can insert the SIM card and import the contacts from it.

Import Your Contacts into the Contacts App

Import Contacts Attached to an E-Mail Message

1. In the Gmail app, tap the message to open it.

2. Tap the attachment icon (📄).

Note: If the Open With dialog box opens, prompting you to choose the app with which to open the file, tap **Contacts** (👤) and then tap **Always**.

The Contacts app displays the contacts in the file.

3. Tap **Save**.

The Save Contact To dialog box opens.

4. Tap the account to which you want to add the contacts.

The Gmail app appears again.

Ⓐ Android imports the contacts to the account that you chose.

5. Tap **Back** (◄) or **Back** (↩).

Your Inbox appears.

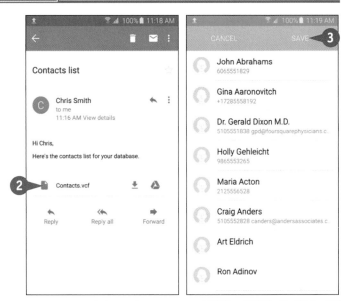

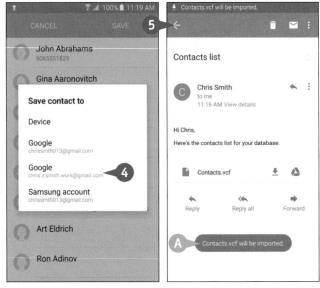

Import Contacts from a File

1 Copy the file to the Download folder on your Galaxy S6 using File Explorer, Android File Transfer, or another file-management app.

2 In the Contacts app, tap **More**.

The menu opens.

3 Tap **Settings**.

The Contacts Settings screen appears.

4 Tap **Import/Export contacts**.

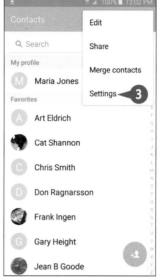

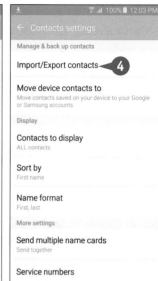

The Import/Export Contacts screen appears.

5 Tap **Import**.

The Import Contacts From dialog box opens.

6 Tap **Device storage**.

The Save Contact To dialog box opens.

7 Tap the account to which you want to save the contacts.

The Contacts app imports the contacts.

TIP

How do I create vCard files containing my contacts?

In Windows, first open the Contacts folder in a File Explorer or Windows Explorer window. Select the contacts to export and then click **Export** on the toolbar. In the Export Windows Contacts dialog box, click **vCards (folder of .vcf files)** and then click **Export**. On the Mac, click **Contacts** (■) if it appears on the Dock; otherwise, click **Launchpad** (●) on the Dock and then click **Contacts** (■) on the Launchpad screen. In the Contacts app, select the contacts to export and then drag them to the desktop or to a Finder window.

Choose S Planner Notifications and Reminders

The S Planner app helps you track your time commitments on your Galaxy S6. You can easily add your events to S Planner, send invitations to other people for meetings and shared appointments, and accept invitations to events other people create.

To help you remember your plans, S Planner can notify you of upcoming events by playing sounds, vibrating, and displaying pop-up messages. You can choose your notifications and control when they appear by working on the Settings screen for S Planner.

Choose S Planner Notifications and Reminders

1 Press **Home**.

The Home screen appears.

2 Tap **Apps** (▦).

The Apps screen appears.

Note: If S Planner (🗓) is not on the Apps screen that appears first, scroll right or left until you find it.

3 Tap **S Planner** (🗓).

The S Planner app opens.

4 Tap **More**.

The menu opens.

5 Tap **Settings**.

The Settings screen appears.

6 Tap **Notification**.

The Notification screen appears.

7 Set the **Notification** switch to On (changes to) to receive notifications. This is usually helpful.

8 Tap **Notification sound**.

The Notification Sound screen appears.

9 Tap the ringtone you want to hear (changes to).

10 When you have chosen your ringtone, tap **Back** (←) or **Back** (⤺).

The Notification screen appears again.

11 Set the **Vibration** switch to On (changes to) if you want your Galaxy S6 to vibrate when S Planner raises a notification.

12 Tap **Back** (←) or **Back** (⤺).

The S Planner Settings screen appears.

13 Tap **Back** (←) or **Back** (⤺).

The S Planner screen appears.

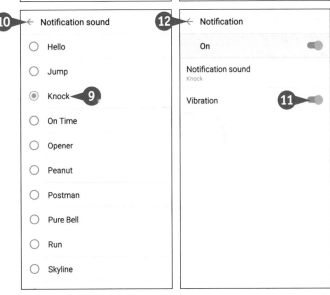

TIP

What does the 7-Day Weather Forecast command do?

The 7-Day Weather Forecast command makes S Planner display a weather symbol on the next seven days indicating the daily weather forecast for those days. Using this feature requires S Planner to share your location with the source of the weather information — as you would most likely expect.

Choose Week and Time Zone Settings

S Planner enables you to choose whether to display the week number in the year — from Week 1 to Week 52 — for reference. You can also choose which day to use as the start of the week: Saturday, Sunday, Monday, or the default for the locale you are using.

If you travel to different time zones, you may need to specify in which time zone S Planner should show event dates and times. Otherwise, S Planner uses your current location's time zone for your events.

Choose Week and Time Zone Settings

① Press **Home**.

The Home screen appears.

② Tap **Apps** (⊞).

The Apps screen appears.

Note: If S Planner (🗓) is not on the Apps screen that appears first, scroll right or left until you find it.

③ Tap **S Planner** (🗓).

The S Planner app opens.

④ Tap **More**.

The menu opens.

⑤ Tap **Settings**.

The Settings screen appears.

6 Set the **Show week numbers** switch to On (changes to) if you want to display the week numbers.

7 Tap **First day of week**.

The pop-up menu opens.

8 Tap the appropriate option, such as **Monday**.

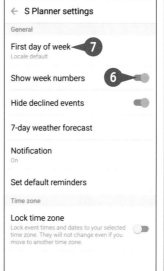

9 Set the **Lock time zone** switch to On (changes to) if you want to lock your event times and dates to a particular time zone.

10 Tap **Select time zone**.

The Time Zone screen appears.

11 Tap the time zone you need.

The Settings screen appears again.

12 Tap **Back** (←) or **Back** (↰).

The S Planner screen appears.

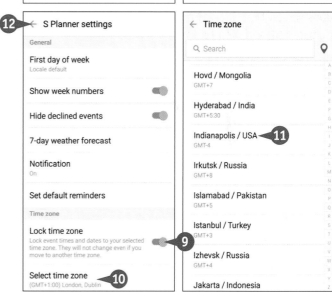

TIP

What does the Hide Declined Events option do?
Set the **Hide declined events** switch to On (changes to) if you want to prevent events to which you were invited but you declined from appearing in your calendar. Depending on your business life and social life, you may find it helpful to see those events you have declined as well as those you have accepted; if so, set the **Hide declined events** switch to Off (changes to).

CHAPTER 5

Networking and Communicating

Your Galaxy S6 can connect to cellular networks, wireless networks, and wireless hotspots. It can also connect via Bluetooth, transfer data wirelessly using the Android Beam and S Beam features, and make payments using the Tap and Pay feature.

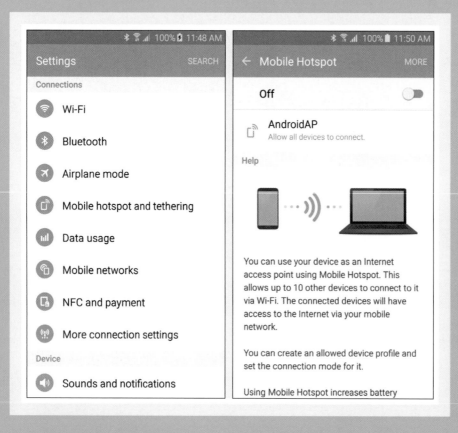

Control Wi-Fi, Bluetooth, and Cellular Access 114

Connect Bluetooth Devices 116

Control Data Roaming and Cellular Usage 118

Connect to a Wi-Fi Direct Device 120

Using USB Tethering 122

Using Mobile Hotspot 124

Manage Your Wireless Networks. 128

Log In to Wi-Fi Hotspots 130

Transfer Data Using Android Beam 132

Make Payments with Tap and Pay 134

Control Wi-Fi, Bluetooth, and Cellular Access

Your Galaxy S6 can connect to cellular networks, Wi-Fi networks, and Bluetooth devices. When you do not need or may not use the cellular network, you can turn on Airplane Mode to cut off all connections. Turning on Airplane Mode turns off Wi-Fi and Bluetooth connections as well, but you can also turn Wi-Fi and Bluetooth on and off independently when necessary.

Control Wi-Fi, Bluetooth, and Cellular Access

Turn On Airplane Mode

1 Pull down from the top of the screen.

The Notification panel opens.

2 Scroll the Quick Settings buttons left.

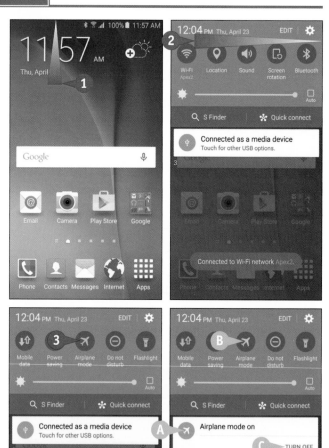

3 Tap **Airplane mode** (✈ changes to ✈).

A The *Airplane mode on* notification appears.

B You can turn Airplane Mode off by tapping **Airplane mode** (✈ changes to ✈).

C You can also turn Airplane Mode off by tapping **Turn Off** in the *Airplane mode on* notification.

Turn On Wi-Fi

D When Airplane Mode is on, the Airplane mode icon (✈) appears in the status bar.

1 Pull down from the top of the screen.

The Notification panel appears.

2 Tap **Wi-Fi** (📶).

Your Galaxy S6 turns Wi-Fi on (📶 changes to 📶) and connects to a known Wi-Fi network if one is available.

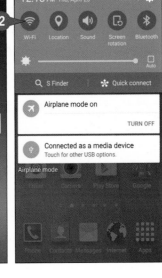

Turn On Bluetooth

E When Wi-Fi is on, the Wi-Fi icon (📶) appears in the status bar.

1 Pull down from the top of the screen.

The Notification panel appears.

2 Tap **Bluetooth** (❋ changes to ❋).

Your Galaxy S6 turns on Bluetooth.

Note: When Bluetooth is on, the Bluetooth icon (❋) appears in the status bar.

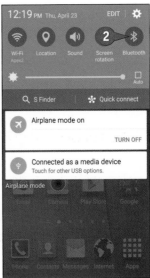

TIPS

When should I use Airplane Mode?
Airplane Mode is designed for use on airplanes, but you can also use it any other time you want to take your Galaxy S6 offline, such as in movie theaters or during important meetings.

Should I turn Bluetooth on or leave it off?
Turn Bluetooth on when you want to use Bluetooth devices with your Galaxy S6. If you use Bluetooth devices frequently, leave Bluetooth on. Otherwise, turn Bluetooth off to save battery power and avoid unintentional Bluetooth connections.

Connect Bluetooth Devices

Your Galaxy S6 enables you to extend its functionality by connecting devices that communicate using the wireless Bluetooth technology. Bluetooth is a networking protocol that is limited to short distances — typically up to about 30 feet — and modest transfer speeds. For example, you can connect a Bluetooth headset and microphone so that you can listen to audio and make and take phone calls. Alternatively, you can connect a Bluetooth keyboard so that you can quickly type e-mail messages, notes, or documents.

Connect Bluetooth Devices

1 Pull down from the top of the screen.

The Notification panel opens.

2 Tap and hold **Bluetooth** (🔵 or 🔵).

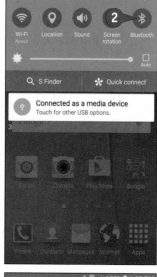

The Bluetooth screen appears.

3 If the **Bluetooth** switch is set to Off (⚪), set it to On (⚪ changes to 🔵).

Ⓐ By default, your Galaxy S6 is visible to other Bluetooth devices while Bluetooth is turned on and you are working on the Bluetooth screen.

4 Turn on the Bluetooth device and make it visible.

5 Tap **Scan**.

The Available Devices list shows available Bluetooth devices.

6 Tap the device to which you want to connect.

Note: When connecting a keyboard, type the code shown in the Bluetooth Pairing Request dialog box.

Your Galaxy S6 pairs with the device, and the device moves to the Paired Devices list.

7 Tap **Settings** (⚙) for the device.

The Paired Device screen appears.

8 In the Use For section, set the switch for each option you want to use to On (⬜ changes to ⬤).

B You can tap **Unpair** if you want to remove the device's pairing.

9 Tap **Rename**.

The Rename dialog box opens.

10 Type a descriptive name that will help you identify the device.

11 Tap **Rename**.

The device receives the new name.

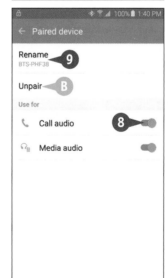

What else can I do with Bluetooth?
You can connect your Galaxy S6 to a Bluetooth-enabled computer or another Bluetooth-enabled device so you can transfer files from one to the other. File transfer via Bluetooth is slow compared to Wi-Fi, but it can be handy if the files are not too large.

Where do I find the files I receive via Bluetooth?
Pull down from the top of the screen to open the Notification panel, and then tap the File Received notification for a file. The Inbound Transfers screen appears, showing the files you have received.

Control Data Roaming and Cellular Usage

Your Galaxy S6 has a data-roaming feature that enables you to access the Internet using carriers other than your regular cellular carrier. With data roaming, you can use your Galaxy S6 in a location where your carrier does not provide Internet service. Using data roaming may incur extra charges, especially when you use it in a different country, so you would normally keep data roaming turned off and turn it on only when you need it.

Control Data Roaming and Cellular Usage

1 Pull down from the top of the screen.

The Notification panel opens.

2 Tap **Settings** (⚙).

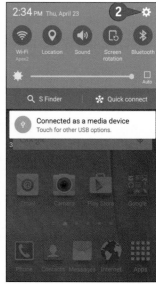

The Settings screen appears.

3 Tap **Mobile Networks** (🕸).

The Mobile Networks screen appears.

4 Set the **Data roaming** switch to On (changes to).

5 Tap **Back** (⬅) or **Back** (⤶).

The Settings screen appears.

6 Tap **Data usage** (📊).

The Data Usage screen appears.

Ⓐ Your data usage for the selected period appears.

7 Set the **Mobile data** switch to On (◯● changes to ●◯) to enable mobile data.

8 Set the **Set mobile data limit** switch to On (◯● changes to ●◯).

The Limit Data Usage dialog box opens.

9 Tap **OK**.

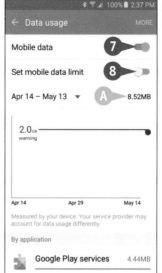

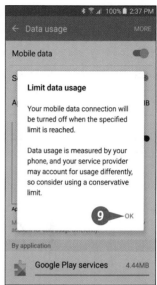

10 Drag the red **Limit** handle (🔴) up or down to set the limit.

11 Drag the black **Warning** handle (⚫) up or down to set the warning level.

12 In the By Application section, tap an app.

The app's Application Data Usage screen appears.

Ⓑ You can examine the *Foreground* and *Background* readouts.

Ⓒ You can set the **Restrict background data** switch to On (◯● changes to ●◯) to prevent the app from using background data.

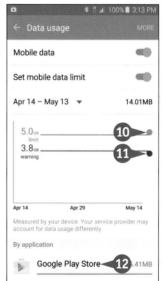

What is background data and why might I turn it off?
Background data is data an app transfers when it is in the background and you are not using it — for example, the Gmail app synchronizing your e-mail while you are using another app in the foreground. You might turn off background data to protect your cellular data allowance from surreptitious predation.

How can I turn off cellular data altogether?
On the Data Usage screen, set the **Mobile data** switch to Off (●◯ changes to ◯●) and then tap **OK** in the Mobile Data dialog box. If you exhaust your cellular data allowance, you might want to turn off cellular data until the start of the next billing period.

Connect to a Wi-Fi Direct Device

Your Galaxy S6 supports the Wi-Fi Direct standard for establishing wireless devices directly instead of connecting through a wireless access point. You can quickly connect your Galaxy S6 to another Wi-Fi Direct–enabled device, such as a tablet, and share data or transfer files.

Wi-Fi Direct in effect turns one of the devices into a miniature access point for the wireless network. Your Galaxy S6 can connect to multiple devices simultaneously via Wi-Fi Direct.

Connect to a Wi-Fi Direct Device

Connect to Another Wi-Fi Direct Device

1 Pull down from the top of the screen.

The Notification panel opens.

2 Tap and hold **Wi-Fi** (📶).

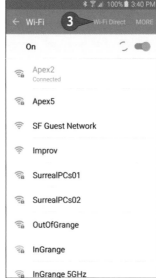

The Wi-Fi screen appears.

3 Tap **Wi-Fi Direct**.

The Wi-Fi Direct screen appears.

Your Galaxy S6 automatically scans for other Wi-Fi Direct devices.

4 Start Wi-Fi Direct on the device to which you want to connect.

Note: If your Galaxy S6 stops scanning before Wi-Fi Direct is ready on the other device, tap **Scan** to scan again.

5 Tap the device to which you want to connect.

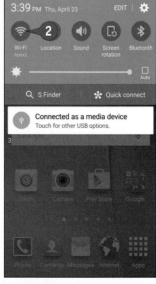

120

Your Galaxy S6 establishes the connection.

6 Share files with the other device.

Note: For example, open a photo, tap **Share** (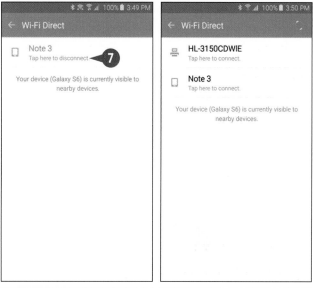), and then tap **Wi-Fi Direct** (⊚) in the Share panel.

7 When you finish using Wi-Fi Direct, tap **Tap here to disconnect**.

Your Galaxy S6 ends the connection.

You can establish another connection or tap **Back** (⬅) or **Back** (⤺) to go back to the Wi-Fi screen.

Accept a Wi-Fi Direct Connection from Another Device

1 Go to the Wi-Fi Direct screen.

When you receive a request for a connection, the Invitation to Connect dialog box opens.

2 Tap **Connect**.

Settings establishes the connection.

3 When you finish using Wi-Fi Direct, tap **Tap here to disconnect**.

Your Galaxy S6 ends the connection.

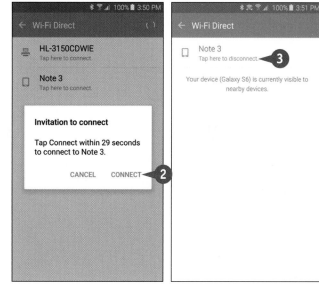

TIP

How else can I connect to other devices wirelessly?
You can also connect by using the Quick Connect feature, explained in the section "Play Music Through Other Devices" in Chapter 11, and by using the Android Beam feature, covered in the section "Transfer Data Using Android Beam" later in this chapter.

Using USB Tethering

Your Galaxy S6 can share its cellular connection with your computer or other devices. You can connect a single computer to your Galaxy S6 via USB tethering to share the phone's connection. Alternatively, you can turn your Galaxy S6 into a mobile Wi-Fi hotspot, as discussed in the following section, "Using Mobile Hotspot," or use Bluetooth tethering to share the connection with multiple devices.

Using USB Tethering

Turn Tethering On or Off

1. Connect your Galaxy S6 to your computer via USB.

2. Pull down from the top of the screen.

   The Notification panel opens.

3. Tap **Settings** (⚙).

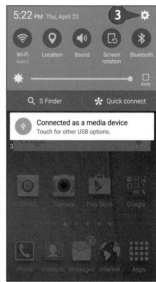

The Settings screen appears.

4. In the Connections section, tap **Mobile hotspot and tethering** (⚙).

   The Mobile Hotspot and Tethering screen appears.

5. Set the **USB tethering** switch to On (changes to).

A. The *Tethering or hotspot active* message appears in the status bar.

   Your computer starts using your Galaxy S6's Internet connection across the USB cable.

Note: Windows usually picks up the Internet connection seamlessly, but you may need to set a Mac to use the connection, as explained in the next subsection.

6. Press **Home**.

The Home screen appears.

Ⓑ The Tethering or Hotspot Active icon (🔱) appears in the status bar.

❼ When you are ready to turn off USB tethering, pull down from the top of the screen.

The Notification panel appears.

❽ Tap **Tethering or hotpot active**.

The Tethering and Wi-Fi Hotspot screen appears.

❾ Set the **USB tethering** switch to Off (⚫━ changes to ━⚫).

Set Your Mac to Use a Tethered Connection

❶ On your Mac, Control+click **System Preferences** (⚙) on the Dock.

The contextual menu opens.

❷ Click **Network**.

The System Preferences window opens, showing the Network preferences pane.

❸ In the left pane, click your Galaxy S6.

❹ Click **Apply** if the button is active rather than dimmed and unavailable.

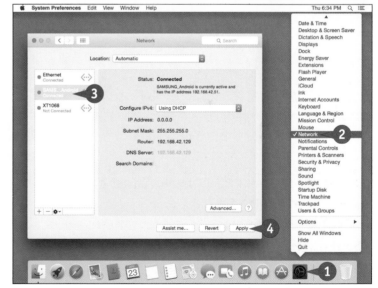

TIP

Why does my Galaxy S6 not appear in Network preferences on my Mac?

You may need to install a driver, a piece of software that enables your Mac to use the USB connection on your Galaxy S6. The HoRNDIS driver available at http://joshuawise.com/horndis enables OS X to use your Galaxy S6 this way.

To install HoRNDIS, you must allow apps downloaded from anywhere. Click **System Preferences** (⚙) on the Dock, click **Security & Privacy**, click **General**, and then click **Anywhere** in the Allow Applications Downloaded From area. You may need to click the lock icon and type your password to make these changes.

Using Mobile Hotspot

When your Galaxy S6 has a connection to the cellular network, you can use the Mobile Hotspot feature to share that Internet access with your computer and other devices. In order for your phone to use Mobile Hotspot, your cellular carrier must permit it. Many carriers charge an extra monthly fee for using your phone as a mobile hotspot, so before you try it, read your carrier's policy and be careful not to exceed your cellular data allowance.

Using Mobile Hotspot

1 Pull down from the top of the screen.

The Notification panel appears.

2 Tap **Settings** (⚙).

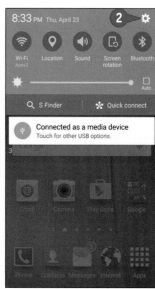

The Settings screen appears.

3 Tap **Mobile hotspot and tethering** (📱).

The Mobile Hotspot and Tethering screen appears.

4 Tap **Mobile Hotspot.**

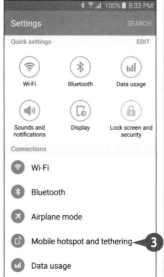

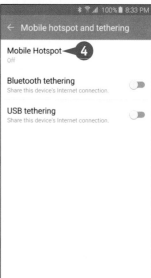

The Mobile Hotspot screen appears.

5 Tap **More**.

The More menu opens.

6 Tap **Allowed devices**.

The Allowed Devices screen appears.

7 Tap **Add**.

The Add to Allowed Devices dialog box opens.

8 Tap **Device name** and type the name for the device.

9 Tap **MAC address** and type the Media Access Control (MAC) address of the device's wireless network adapter.

Note: The MAC address is six pairs of hexadecimal (0–9, A–F) characters, separated by colons or hyphens, such as f8:a9:d0:82:4b:5a.

10 Tap **OK**.

The Add to Allowed Devices dialog box closes.

11 Tap **Back** (⬅) or **Back** (↩).

TIP

How do I find the MAC address for a device?

On Windows, right-click **Start**, click **Command Prompt**, type **ipconfig /all** and press Enter, and then look at the *Physical Address* readout for the wireless adapter.

On the Mac, Option +click **Wi-Fi** (🛜) on the menu bar and look at the *Address* readout.

On iOS, tap **Settings** (⚙), tap **General** (⚙), tap **About**, and look at the *Wi-Fi Address* readout.

On Android, tap **Apps** (▦), tap **Settings** (⚙), tap **About phone** or **About tablet** (ⓘ), tap **Status**, and then look at the *Wi-Fi MAC Address* readout.

continued ▶

While it is possible to simply turn on Mobile Hotspot using its default network name, AndroidAP, and no security, you will normally want to change the hotspot's name and implement security. By giving the hotspot a distinctive name, you can differentiate it from other Android-based hotspots that use default settings. By implementing security, you can limit hotspot use to people and devices you intend to use it.

Using Mobile Hotspot (continued)

The Mobile Hotspot screen appears.

⑫ Tap **More**.

The More menu opens.

⑬ Tap **Configure Mobile Hotspot**.

The Configure Mobile Hotspot dialog box opens.

⑭ Tap **Network name** and type the name you want to use.

Ⓐ You can tap **Hide my device** (☐ changes to ☑) to hide the wireless hotspot.

⑮ Tap **Security** and tap the security method, such as WPA2 PSK.

⑯ Tap **Password** and type the password.

⑰ Tap **Save**.

The Configure Mobile Hotspot dialog box closes.

⑱ Tap **More**.

The More menu opens.

⑲ Tap **Timeout settings**.

The Timeout Settings dialog box opens.

⑳ Tap the timeout interval you want, such as **20 minutes** (◯ changes to ◉).

The Timeout Settings dialog box closes.

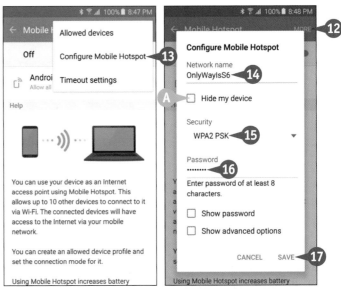

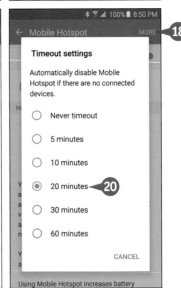

21 Tap the hotspot's button.

The pop-up menu opens.

22 Tap **Allow all devices** or **Allowed devices only**, as needed.

23 Set the **Mobile Hotspot** switch to On (⚪ changes to ⚫).

The Attention dialog box opens, warning you that turning on Mobile Hotspot will turn off Wi-Fi.

24 Tap **OK**.

Android turns on Mobile Hotspot.

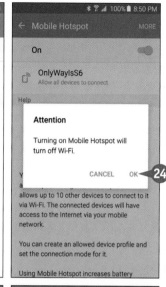

Ⓑ The *Tethering or hotspot active* readout appears briefly in the status bar.

Ⓒ The Mobile Hotspot Active icon (📶) appears in the status bar while Mobile Hotspot is on.

Ⓓ Connected devices appear in the Connected Devices list.

Ⓔ You can tap **Add** (➕) to open the Add to Allowed Devices dialog box with the device's MAC address already entered. You can then type the device name and tap **OK**.

25 When you need to turn Mobile Hotspot off, set the **Mobile Hotspot** switch to Off (⚫ changes to ⚪).

TIP

Why would I use the Hide My Device option?

You can select **Hide my device** (☐ changes to ☑) to prevent Mobile Hotspot from broadcasting the network name. This means that anyone connecting a device to the network must provide the network name.

Hiding the network provides only marginal security, because anybody using a network scanner can detect the network. If you need to prevent unauthorized access, secure the hotspot with a strong password and allow only specific devices by MAC address.

Manage Your Wireless Networks

To conserve your cellular data allowance, you should use wireless networks whenever possible. Your Galaxy S6 can connect both to wireless networks that broadcast their network names and to *closed* networks, ones that do not broadcast their names. Your Galaxy S6 can switch automatically between Wi-Fi networks and cellular networks.

The first time you connect to a Wi-Fi network, you provide the network's password. Your Galaxy S6 then stores the password for future connections.

Manage Your Wireless Networks

Connect to an Open Wireless Network

1 Pull down from the top of the screen.

The Notification panel opens.

2 If Wi-Fi is off (![icon]), tap **Wi-Fi** (![icon] changes to ![icon]).

3 Tap and hold **Wi-Fi** (![icon]).

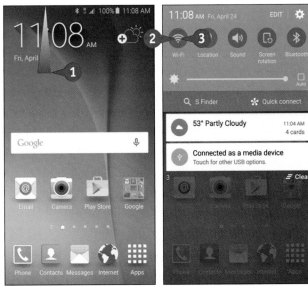

The Wi-Fi screen appears.

4 Tap the network to which you want to connect.

Note: If the network has no password, your Galaxy S6 connects to it without prompting you for one.

A dialog box for connecting to the network opens.

5 Type the password.

Ⓐ You can tap **Show password** (☐ changes to ☑) to view the password.

6 Tap **Connect**.

Your Galaxy S6 connects to the network.

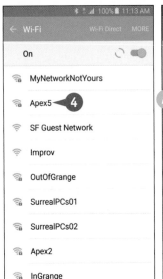

Connect to a Closed Wireless Network

1 On the Wi-Fi screen, tap **More**.

The More menu opens.

2 Tap **Add network**.

The Add Network dialog box opens.

3 Tap **Network name** and type the network name.

4 Tap **Security** and select the security type, such as **WPA/WPA2/FT PSK**.

5 Tap **Password** and type the password.

6 Tap **Connect**.

Your Galaxy S6 connects to the network.

Make Your Galaxy S6 Forget a Wireless Network

1 On the Wi-Fi screen, tap the network's name.

A dialog box opens. The dialog box's title bar shows the network's name.

2 Tap **Forget**.

Your Galaxy S6 forgets the network.

Note: After telling your Galaxy S6 to forget a network, you can join the network again, but you will need to enter its password.

TIP

What is Smart Network Switch, and should I use it?

Smart Network Switch is a feature that enables your Galaxy S6 to switch automatically to a cellular connection if the Wi-Fi connection becomes unstable or disappears. When your Galaxy S6 is using a patchy or intermittent Wi-Fi connection and you can afford to use your cellular connection instead, turn on Smart Network Switch by tapping **More** on the Wi-Fi screen, tapping **Smart network switch** on the More menu, and then tapping **On** (○ changes to ◉) in the Smart Network Switch dialog box. When you are using a reliable Wi-Fi network, it is best to keep Smart Network Switch turned off.

Log In to Wi-Fi Hotspots

hen you are in town or on the road, you can log in to Wi-Fi hotspots to enjoy fast Internet access without using your Galaxy S6's data allowance. You can find Wi-Fi hotspots at many locations, including coffee shops and restaurants, hotels, airports, municipal areas, and even parks and highway rest stops.

Some Wi-Fi hotspots charge for access, whereas others are free. If you travel extensively, sign up for a plan that provides long-term access to Wi-Fi hotspots.

Log In to Wi-Fi Hotspots

1 Pull down from the top of the screen.

The Notification panel opens.

2 If Wi-Fi is off (📶), tap **Wi-Fi** (📶 changes to 📶).

3 Tap and hold **Wi-Fi** (📶).

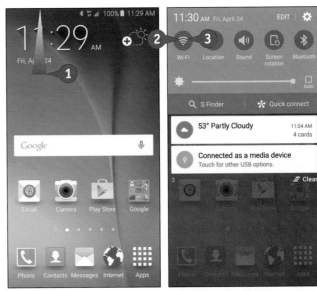

The Wi-Fi screen appears.

4 Tap the network to which you want to connect.

5 Tap **Connect**.

Your Galaxy S6 connects to the network.

6 Press **Home**.

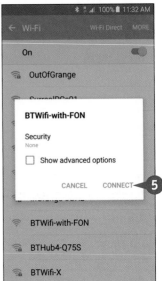

The Home screen appears.

7 Tap **Internet** (🌐).

The Internet app opens and displays a login page for the hotspot.

8 Type the login information.

9 Tap the button for logging in.

Your Galaxy S6 logs in to the hotspot, and you can begin using the Internet connection.

10 When you finish using the hotspot, pull down from the top of the screen.

The Notification panel opens.

11 Tap and hold **Wi-Fi** (🛜).

The Wi-Fi screen appears.

12 Tap the wireless network's name.

The network's dialog box opens.

13 Tap **Forget**.

Your Galaxy S6 forgets the network.

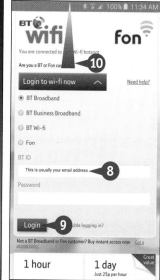

TIP

What precautions should I take when using Wi-Fi hotspots?

The main danger is that you may connect to a malevolent network. To stay safe, connect only to hotspots provided by reputable establishments — for example, national hotel chains or restaurant chains — and avoid hotspots run by unknown operators. Even then, it is best not to transmit any private information that may interest eavesdroppers. An attacker can create a malevolent hotspot that mimics a real hotspot, causing your device to connect to the wrong hotspot and compromising its security.

Transfer Data Using Android Beam

Android includes a feature called *Android Beam* that enables you to transfer files wirelessly between your Galaxy S6 and other Android devices. Android Beam uses a technology called *Near Field Communications* (NFC), which allows NFC-enabled smartphones and tablets to automatically establish a radio connection when you bring them to within a few inches of each other. NFC is great for sharing contacts, photos, and other data quickly and effortlessly.

Transfer Data Using Android Beam

Turn On Android Beam

1 Pull down from the top of the screen.

The Notification panel opens.

2 Tap **Settings** ().

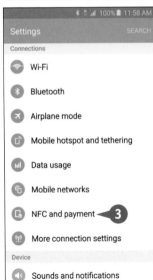

The Settings app opens.

3 In the Connections section, tap **NFC and payment** ().

The NFC and Payment screen appears.

4 Tap **NFC.**

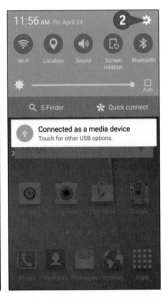

The NFC screen appears.

5 Set the **NFC** switch to On (changes to).

6 Tap **Back** ( ) or **Back** ( ).

The NFC and Payment screen appears.

7 If you need to set the default NFC payment method, tap **More** and then tap **Advanced NFC Settings**.

The Advanced NFC Settings screen appears.

8 Tap **SE SIM card**, **Android operating system**, or **Embedded Secure Element** (changes to), as needed.

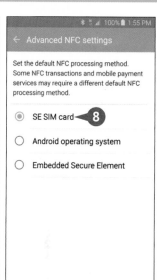

Send a File via Android Beam

1 Open the app that contains the file you want to transfer.

Note: This example uses a photo in the Gallery app.

2 Bring your Galaxy S6 back-to-back with the other NFC-enabled Android phone or tablet.

The *Touch to Beam* prompt appears.

3 Tap **Touch to beam**.

Ⓐ Your Galaxy S6 sends the file.

Touch to beam.

Beaming content...

TIPS

Why can't my Galaxy S6 connect to another Android device via Android Beam?

If you have turned on NFC and enabled Android Beam on both devices, most likely you have not brought the NFC chips close enough to each other. Hold your Galaxy S6 back-to-back with the other device and move it around the other device until both devices vibrate. Android Beam should then work.

What happens when my Galaxy S6 receives data via Android Beam?

Your Galaxy S6 accepts the data, but it may prompt you to decide where to store it. For example, if the Contacts app receives a contact, it may prompt you to choose the account in which to place that contact.

Make Payments with Tap and Pay

The Tap and Pay feature enables you to make payments quickly and easily by bringing your Galaxy S6 into contact with a payment terminal. Tap and Pay uses the NFC chip in your Galaxy S6 to communicate with the payment terminal. Before you can make payments with Tap and Pay, you must install a payment service app, such as Google Wallet; turn on NFC; and select your payment service app.

Install Google Wallet

Unless you have installed another payment service app, start by installing Google Wallet. Press **Home**, tap **Play Store** ( ), and then tap **Apps** on the Google Play home screen. Tap **Search** ( ), type **google wallet**, and then tap **Search** ( ) on the keyboard. Tap the Google Wallet search result, and then tap **Install**. Review the permissions the app requires — they are necessarily extensive — and then tap **Accept** if you want to proceed. Android downloads and installs Google Wallet. You can then open the app either by tapping **Open** on its screen in the Play Store app or by tapping **Wallet** ( ) on the Apps screen.

Configure Google Wallet

The first time you open Google Wallet, you must configure it. First, you create a four-digit Wallet PIN to protect your wallet. Next, you must agree to the Google Wallet Terms of Service and the Privacy Notice; read both carefully, preferably on a larger screen than that of your Galaxy S6. When the main Google Wallet screen appears, tap **Set up tap and pay**, tap **Accept** in the Terms of Use dialog box, and then follow the prompts to add a credit card to pay for your Google Wallet purchases.

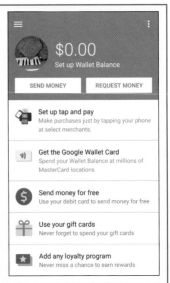

Turn On NFC

After installing Google Wallet, turn on NFC on your Galaxy S6. To do so, pull down from the top of the screen to open the Notification panel, tap **Settings** (⚙), and then tap **NFC and payment** (🔘) in the Connections section. On the NFC and Payment screen, tap **NFC** to display the NFC screen. Set the **NFC** switch to On (⚪ changes to ●). Tap **Back** (⬅) or **Back** (↩) and verify that the Tap and Pay button on the NFC and Payment screen appears in regular dark type instead of being dimmed and unavailable. Leave the NFC and Payment screen displayed for now.

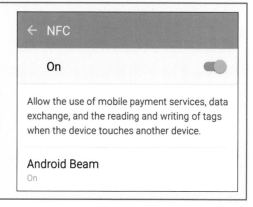

Set Up Your Tap and Pay Method

Still on the NFC and Payment screen, tap **Tap and pay** to display the Tap and Pay screen. Tap **Google Wallet** (⚪ changes to ●) to use Google Wallet for Tap and Pay payments; unless you have multiple payment service apps installed, Google Wallet will already be selected.

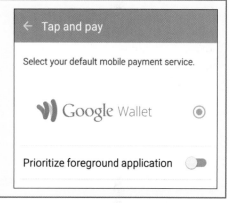

Make Payments with Your Galaxy S6

Now that you have set up Google Wallet and configured Tap and Pay to use as your default mobile payment service, you can make payments by bringing the back of your Galaxy S6 to the contact area on a payment terminal.

When the NFC chips make contact, a tone sounds. Your Galaxy S6 then displays details of the transaction and prompts you to confirm it — for example, by placing your finger on the Home button so that it can verify your fingerprint.

CHAPTER 6

Phoning, Messaging, and Social Networking

Your Galaxy S6 not only enables you to make phone calls anywhere, including easy conference calls, but also to send and receive text messages and multimedia messages, and to enjoy social networking via services such as Google+, Facebook, and Twitter.

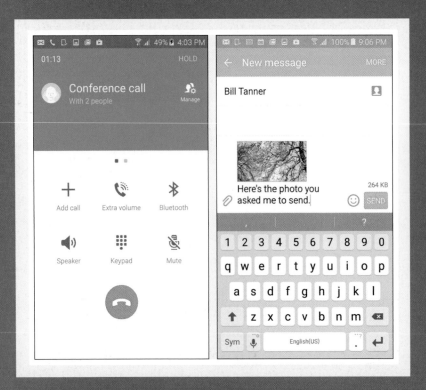

Make Phone Calls. 138

Make a Conference Call 140

Call Using Call Logs and Frequently Contacted 142

Send and Receive Instant Messages 144

Manage Your Instant Messages 146

Set Up Google+ 148

Navigate Google+ 150

Using Facebook and Twitter. 152

Make Phone Calls

Your Galaxy S6 enables you to make phone calls anywhere you have a connection to the cellular network. You can make a phone call by dialing the phone number using the keypad, but you can place calls more easily by tapping the appropriate phone number for a contact or by using your call logs. When you need other people near you to be able to hear both ends of the phone call you are making, you can turn on the speaker.

Make Phone Calls

Open the Phone App

1 Press **Home**.

The Home screen appears.

2 Tap **Phone** (📞).

The Phone app opens and displays the screen you used last, such as Contacts.

Note: You can also place a call quickly to a phone number Android has identified. For example, you can tap an underlined phone number that represents a link on a web page.

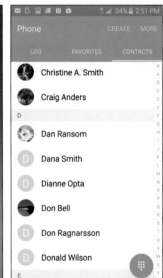

Dial a Call Using the Keypad

1 Tap **Keypad** (⌗).

The Keypad screen appears.

2 Tap the number keys to dial the number.

A You can tap **Add to Contacts** to add this phone number to your contacts.

B You can tap **More** and then tap **Add 2-sec pause (;)** or **Add wait (,)**.

3 Tap **Dial** (📞).

Your Galaxy S6 places the call.

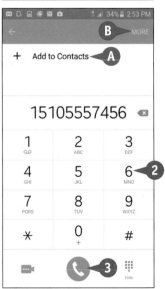

Dial a Call to a Contact

1 Tap **Contacts**.

The Contacts list appears.

2 Tap the contact you want to call.

The contact's details open.

3 Tap **Call** (📞) for the phone number you want to call.

Your Galaxy S6 places the call.

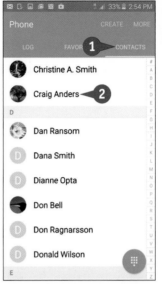

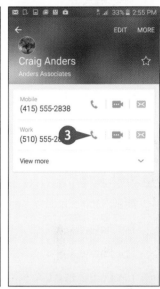

End a Phone Call

1 Tap **End Call** (📞).

Your Galaxy S6 ends the call.

C The *Call ended* message appears for a moment.

Your Galaxy S6 then displays the screen from which you placed the call — for example, the Contacts screen.

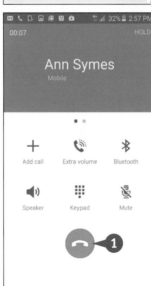

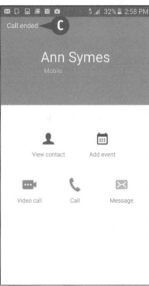

TIP

Can I use my Galaxy S6 as a speakerphone?

Yes. Tap **Speaker** (🔊 changes to 🔊) on the control panel that appears while you are making a phone call. Your Galaxy S6 starts playing the call through the main speaker rather than the ear speaker, acting as a speakerphone. Tap **Speaker** again (🔊 changes to 🔊) when you want to switch off the speaker. If you need greater volume than the internal speaker can produce, try connecting your Galaxy S6 to a Bluetooth speaker.

Make a Conference Call

When you need to talk to more than one person at a time, you can make a conference call using your Galaxy S6. This capability is useful for both business calls and social calls. To make a conference call, you simply call the first participant and then add each other participant in turn.

During a conference call, you can talk in private to individual participants as needed. You can also drop a participant from the call without affecting the other participants.

Make a Conference Call

1 Press **Home**.

The Home screen appears.

2 Tap **Phone** (📞).

The Phone app opens.

3 Tap **Contacts**.

The Contacts screen appears.

4 Tap the contact you want to call first.

The contact's information appears.

5 Tap **Call** (📞) for the phone number you want to call.

Your Galaxy S6 places the call.

6 After the contact answers the call, tap **Add call** (+).

The Keypad screen appears.

7 Tap **Contacts**.

The Contacts screen appears.

8 Tap the contact.

The contact's information appears.

9 Tap **Call** (📞) for the appropriate phone number.

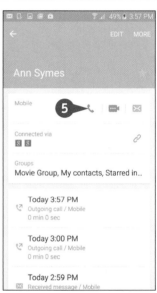

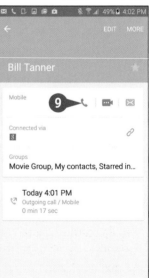

The Phone app places the first call on hold and places the second call.

Ⓐ The first call is on hold.

⑩ Tap **Merge** (🔗).

The Phone app merges the calls and displays the Conference Call readout.

You can add another participant by repeating steps **6** to **10**.

⑪ Tap **Manage** (📇).

The list of participants appears.

Ⓑ You can tap **Split** (🔀) to speak privately to a participant.

Ⓒ You can tap **Hang Up** (📞) to hang up on a participant.

⑫ When you are ready to end the call, tap **End call** (📞).

The Phone app ends the call.

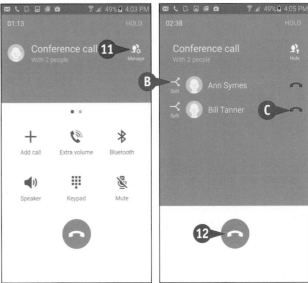

TIPS

How many participants can I include in a conference call?

This depends on your cellular carrier. Contact your carrier's support department to find out the limit.

How do I use other apps during the conference call?

Press **Home** to display the Home screen and then launch an app from there or from the Apps screen. Alternatively, tap **Recents** (🗔) to display the Recents screen and then tap the app to which you want to switch. The status bar shows a green shade to indicate the call is continuing. To return to the call, pull open the Notification panel and then tap the Phone card in the Notifications list.

Call Using Call Logs and Frequently Contacted

To help you make phone calls quickly and easily, the Phone app provides call logs that track the calls you place and receive, a Favorites list to which you can add people, and a Frequently Contacted list.

You can filter the call logs to show only calls you have missed, only outgoing calls, or only incoming calls. The Frequently Contacted list automatically gathers the contacts whom you call and who call you most often.

Call Using Call Logs and Frequently Contacted

Call Using Call Logs

1 Press **Home**.

2 Tap **Phone** (📞).

3 Tap **Log**.

The Log screen appears.

4 Tap **More**.

The More menu opens.

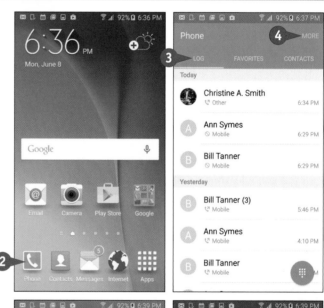

5 Tap **Filter by**.

The Filter By dialog box opens.

6 Tap **All calls**, **Missed calls**, or **Rejected calls** (○ changes to ◉) to choose which log to view.

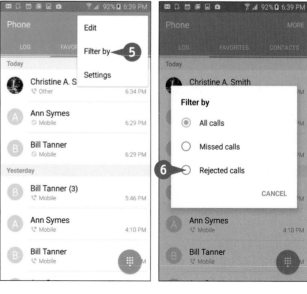

The call log appears.

7 Tap the contact.

The contact's information appears.

8 Tap **Call** ( ).

The Phone app places the call.

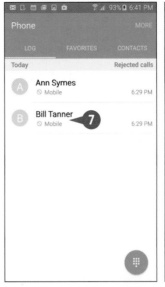

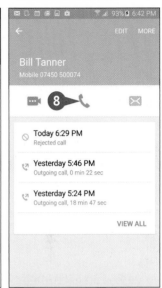

Call Using Your Favorites and Frequently Contacted List

1 In the Phone app, tap **Favorites**.

The Favorites screen appears.

A The upper section of the Favorites screen shows the Favorites list.

B The Frequently Contacted list appears below the Favorites list.

2 Tap the contact you want to call.

Note: If the Make Call To dialog box opens, tap the appropriate number. You can then tap **Mark as Default** to use the number as the default or tap **Just Once** to use the number this time only.

C You can tap **Information** ( ) to display the contact's information instead of placing a call.

The Phone app places the call.

TIP

How do I turn a contact into a favorite?

Tap the contact's name on the Contacts screen to display the contact record and then tap the **Favorites** star (changes to).

To remove a contact from the Favorites list, you can display the contact record and tap the **Favorites** star (changes to). Alternatively, display the Favorites screen and then tap and hold a favorite you want to remove. Phone displays a check box for each favorite. Tap each favorite you want to remove (changes to) and then tap **Remove**.

Send and Receive Instant Messages

Your Galaxy S6 enables you to send instant messages to other smartphone users. The messages can use either SMS or MMS. SMS stands for *Short Message Service* and transmits text-only messages. MMS stands for *Multimedia Messaging Service* and transmits messages that can contain text, photos, videos, sounds, or other data.

The Messages app automatically switches between SMS and MMS. Messages uses SMS for each new message. If you add a photo, Messages changes the message seamlessly to MMS.

Send and Receive Instant Messages

1 Press **Home**.

The Home screen appears.

2 Tap **Messages** (⬛).

A If Messages (⬛) does not appear on the Home screen, tap **Apps** (▦) and then tap **Messages** (⬛).

The Messages app opens.

3 Tap **New Message** (⬛).

The New Message screen appears.

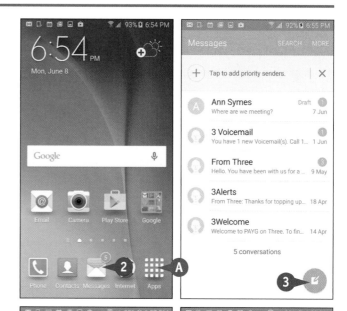

4 Tap the To field, which has the prompt *Enter recipients*, and start typing the contact's name or phone number.

A list of matching contacts appears.

5 Tap the contact you want.

B The contact's name appears in the To field.

6 Tap the text field, which has the prompt *Enter message*, and type the message.

7 To add pictures, video, or audio to the message, tap **Attach** (⬛).

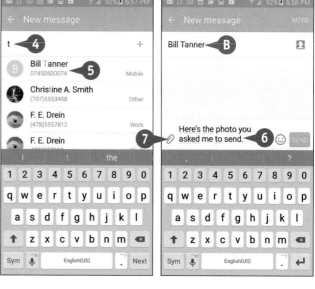

The Attach dialog box opens.

8 Tap the type of item you want to attach. This example uses **Image** (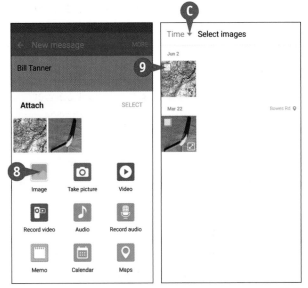).

Note: If the Complete Action Using dialog box opens, tap the appropriate app. For example, tap **Gallery** for attaching an image. Then tap **Always** if you want to use this app each time, or tap **Just once** to use the app only this time.

The appropriate app opens, such as Gallery.

C You can tap the pop-up menu and then tap **Time** or **Albums** to change views.

9 Tap the check box (☐ changes to ✓) for each photo you want to send.

10 Tap **Done**.

D The photo appears in the message.

11 Tap **Send**.

Messages sends the text.

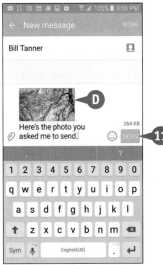

TIP

Why do videos I send via MMS look so jerky and grainy?

MMS messages are limited in size, so you can send only a small amount of video that uses a low resolution and high compression. If you record a video, the Camera app limits it to 295 kilobytes, which typically records between 10 and 20 seconds, depending on the subject. Similarly, the Voice Recorder app limits an audio recording to 295 kilobytes, which records around three minutes of audio at moderate quality. To transfer longer or higher-quality audio or video, use a different means, such as Dropbox.

Manage Your Instant Messages

If you send and receive many instant messages, you may find the Messages app's interface soon becomes full of messages, making it difficult to navigate among them. To keep your messages under control, you can forward messages to others and delete messages you do not need to keep. You can either delete individual messages from a conversation, leaving the other messages, or delete an entire conversation you no longer need.

Manage Your Instant Messages

Forward or Delete a Message

1 Press **Home**.

The Home screen appears.

2 Tap **Messages** ( ).

A If Messages ( ) does not appear on the Home screen, tap **Apps** (▦) and then tap **Messages** ( ).

The Messages app opens.

3 Tap the conversation that contains the message.

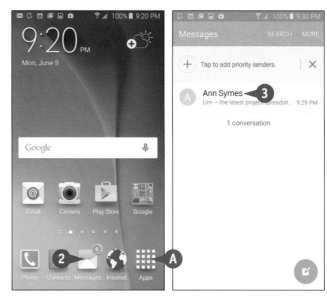

The conversation appears.

4 Tap and hold the message you want to forward or delete.

The Message Options dialog box opens.

5 Tap **Delete** or tap **Forward**, as needed.

If you tap **Forward**, Messages starts a new message containing the forwarded message. You can then address the message and tap **Send**.

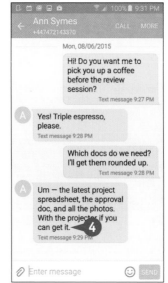

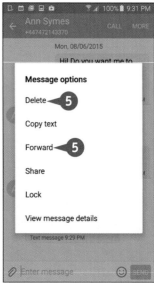

Delete Conversations

1 Press **Home**.

The Home screen appears.

2 Tap **Messages** (📧).

B If Messages (📧) does not appear on the Home screen, tap **Apps** (▦) and then tap **Messages** (📧).

The Messages app opens.

3 Tap and hold the conversation you want to delete.

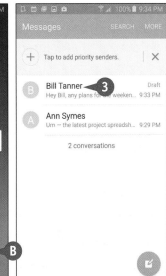

A check box appears to the left of each conversation.

C The check box for the conversation you tapped is selected (☑).

D You can tap another conversation to select it (☐ changes to ☑).

E You can tap **All** (☐ changes to ☑) to select all conversations.

4 Tap **Delete**.

The Delete Conversation dialog box opens.

5 Tap **Delete**.

The Messages app deletes the selected conversations.

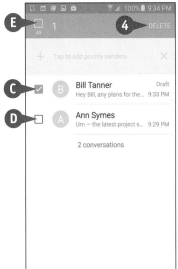

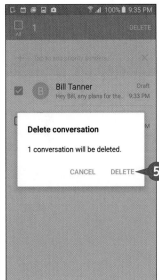

TIP

How do I save a photo I receive in a message?

1 On the message screen, tap and hold the photo to display the Message Options dialog box.

2 Tap **Save attachment** to display the Save Attachment dialog box.

3 Tap the name of the file (☐ changes to ☑).

4 Tap **Save**.

Android saves the photo in the Download folder, which you can access through the Gallery app.

Set Up Google+

By setting up Google+ on your Galaxy S6, you can log in to Google's social network and stay connected to your contacts wherever you go.

Google+ includes a range of social networking features. You can use the Google Circles feature to organize your contacts into groups for easy communication; share your photos in moments using the Instant Upload feature; and chat with your family, friends, and colleagues using Google Hangouts.

Set Up Google+

1 Press **Home**.

The Home screen appears.

2 Tap **Google** (▦).

The Google folder opens.

3 Tap **Google+** (8+).

Note: If the Choose Account dialog box opens, tap the account for which you want to set up Google+.

The Your Contacts screen appears.

4 Tap **Keep my address book up to date** (☑ changes to ☐) if you do not want to add your Google+ connections to your Android contacts.

5 Tap **Improve suggestions** (☑ changes to ☐) if you do not want Google to monitor your communications so that it can make more accurate suggestions.

6 Tap **Next**.

Your Home screen appears.

7 Tap **Menu** (⋮).

The menu opens.

8 Tap **Settings**.

The Settings screen appears.

A You can tap **Auto Backup** to set up automatic backups for your photos and videos. See the tip for details.

B You can tap **Conserve data usage** (☐ changes to ☑) to reduce data usage by downloading lower-quality images.

9 In the Account Settings section, tap your account name.

The settings screen for the account appears.

10 Tap **Notifications**.

11 Set the **Notifications** switch to On (⬤ changes to ⬤) to receive notifications.

12 Tap **Ringtone** and select the ringtone.

13 Tap **Vibrate** (☐ changes to ☑) if you want vibrations for notifications.

14 Tap **Who can notify me** and select who can notify you.

15 Tap the Posts and Mentions options (☐ changes to ☑) to control which notifications you receive.

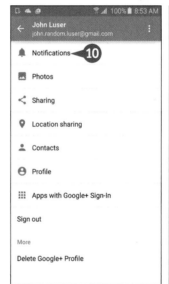

TIP

What is the Auto Backup feature?

The Auto Backup feature enables you to automatically back up your new photos and videos to the Google Photos service. To enable this feature, tap **Auto Backup** on the Settings screen, and then set the **Auto Backup** switch to On (⬤ changes to ⬤). You can then tap **Photo size** to choose whether to store photos at their full size, for which Google Photos gives you 15GB of space, or at the standard size of 2048 pixels, for which Google Photos gives you unlimited free storage. You can also choose options to control when to back up photos and videos or tap **Back up all** to back them all up immediately.

Navigate Google+

After you have set up Google+ on your Galaxy S6, you can run the Google+ app to enjoy social networking. From the Circles screen that Google+ displays at launch, you can easily view the posts for one or more circles, comment on posts, or post your own photos. You can write posts, share moods, and even shoot new videos and post them immediately.

Navigate Google+

1 Press **Home**.

The Home screen appears.

2 Tap **Google** (⊞).

The Google folder opens.

3 Tap **Google+** (8+).

The Google+ Home screen appears.

4 Tap the **Circles** pop-up menu (▼).

The Circles list appears.

5 Tap **Circles**.

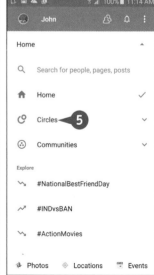

The list of circles appears.

6 Tap the circle you want to display. This example uses **Friends**.

The posts for that circle appear, and you can browse through them.

7 Tap **Compose** (✐).

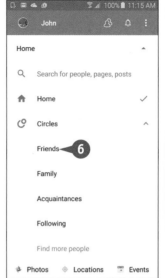

The screen for creating a new post appears.

8 Tap the current circles and then tap the circles for the post, such as **Your Circles**.

A You can tap **Add your location** (📍) to add your location to the post.

9 Tap a photo to include it in the post. To see more photos, scroll down or tap **All photos** (🔁).

10 Tap **Write something** and type the text for the post.

11 Tap **Post** (➤).

Google+ posts your new post.

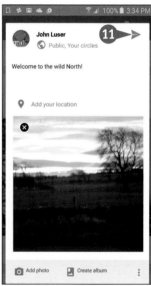

TIP

What are Google+ circles?

On Google+, circles are separate groups within your social network. Google+ provides circles called Friends, Family, Acquaintances, and Following to get you started, enabling you to associate your contacts with different groups. You can also access the What's Hot circle and the Nearby circle, create your own custom circles, and share data only with particular circles. For example, you may want to share some items with your friends but not with your family or acquaintances.

Using Facebook and Twitter

To enjoy social networking on your Galaxy S6, you will likely want to use the Facebook app to access the Facebook social network and the Twitter app to access the Twitter micro-blogging service. You may need to install the Facebook app and the Twitter app on your phone.

You can access Facebook and Twitter through a web browser such as Internet or Chrome, but the dedicated apps are designed to make better use of the limited amount of space on smartphone screens, so they normally give you a fuller experience.

Install the Facebook App and the Twitter App

If the Facebook app and the Twitter app are not already installed on your Galaxy S6, you can install them quickly by using the Play Store app.

Press **Home** to display the Home screen, and then tap **Play Store** ( ) to launch the Play Store app; if Play Store ( ) does not appear on the Home screen, tap **Apps** ( ) and then tap **Play Store** ( ).

On the Google Play screen, tap **Apps**, tap **Search** ( ), and then type **facebook**. Tap the **Facebook** ( ) result to display the app's information, and tap **Install** to install it. Be sure to review the many permissions that the app requires before you tap **Accept** to proceed.

Next, repeat the search and installation steps to install the Twitter app.

Launch Facebook and Log In

After installing Facebook, press **Home** to display the Home screen, and then tap **Facebook** ( ) on the Home screen; if the app does not appear there, tap **Apps** ( ) and then tap **Facebook** ( ).

Facebook enables you to log in using either your phone number or your e-mail address. The Login screen automatically fills in your phone number for you; to use your e-mail address instead, tap the phone number and tap **Delete** ( ) on the on-screen keyboard to delete it. Type your e-mail address and password, and then tap **Log In**.

Navigate Facebook

Once you have logged in to Facebook, you can navigate the app easily by using the controls at the top of the screen.

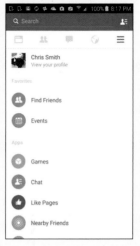

Tap **Status** (▣) to display the Status screen, on which you can post your status, post a photo, or check in with your current location.

Tap **Friend Requests** (👥) to see who has requested you as a friend. You can also send friend requests by tapping the **Add Friend** buttons in the People You May Know list.

Tap **Messages** (💬) to see your current messages. Depending on your phone and location, you may need to install Facebook's Messenger app to send and receive messages.

Tap **Explore** (🌐) to see Facebook's suggestions of people you may know.

Tap **Menu** (☰) to display the menu panel, which provides a wide range of commands. Scroll up and down as needed.

Launch Twitter and Sign In

After installing Twitter, press **Home** to display the Home screen, and then tap **Twitter** (🐦) on the Home screen; if the app does not appear there, tap **Apps** (▦) and then tap **Twitter** (🐦).

Twitter enables you to log in using your phone number, your e-mail address, or your username. On the Login screen, type the appropriate identifier, type your password, and tap **Log in**.

If Twitter prompts you to allow it to use your current location "to customize your experience," tap **Don't Allow** or **OK**, as appropriate.

The Twitter Home screen then appears, and you can start using Twitter.

Navigate Twitter

After logging in to Twitter, you can easily navigate the app by using the controls at the top of the screen.

Tap **Notifications** (🔔) to view all your new notifications.

Tap **Messages** (✉) to display your messages.

Tap **Find People** (👥) to display the Find People screen. Here, you can use the Tailored tab or the Popular tab to browse for Twitter accounts you may want to follow.

Tap **Search Twitter** (🔍) to search Twitter using keywords.

Tap **Menu** (⋮) to display the menu, which gives you access to your lists, drafts, accounts, and settings.

Tap **Home** (🐦) to return to the Home screen.

CHAPTER 7

Working with Apps

An *app* is software that provides specific functionality on a computer. Your Galaxy S6 comes with many apps built in, and you can install further apps to make your phone perform the tasks that you need. You can download apps from Google's Play Store or other sources, run them as needed, and switch quickly from app to app. You also can update your apps to keep them running well.

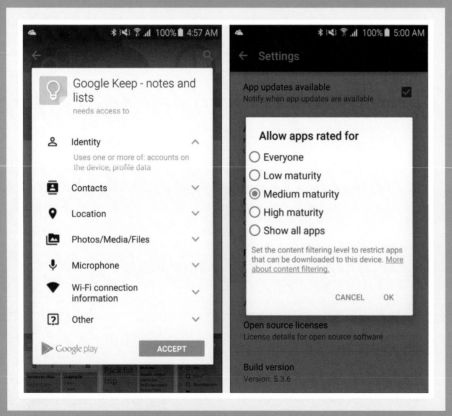

Switch Quickly from One App to Another 156

Pin a Window to the Screen. 158

Find and Download Apps from Google Play 160

Update Your Apps 162

Remove an App 164

Choose Which Apps to Update Automatically 166

Install an App Manually 168

Understanding the Galaxy Apps. 170

Switch Quickly from One App to Another

When you need to use an app on your Galaxy S6, you run the app. You can run any app from the Apps screen, but you can also put apps on the Home screen for quick access.

Your Galaxy S6 can run many apps simultaneously. Each app appears full screen by default, so you work in a single app at a time, but you can switch from app to app as needed.

Switch Quickly from One App to Another

Launch Multiple Apps

1 Press **Home**.

The Home screen appears.

2 Tap **Apps** (▦).

The Apps screen appears.

3 Tap the first app you want to open.

Note: This example uses **Clock** (⏲).

Note: You can also run apps in Multi Window, as explained in Chapter 1.

The app opens.

4 Press **Home**.

The Home screen appears.

5 Tap **Apps** (▦).

The Apps screen appears.

Note: If necessary, swipe left or right to display the icons for other apps.

6 Tap the second app you want to open.

Note: This example uses **Calculator** (▦).

The app opens.

Switch Quickly Among Running Apps

1 With a running app displayed, tap **Recents** (⬜).

The Recents screen appears, showing the apps and windows you have used recently.

The apps and windows at the bottom of the list are the ones you have used most recently.

2 If necessary, pull down to scroll the list to display other apps and windows.

3 Tap the app or window you want to use.

The window appears, and you can start using the app.

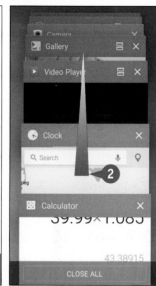

TIP

What other actions can I take on the Recents screen?

You can take four actions:

- Tap **Multi Window** (≣) to switch that app or screen to Multi Window.
- Tap **Pin window** (⊙) to pin the window to the screen. See the next section for details.
- Tap **Close** (✖) to close the app or window. You can close an app or window by swiping its thumbnail off the list to the left or right.
- Tap **Close All** to close all apps and windows.

Pin a Window to the Screen

Sometimes you may want to hand your Galaxy S6 to someone else so that she can view what is on the screen — but without her being able to access other information. Android enables you to share your phone safely by *pinning* — fixing — the front window to the screen. Before you can pin a window, window pinning must be turned on; see the following tip for instructions. You can then pin the front window from the Recents screen.

Pin a Window to the Screen

Pin an App

1 Press **Home**.

The Home screen appears.

2 Tap **Apps** (▦).

The Apps screen appears.

3 Tap the app you want to open. This example uses **Maps** (▒).

Note: If the app is already running, you can tap **Recents** (▭) and then tap the appropriate window to switch to it.

The app opens.

4 Display the content you want to share. For example, in Maps, navigate to the appropriate place.

Note: You can pin only the front window — the window you used last.

5 Tap **Recents** (▭).

The Recents screen appears.

6 Tap the bottom thumbnail and pull up.

The entire thumbnail appears.

7 Tap **Pin window** (📌).

The window appears.

The Turn on Pin Windows dialog box opens.

8 Tap **Ask for Fingerprint before unpinning** (☐ changes to ☑).

Note: If you have not set up fingerprint recognition, the Ask for PIN Before Unpinning check box appears instead.

9 Tap **Start**.

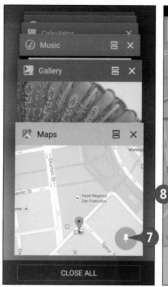

The Turn On Pin Windows dialog box closes.

A The *Application locked on screen* message appears briefly.

10 Hand your device to the other person. She can use only the pinned window.

11 When you are ready to stop pinning, tap and hold **Back** (⤺) and **Recents** (▭) together.

The lock screen appears if you required a fingerprint or PIN.

B The *Application no longer locked on screen* message appears briefly.

12 Unlock the screen as usual. For example, place your finger on the Home button to scan your fingerprint.

TIP

How do I turn on screen pinning in the Settings app?

1 Press **Home**.

2 Tap **Apps** (▦).

3 Tap **Settings** (⚙).

4 Tap **Lock screen and security** (🔒).

5 Tap **Other security settings**.

6 Tap **Pin windows**.

7 Set the **Pin windows** switch to On (⬤ changes to ⬤).

Find and Download Apps from Google Play

The Play Store app enables you to access Google Play, Google's online service, to find and download media and apps. When you need a particular app, you can search the Apps section of Google Play for it. You can then download and install the app.

During installation, you must review the permissions the app requires on your Galaxy S6. If you are prepared to grant these permissions, you can complete the installation; if not, you can cancel it.

Find and Download Apps from Google Play

1 Press **Home**.

The Home screen appears.

2 Tap **Play Store** ( ).

A If Play Store ( ) does not appear on the Home screen, tap **Apps** (▦) to display the Apps screen and then tap **Play Store** ( ).

The Play Store app opens and displays the Google Play screen.

3 Tap **Apps**.

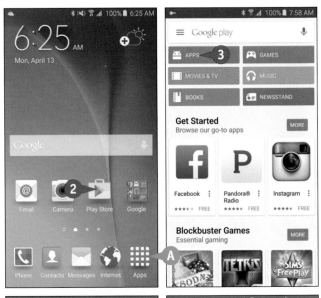

The Apps screen appears, showing the Home list.

4 Tap **Search** ( ).

The Search box and keyboard appear.

B The pop-up menu shows any recent searches you have performed. You can repeat a search by tapping it in the pop-up menu.

C You can search using your voice. Tap **Microphone** ( ) and then speak the terms when the *Speak now* prompt appears.

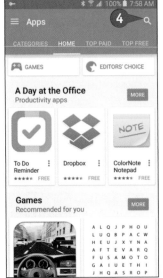

160

5 Type your search terms.

D The pop-up menu displays suggestions.
If one of them is suitable, tap it. Otherwise,
finish typing your search terms and then tap
Search (Q) on the keyboard.

6 Tap the result you want to view.

The app's screen appears.

7 Tap **Read More** to read the description and,
below it, the user reviews.

8 Tap **Install** if you want to install the app.

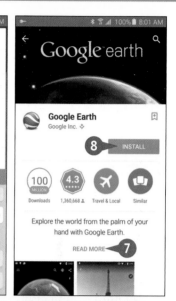

The App Permissions dialog box opens.

9 Read the list of permissions.

10 Tap **Expand** (∨) to expand a permission
category so you can see its details.

11 Tap **Collapse** (∧) to collapse a permission
category again.

12 Tap **Accept** if you want to complete the
installation. Otherwise, tap **Back** (⤶) to cancel
the installation.

Android downloads and installs the app.

13 Tap **Open**.

The app opens.

TIPS

**What permissions should I grant
to an app?**

This depends on the app, so you must
decide depending on what the app does.
Be suspicious of any app that demands
access to sensitive data such as your
contacts without a compelling reason.

**How can I see which apps I have previously bought on
Google Play?**

Press **Home**, tap **Play Store** ( ), tap **Menu** (≡), and then tap
My apps. The My Apps screen appears, showing your Installed
list first. Tap the **All** tab to display the All list, which shows
all the apps you have bought, including apps you have not
installed on your Galaxy S6.

Update Your Apps

To keep your apps running well, you should install app updates when they become available. Most updates for paid apps are free, but you must usually pay to upgrade to a new version of an app.

You can update all your apps at once or update a single app at a time. Normally, updating all your apps is most convenient, but you may sometimes need to update a single app without downloading all the available updates.

Update Your Apps

Display the My Apps Screen

1 Press **Home**.

The Home screen appears.

2 Tap **Play Store** ( ).

A If Play Store does not appear on the Home screen, tap **Apps** (▦) to display the Apps screen and then tap **Play Store** ( ).

The Play Store app opens.

3 Tap **Menu** (≡).

The menu opens.

4 Tap **My apps**.

The My Apps screen appears.

Update a Single App

1 Tap the button for the app, such as **Maps** ( ).

The app's screen appears.

B You can view the What's New section to see what is new in this version of the app, read user reviews, and decide whether to install the update.

2 Tap **Update**.

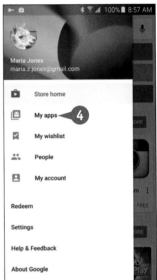
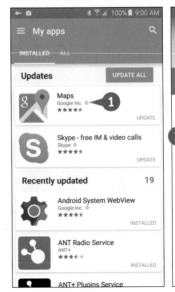

The App Permissions dialog box opens.

3 Read the permissions.

Note: Look for a *New* readout, which marks a change in permissions from the previous version.

C You can tap **Expand** (∨) to expand a permissions category.

D You can tap **Collapse** (∧) to collapse a permissions category.

4 Tap **Accept**.

The app's screen appears again.

The Play Store app downloads and installs the update.

E You can tap **Open** to open the updated app.

5 Tap **Back** (⬅) or **Back** (↰).

The My Apps screen appears.

Update All Installed Apps

1 Tap **Update All**.

The Play Store app downloads and installs all the updates.

The App Permissions dialog box opens for each app in turn.

2 Review the permissions.

3 Tap **Accept** if you want to proceed.

The updated apps appear in the Recently Updated list.

You can now press **Home** to return to the Home screen.

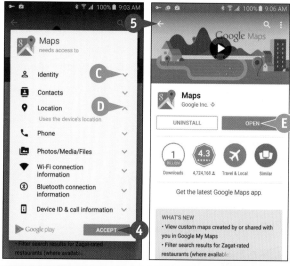

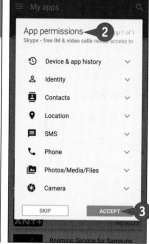

TIP

Should I tap OK or Not Now in the Update Apps Automatically When on Wi-Fi? dialog box?

If the Update Apps Automatically When on Wi-Fi? dialog box opens, you have two choices: Tap **OK** if you want to enable automatic updating for all apps when your Galaxy S6 is connected to a wireless network or tap **Not Now** to defer the decision.

Automatic updates can be helpful, but you may sometimes want to skip particular updates that turn out to be less stable or have fewer features than the versions they replace. If you want to retain control over updates, tap **Not Now**.

Remove an App

Each app you install takes up some storage space. When you no longer need an app that you have installed, you can remove it. The app remains available to you on Google Play, so you can reinstall it later if necessary. You can remove an app either by using the Apps screen or by using the App Info screen for the app. You cannot remove apps considered essential to Android, but you can remove some preinstalled apps and disable others.

Remove an App

Remove an App by Using the Apps Screen

1 Press **Home**.

The Home screen appears.

2 Tap **Apps** (⊞).

The Apps screen appears.

Note: If the Apps screen that appears at first does not contain the app you want to remove, scroll left or right until the screen appears that contains the app.

3 Tap **Edit**.

A The Remove icon (⊖) indicates an app that you can uninstall or disable.

4 Tap the app that you want to remove or disable.

The Uninstall App dialog box opens.

5 Tap **Uninstall**.

Android removes the app.

6 Tap **Done**.

7 Press **Home**.

The Home screen appears.

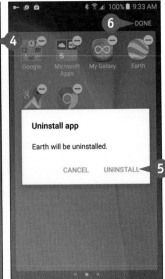

Remove an App by Using Its App Info Screen

1 Press **Home**.

The Home screen appears.

2 Tap **Play Store** ( ).

B If Play Store ( ) does not appear on the Home screen, tap **Apps** (▦) to display the Apps screen and then tap **Play Store** ( ).

The Play Store app opens.

3 Tap **Menu** (≡).

4 Tap **My apps**.

The My Apps screen appears.

5 Tap **Installed**.

The list of apps installed on your Galaxy S6 appears.

6 Tap the app you want to remove.

The app's screen appears.

7 Tap **Uninstall**.

A confirmation dialog box opens.

8 Tap **OK**.

The Play Store app uninstalls the app.

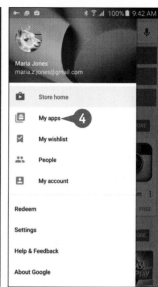
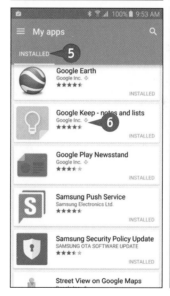

TIP

How do I reinstall an app I have removed?

Press **Home** and tap **Play Store** ( ) to open the Play Store app. Tap **Menu** (≡) and then tap **My apps** to display the My Apps screen. Tap **All** to display the All list, tap the app to display its screen, and then tap **Install**. As usual, review the app's permissions carefully before tapping **Accept**.

Choose Which Apps to Update Automatically

Your Galaxy S6 enables you to update apps either manually or automatically. Updating apps automatically makes it easy to take advantage of the bug fixes and new features that developers add to their apps. You can update all apps automatically or just some apps.

Automatic updates may involve downloading large amounts of data, so unless you have an unlimited cellular plan, set your Galaxy S6 to download updates only when connected to Wi-Fi.

Choose Which Apps to Update Automatically

Control Updates for Individual Apps

1 Press **Home**.

The Home screen appears.

2 Tap **Play Store** ( ).

A If Play Store ( ) does not appear on the Home screen, tap **Apps** (⊞) to display the Apps screen and then tap **Play Store** ( ).

The Play Store app opens.

3 Tap **Menu** (≡).

4 Tap **My apps**.

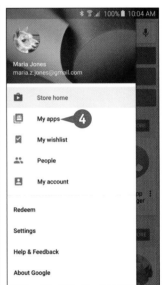

The My Apps screen appears.

5 Tap **Installed**.

The Installed list appears.

6 Tap the app.

The app's App Info screen opens.

7 Tap **Menu** (⋮).

The menu opens.

8 Tap **Auto-update** (☐ changes to ☑).

9 Tap **Back** (⬅) or **Back** (↩).

The My Apps screen appears again.

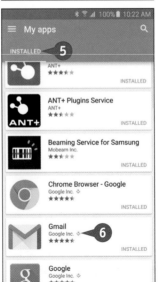

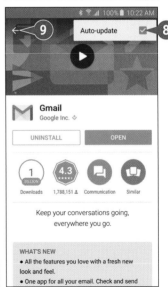

Set All Your Apps to Update Automatically

1 On the My Apps screen, tap **Menu** (≡).

The menu panel opens.

2 Tap **Settings**.

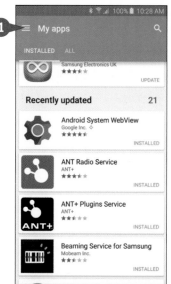
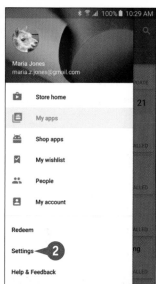

The Settings screen appears.

3 Tap **Auto-update apps**.

The Auto-Update Apps dialog box opens.

4 Tap **Auto-update apps over Wi-Fi only** (◯ changes to ◉).

Ⓑ Tap **Auto-update apps at any time. Data charges may apply** (◯ changes to ◉) only if you have an unlimited data plan.

5 Tap **Back** (⬅) or **Back** (⤺).

The My Apps screen appears.

TIP

What other settings can I choose on the Settings screen in the Play Store app?

Tap **Add icon to Home screen** (☐ changes to ☑) if you want each app you install to add its icon to the Home screen.

Tap **Content filtering** to display the Allow Apps Rated For dialog box. You can then tap the appropriate radio button (◯ changes to ◉): **Everyone**, **Low maturity**, **Medium maturity**, **High maturity**, or **Show all apps**.

Tap **Require authentication for purchases** to open the Require Authentication dialog box. You can then tap **For all purchases through Google Play on this device**, **Every 30 minutes**, or **Never** (◯ changes to ◉).

Install an App Manually

I f an app is available on the Google Play service, you can easily install it on your Galaxy S6 by using the Play Store app. But you can also install an app manually by using a technique called *sideloading*. To sideload, you first acquire a package file containing the app that you want to install. You then transfer the package file to your Galaxy S6, enable the installation of apps from unknown sources, and finally install the app.

Understanding When to Use Manual Installation

Sideloading is primarily useful for installing apps that are not available on the Google Play service. For example, you may need to sideload an app that your company or organization provides. Sideloading can also be useful for installing an app that is available for other Android

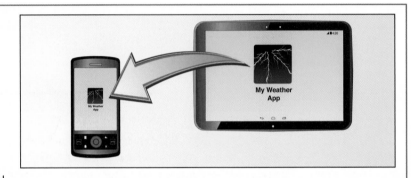

devices but not for your Galaxy S6. Be aware that apps that you download from sources other than Google Play may contain malevolent code. It is wise to search the web for reviews of an app before installing it.

Install an App That Enables Sideloading

To sideload apps, you need a suitable file-management app on your Galaxy S6. You use this app to install the app that you are sideloading. To get your Galaxy S6 ready to sideload, open the Play Store app and install a file-management app such as ES File Explorer, shown here, or Astro File Manager. Both these apps are free and are easy to use.

Get the Package File for the App That You Will Sideload

You can find many apps for sideloading on your Galaxy S6 to add functionality. Each app comes in a distribution file called a *package file* from which you install the app. You can acquire a package file in several ways. If you already have the app on another Android device, use a file-management app such as ES File Explorer or Astro File Manager to copy the file to a backup, creating a package file. For an app

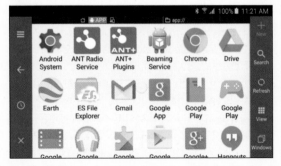

provided by your company or organization, download the package file from the company's or organization's site. For other apps, download the package file from an online repository, but be wary of malevolent content.

Transfer the Package File to Your Galaxy S6

After acquiring the package file for the app that you want to sideload, you need to transfer the file to your Galaxy S6. You can transfer the file in several ways. If the package file is on your computer, use File Explorer or Windows Explorer on Windows or Android File Transfer on the Mac to copy or move the file to your Galaxy S6. Otherwise, use an online storage service such as Dropbox. If the package file is small, you can also transfer it via e-mail or Bluetooth.

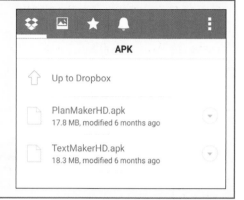

Enable Installation of Apps from Unknown Sources

By default, Android prevents you from installing apps from sources other than Google Play. So before you can sideload an app on your Galaxy S6, you must set Android to allow the installation of apps from unknown sources. Press **Home**, tap **Apps** (▦), and then tap **Settings** (○) to open the Settings app. Tap **Lock screen and security** to display the Lock Screen and Security screen, and then set the **Unknown sources** switch to On (⬭ changes to ⬤). In the Unknown Sources dialog box that opens, tap **Allow this installation only** (☐ changes to ☑) to allow the installation of only one app, and then tap **OK**.

Sideload the App

After copying the package file to your Galaxy S6 and setting Android to allow the installation of apps from unknown sources, you can sideload the app. Open the file-management app that you installed, such as ES File Explorer or Astro File Manager, and then tap the package file. When the screen listing the app's required permissions appears, read the permissions carefully and decide whether to proceed with the installation. After you install the app, you can run it from the Apps screen like any other app.

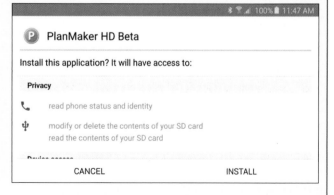

Understanding the Galaxy Apps

Samsung produces a range of apps specifically for its Galaxy devices, which include the Galaxy S6, the Galaxy Note 4, and the Galaxy Note and Galaxy Tab tablets. Samsung now refers to these apps as Samsung Galaxy Apps, or Galaxy Apps for short; an earlier name for them was Samsung Apps.

The Galaxy Apps provide extra features and functionality for Galaxy devices. You can browse and install these apps by using the Galaxy Apps app, which is included on your Galaxy S6. This section introduces you to two useful Galaxy Apps, the Kids Mode app and the Car Mode app.

Launch the Galaxy Apps App

To launch the Galaxy Apps app, first press **Home** to display the Home screen. Tap **Apps** (⊞) to display the Apps screen, and then touch **Galaxy Apps** (⬡).

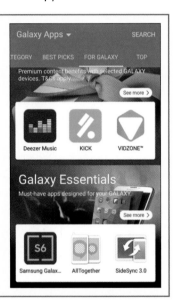

The Galaxy Apps app opens and displays the For Galaxy screen of the Galaxy Apps store. This screen presents selected third-party apps and the Galaxy Essentials section, which contains what Samsung describes as "must-have apps" for your Galaxy device.

You can tap **See more** to explore the apps available.

Explore the Galaxy Apps Available

You can explore the Galaxy Apps in several ways:

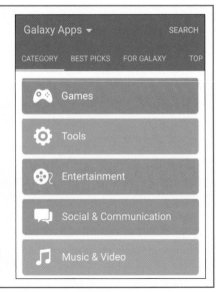

- Tap **Category** at the top of the screen, or swipe right twice, to display the category screen. From here, you can tap **Games**, **Tools**, **Entertainment**, **Social & Communication**, **Music & Video**, **Personalization**, **Productivity**, **Photography**, **Education & e-Book**, or **Lifestyle** to view the category of apps that interests you.

- Tap **Best Picks** at the top of the screen to view selections such as Editor's Choice and Hot & New.

- Tap **Top** at the top of the screen to display a screen of top-rated apps. Tap the pop-up menu and then tap **Top free**, **Top paid**, or **Top new** to display the list you want to view.

- Tap **Search** and type your search terms. If you know the name of the app you are looking for, searching can be the quickest way to locate it.

Download and Install an App

After locating an app you want to use on your Galaxy S6, tap **Install** to download and install it. As when you are using the Play Store app to install an app from Google Play, you must accept the permissions in the App Permissions dialog box in order to install an app from the Galaxy Apps store.

Read through the required permissions carefully to make sure they are acceptable to you. If so, tap **Accept and Download**.

After installing an app, you can run it either by tapping the **Open** button on the app's Details screen in the Galaxy Apps app or by tapping the app's icon on the Apps screen or the Home screen, as usual.

Using Kids Mode

If you want to be able to share your Galaxy S6 with a child, invest in a highly protective case and install the Kids Mode app from the Galaxy Apps store. Kids Mode enables you to restrict the apps and content that a user can access. As its name suggests, Kids Mode is primarily intended for children, and its design reflects this.

Kids Mode has an oddity in that what you download from the Galaxy Apps store is only an installer for the app. When you run this installer, it downloads the rest of Kids Mode and installs it.

You can then run Kids Mode, set a PIN to lock it, and create a profile for the child who will use it.

Using Car Mode

If you want to use your Galaxy S6 with your car, you can take advantage of the Car Mode app. Car Mode, previously known as *hands-free mode* or *driving mode,* can accept voice commands and can automatically read out the details of incoming calls and the text of new notifications. You can turn Car Mode on at any time, but it is primarily useful in situations when you cannot use your hands to manipulate the phone, such as when you are driving a vehicle.

CHAPTER 8

Browsing the Web and E-Mailing

For browsing the Web, your Galaxy S6 includes the Internet app and the Chrome app. For sending and receiving e-mail, your Galaxy S6 provides the Gmail app for personal accounts and the Email app for corporate accounts.

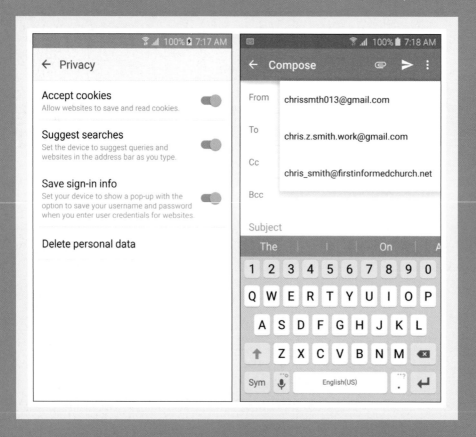

Browse the Web 174

Create Bookmarks for Web Pages 176

Using Bookmarks, Saved Pages, and History 178

Search for Information 180

Fill in Forms Using Auto Fill 182

Tighten Up Your Browsing Privacy Settings 184

Read Your E-Mail Messages with Gmail 186

Reply to or Forward a Message with Gmail. 188

Write and Send E-Mail Messages with Gmail 190

Send and Receive Files with Gmail 192

Label and Archive Your Messages with Gmail 194

Browse by Label and Search with Gmail 196

Browse the Web

Your Galaxy S6 includes two apps for browsing the web: Samsung's Internet app and Google's Chrome app. Both browsers are full featured. This chapter shows Internet, but you likely want to explore Chrome as well.

Using Internet, you can quickly go to a web page by entering its address in the address box or by following a link from another page. You can browse by opening a single web page at a time or by opening multiple pages in separate tabs.

Browse the Web

Open the Internet App and Navigate to Web Pages

1. Press **Home**.

   The Home screen appears.

2. Tap **Internet** (🌐).

   Ⓐ If Internet (🌐) does not appear on the Home screen, tap **Apps** (▦) and then tap **Internet** (🌐).

   The Internet app opens.

   Your home page appears.

3. Tap the address box.

   Note: If the address box does not appear, drag your finger down the screen a short distance.

4. Type the address of the page you want to open.

5. Tap **Go**.

   Internet displays the page.

6. Tap a link on the page.

   Internet displays the linked page.

   Ⓑ After going to another page, you can tap **Back** (❮) to go back to the previous page. After going back, you can tap **Forward** (❯) to go forward again.

   Ⓒ You can tap **Home** (🏠) to display your home page.

Open Multiple Web Pages and Navigate Among Them

① In Internet, tap **Tabs** (▤).

Note: The number on the Tabs button (▤) shows how many tabs are open.

The Tabs screen appears, showing thumbnails of your open tabs — in this case, a single tab.

② Tap **New Tab**.

Internet opens a new tab and displays your home page, such as the Quick Access page.

③ Tap the address box and go to the page you want.

Ⓓ You can tap **www.** to start typing a web address quickly.

Note: After typing most of a web address, you can tap **.com** on the keyboard to enter the .com domain extension. Tap and hold **.com** to display a pop-up panel of other domain extensions.

④ To switch to another web page, tap **Tabs** (▤).

The Tabs screen appears.

Ⓔ You can tap **Close** (✕) to close a tab.

⑤ Tap the tab containing the page you want to display.

The tab appears full screen.

TIPS

How do I get the full version of a web page instead of the mobile version?

You can display the regular version of the current web page by tapping **More** and then tapping **Desktop view**. Some pages are programmed to prevent mobiles from requesting the desktop version of the page, so this does not always work. To get the mobile version of the page again, tap **More** and then tap **Mobile view**.

What else can I do from the Tabs screen?

You can close a window by swiping its thumbnail off the screen to the right. You might find this move easier than tapping **Close** (✕).

Create Bookmarks for Web Pages

The Internet app enables you to create a bookmark for any web page you want to be able to access again easily. When you return to the bookmarked page, Internet displays the current version of the page, which may have changed since you bookmarked it.

You can give each bookmark a descriptive name to help yourself identify the web pages, and you can organize your bookmarks into folders to keep them in a logical order.

Create Bookmarks for Web Pages

1 Press **Home**.

The Home screen appears.

2 Tap **Internet** (🌐).

A If Internet (🌐) does not appear on the Home screen, tap **Apps** (▦) and then tap **Internet** (🌐).

Internet displays the last page you visited.

3 Navigate to the web page you want to bookmark.

4 Tap **Bookmarks** (🔖).

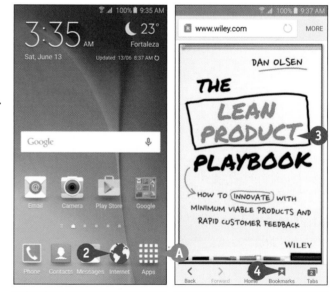

The Bookmarks screen appears.

5 Tap **Add**.

The Add Bookmark screen appears.

6 Tap **Title** and type the name for the bookmark.

Note: You can accept the default name, but it is often helpful to type a more descriptive name.

7 If the folder bar shows the folder in which you want to store the bookmark, go to step **13**. Otherwise, tap the folder bar.

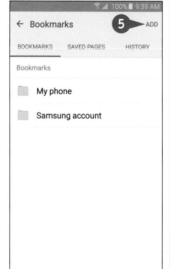

The Select Folder screen appears.

8 If the folder you want to use already exists, tap it and go to step **13**. If not, tap **Create**.

The New Folder screen appears.

9 Type the name for the new folder.

10 Tap the existing folder in which to store the new folder (○ changes to ◉).

11 Tap **Save**.

The Select Folder screen appears.

The new folder appears in the list.

12 Tap the new folder.

The Add Bookmark screen appears, now showing the folder you selected.

13 Tap **Save**.

Internet saves the bookmark.

The Bookmarks screen appears.

14 Tap **Back** (←) or **Back** (⤺).

The web page appears again.

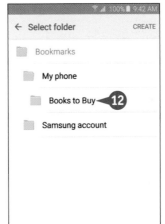

TIP

How do I delete a bookmark?

1 In the Internet app, tap **Bookmarks** (🔖) to display the Bookmarks screen.

2 Navigate to the bookmark by tapping the folder or folders that contain it.

3 Tap **More** to open the menu and then tap **Edit** to display the Select Items screen.

4 Tap each bookmark you want to delete (☐ changes to ☑).

5 Tap **Delete**.

Internet deletes the bookmark.

Using Bookmarks, Saved Pages, and History

To reduce the number of web addresses you have to type, the Internet app provides bookmarks, saved pages, and the history. As explained in the preceding section, "Create Bookmarks for Web Pages," you can create a bookmark for any web page. You also can save a web page in its current state for future reading. The history records the web pages you visit, creating a log that enables you to return to any of the pages, unless you turn on Incognito Mode.

Using Bookmarks, Saved Pages, and History

Open a Bookmarked Web Page

1 Press **Home**.

The Home screen appears.

2 Tap **Internet** (🌐).

A If Internet (🌐) does not appear on the Home screen, tap **Apps** (▦) and then tap **Internet** (🌐).

Internet displays the last page you visited.

3 Tap **Bookmarks** (🔖).

The Bookmarks screen appears.

4 Navigate to the appropriate bookmarks folder by tapping the folder.

5 Tap the bookmark.

Internet displays the web page.

Save a Web Page for Future Reading

1 In the Internet app, navigate to the page you want to save.

2 Tap **More**.

The menu opens.

3 Tap **Save web page**.

Internet saves the page.

B You can tap **Add to Bookmarks** to start creating a bookmark for the page.

C You can tap **Add to Quick access** to add the page to the Quick Access screen as a bookmark.

D You can tap **Add shortcut on Home screen** to add a shortcut to the page to the Galaxy S6 Home screen.

Open a Saved Page

1 In the Internet app, tap **Bookmarks** (🔖).

The Bookmarks screen appears.

2 Tap **Saved Pages**.

The Saved Pages screen appears.

3 Tap the saved page you want to view.

The saved page appears.

Note: To delete saved pages, tap **More** and then tap **Edit**. On the Select Saved Pages screen, tap each saved page (☐ changes to ☑) you want to delete, and then tap **Delete**.

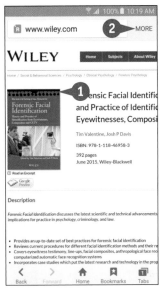

How can I browse the web without the history recording the pages I visit?

You can turn on Secret Mode, which prevents the history from recording the list of pages. In the Internet app, tap **Tabs** (🔲) to display the Tabs screen, tap **More** to open the menu, and then tap **New secret tab**. The Internet app opens a secret tab, which works in the same way as a regular tab, but it has a darker color scheme to help you distinguish it.

When you finish using Secret Mode, tap **Tabs** (🔲) to display the Tabs screen and then close the Secret Mode tab by tapping **Close** (✕) or by swiping it to the right off the list of tabs.

Search for Information

To find information with the Internet app, you often need to search using a search engine. The Internet app enables you to search directly from the address box.

When you search, the Internet app uses your default search engine. You can change the default search engine from the Internet Settings screen. Your choice of search engines may vary depending on your country or region, but many Galaxy S6 models offer Google Search, Yahoo!, and Bing.

Search for Information

1 Press **Home**.

The Home screen appears.

2 Tap **Internet** (🌐).

A If Internet (🌐) does not appear on the Home screen, tap **Apps** (▦) and then tap **Internet** (🌐).

Internet displays the last page you visited.

3 Tap the address box.

The current address becomes selected.

The Quick Access list appears.

4 Type your search terms.

Internet displays suggested searches based on the search terms.

5 If a suggested search is suitable, tap it. Otherwise, finish typing, and then tap **Go** on the keyboard.

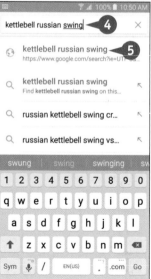

The search results appear.

⑥ To restrict the search to a particular type of result, tap a link at the top, such as **Images**.

The matching search results appear.

Note: You can tap a search result to view the web page in the same tab. But often it is better to open results in separate tabs so you can return to the search results if needed.

⑦ Tap and hold a search result.

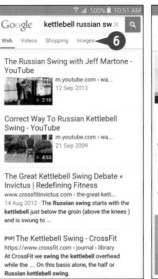

The Actions dialog box opens.

⑧ Tap **Open in new tab**.

Internet opens the web page in a new tab.

TIPS

How can I change the search engine the Internet app uses?

In the Internet app, tap **More** and then tap **Settings** to display the Settings screen. Tap **Default Search Engine** to display the Default Search Engine screen, and then tap the search engine you want, such as **Yahoo!** (○ changes to ◉).

How can I search using a search engine that does not appear on the pop-up menu?

Open a web page to the search engine and then perform the search using the tools on the page. If you plan to use this search engine frequently, create a bookmark for it or tap **More**, and then tap **Add shortcut on Home screen** to add the page to your Home screen.

Fill in Forms Using Auto Fill

If you fill in web forms on your Galaxy S6, you can save time by turning on the Auto Fill feature and setting it up to suit your needs. Auto Fill can automatically fill in standard form fields, such as name and e-mail address, using the information from the profile you enter.

Fill in Forms Using Auto Fill

1 Press **Home**.

The Home screen appears.

2 Tap **Internet** (🌐).

Ⓐ If Internet (🌐) does not appear on the Home screen, tap **Apps** (▦) and then tap **Internet** (🌐).

Internet displays the last page you visited.

3 Tap **More**.

The menu opens.

4 Tap **Settings**.

The Internet Settings screen appears.

5 Tap **My Auto fill profile**.

The My Auto Fill Profile screen appears.

6 Tap **Set my profile**.

The Set My Profile screen appears.

7 Type your name.

8 Type your phone number.

9 Type your e-mail address.

10 Tap **Save**.

The My Auto Fill Profile screen appears.

B You can tap **Edit** if you need to change the information.

11 Tap **Back** (←) or **Back** (⤺).

The Internet Settings screen appears.

12 Tap **Back** (←) or **Back** (⤺).

The web page appears again.

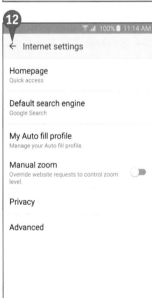

TIP

How do I use Auto Fill to fill out a form?

After turning on the Auto Fill feature and setting up your profiles as shown here, you can navigate to a web page that contains a form with name and address fields. The first time you tap a form field for which your profile contains the appropriate information, the Internet app displays a pop-up button showing that information. Tap the pop-up to insert the information in the field. The Internet app automatically inserts the other available information in the matching fields on the form.

Tighten Up Your Browsing Privacy Settings

The web contains many sites that provide useful information or services, but it also contains sites that try to infect computers with malevolent software — *malware* for short — or lure visitors into providing sensitive personal or financial information. Although Google has built Android to be as secure as possible, it is wise to apply high-security settings. You can choose privacy settings, disable JavaScript, and block pop-ups and cookies.

Tighten Up Your Browsing Privacy Settings

1 Press **Home**.

The Home screen appears.

2 Tap **Internet** (🌐).

A If Internet (🌐) does not appear on the Home screen, tap **Apps** (▦) and then tap **Internet** (🌐).

Internet displays the last page you visited.

3 Tap **More**.

The menu opens.

4 Tap **Settings**.

The Internet Settings screen appears.

5 Tap **Privacy**.

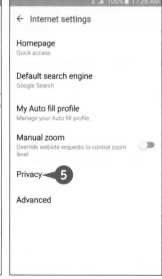

The Privacy screen appears.

6 Set the **Accept cookies** switch to On
(⚪ changes to ⚫) or Off (⚫ changes to ⚪).

7 Set the **Suggest searches** switch to On
(⚪ changes to ⚫) or Off (⚫ changes to ⚪).

8 Set the **Save sign-in info** switch to On
(⚪ changes to ⚫) or Off (⚫ changes to ⚪).

9 Tap **Delete personal data**.

The Delete Personal Data dialog box opens.

10 Tap each item to delete (☐ changes to ☑).

11 Tap **Delete**.

12 Tap **Privacy**.

The Internet Settings screen appears.

13 Tap **Advanced**.

The Advanced screen appears.

14 Set the **Turn on JavaScript** switch to On
(⚪ changes to ⚫) only if you want to
enable JavaScript.

15 Set the **Block pop-ups** switch to On
(⚪ changes to ⚫) if you want to block
pop-up windows.

16 Tap **Back** (←) or **Back** (⭅).

The Internet Settings screen appears.

17 Tap **Back** (←) or **Back** (⭅).

The web page appears again.

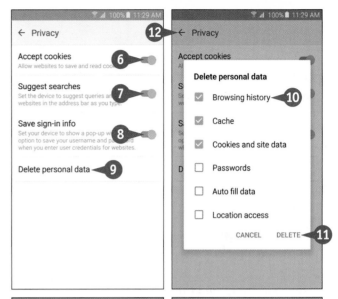

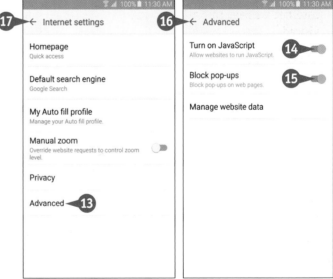

TIP

What are cookies, and what threat do they pose?
A *cookie* is a small text file that a website places on a computer or device to identify it in the future. Cookies are helpful for many sites, such as shopping sites in which you add items to a shopping cart, but when used by malevolent sites, cookies can pose a threat to your privacy. You can set the **Accept cookies** switch to Off (⚫ changes to ⚪) to make the Internet app refuse cookies, but this prevents many legitimate websites from working properly. So normally it is best to set the Internet app to accept cookies.

Read Your E-Mail Messages with Gmail

After setting up your personal e-mail accounts in the Gmail app, as explained in the section "Set Up Your E-Mail Accounts in the Gmail App" in Chapter 4, you can use the Gmail app to send and receive e-mail messages. You can easily read your incoming e-mail messages, reply to messages you have received, and write new messages as needed. If you have set up multiple accounts, you can switch quickly from one account to another.

Read Your E-Mail Messages with Gmail

1 Press **Home**.

The Home screen appears.

2 Tap **Google** (▦).

The Google folder opens.

3 Tap **Gmail** (М).

Your Inbox appears. This is the Inbox for the last account you used in Gmail.

Note: If you have set up only a single e-mail account in the Gmail app, skip steps 4 and 5.

4 Tap **Menu** (≡).

The menu panel opens.

5 Tap the icon for the e-mail account you want to display.

Ⓐ The icon on the left is the current account.

Ⓑ To select the account by name, tap the pop-up menu (◢◣) and then tap the appropriate account.

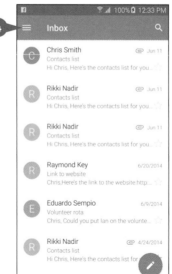

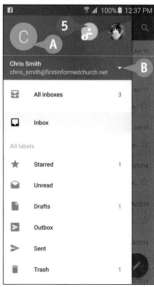

The Inbox for the account you chose appears.

ⓒ Each message preview shows the sender's name, the subject line and time or date, and the first part of the message.

ⓓ The sender and subject of an unread message appear in boldface.

ⓔ The sender and subject of a read message appear in regular font.

⑥ Tap the message you want to read.

The message opens.

⑦ To see the message at a larger size, rotate your Galaxy S6 to landscape orientation.

The message appears in landscape orientation.

Note: You can swipe left to display the previous message or swipe right to display the next message.

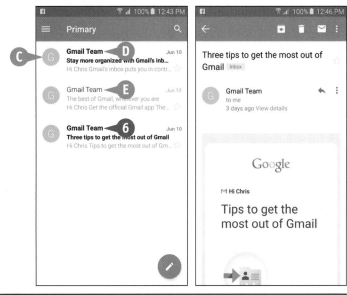

ⓕ You can tap **Delete** (🗑) to delete the message.

⑧ When you finish reading messages, tap **Back** (⬅) or **Back** (↩).

Your Inbox appears.

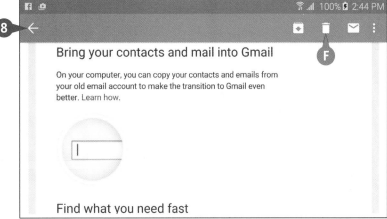

TIP

How do I move a message to a different folder?

In a message you have opened for reading, tap **Menu** (⋮) and then tap **Move to**. In the Move To dialog box that opens, tap the folder to which you want to move the message.

If the account is a Google account, you can use labels to organize your messages instead of moving them to different folders. See the section "Label and Archive Your Messages with Gmail" later in this chapter for details.

Reply to or Forward a Message with Gmail

When replying to an e-mail message sent to multiple people, you can reply only to the message's sender or to the sender and all the other recipients in the To field and the Cc field. The Gmail app automatically adds **Re:** to the beginning of the subject line to indicate the message is a reply.

You can also forward a message you have received. The Gmail app adds **Fwd:** to the beginning of the subject line to indicate the message has been forwarded.

Reply to or Forward a Message with Gmail

Open the Gmail App and a Message

1 Press **Home**.

The Home screen appears.

2 Tap **Google** (📱).

The Google folder opens.

3 Tap **Gmail** (M).

Your Inbox appears.

Note: You can switch to another account by tapping **Menu** (≡) and then tapping the icon for the appropriate e-mail account on the menu panel.

4 Tap the message you want to open.

The message opens.

Ⓐ The To area shows the recipients. You can tap **View details** to display the e-mail addresses.

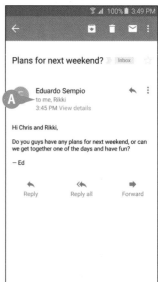

188

Reply to the Message

1. Tap **Reply** (↩), either at the top of the message or at the bottom.

B. You can tap **Reply all** (↩↩) if you want to reply to all To and Cc recipients.

   Gmail creates a reply.

2. Type the text of the reply.

3. Tap **Quote Text** (☑ changes to ☐) if you do not want to include the original message in your reply.

4. Tap **Respond Inline** if you want to respond to the original message paragraph by paragraph.

5. Tap **Send** (➤).

   Gmail sends the message.

Forward the Message

1. Tap **Forward** (➡) at the bottom of the screen.

   Gmail creates a forwarded message.

2. Tap the **To** field and address the message.

3. Tap the **Compose email** field and type any message needed.

C. You can tap **Respond Inline** if you want to compose the forwarded message among the paragraphs of the message you are forwarding.

4. Tap **Send** (➤).

   Gmail sends the message.

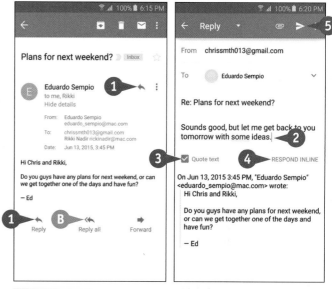

TIP

What is the point of the Respond Inline feature?

Responding inline is useful when you need to answer an e-mail message one point at a time and make clear to which part of the original message your paragraphs refer. When you tap **Respond Inline**, Gmail sets up the reply so that you can edit the original message and add the paragraphs of your reply between the paragraphs of the original message for clarity.

Write and Send E-Mail Messages with Gmail

Using your Galaxy S6, you can send e-mail messages any place and any time. You can send a message using any account you have set up in the Gmail app, and you can either choose recipients from your Contacts list or simply type in their e-mail addresses. You can send a message to either a single recipient or multiple recipients, include carbon-copy (Cc) recipients, and even add blind carbon-copy (Bcc) recipients if necessary.

Write and Send E-Mail Messages with Gmail

1 Press **Home**.

The Home screen appears.

2 Tap **Google** ( ).

The Google folder opens.

3 Tap **Gmail** ( ).

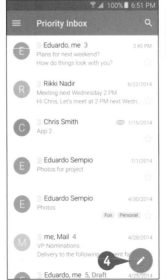

Your Inbox appears.

Note: You can switch to another account by tapping **Menu** ( ) and then tapping the icon for the appropriate e-mail account on the menu panel.

4 Tap **Compose** ( ).

The Compose screen appears, with the insertion point in the To field.

5 Start typing the recipient's name or e-mail address.

A pop-up menu displays possible matches from your Contacts list.

6 Tap the recipient.

The recipient's name appears as a button in the To field.

Note: You can add another recipient by starting to type his or her name or e-mail address.

7 To add Cc or Bcc recipients, tap **Expand** (⌄).

The Cc and Bcc fields appear.

8 Tap the **Cc** or **Bcc** field.

9 Start typing the recipient's name or address.

10 Tap the appropriate match.

11 Tap the **Subject** field and type the subject.

12 Tap the **Compose email** field and type the body of the message.

13 Tap **Send** (➤).

Gmail sends the message.

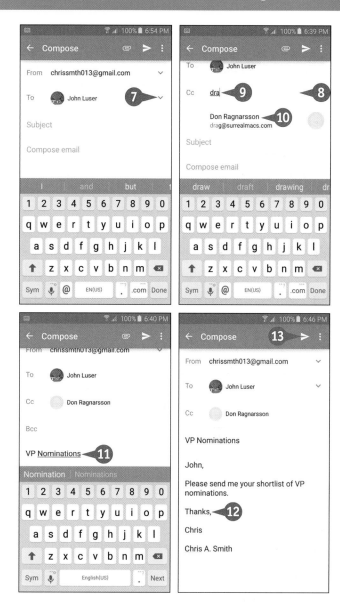

Send and Receive Files with Gmail

Gmail enables you to send and receive files with e-mail messages. You can send files by attaching them to outgoing messages; similarly, you can receive files that others attach to messages they send to you. Sending and receiving files via e-mail is fast and convenient, provided that the total size of files attached to a message is below the size limit for any of the mail servers involved. These limits vary, so it is prudent to err on the side of caution.

Send and Receive Files with Gmail

1 Press **Home**.

The Home screen appears.

2 Tap **Google** (▦).

The Google folder opens.

3 Tap **Gmail** (M).

Your Inbox appears.

Note: You can switch to another account by tapping **Menu** (≡) and then tapping the icon for the appropriate e-mail account on the menu panel.

4 Tap **Compose** (✐).

The Compose screen appears, with the insertion point in the To field.

5 Start typing the recipient's name or e-mail address.

A pop-up menu displays possible matches from your Contacts list.

6 Tap the recipient.

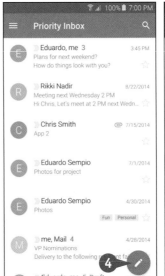

Gmail enters the recipient's name.

7 Tap the **Subject** field and type the subject.

8 Tap the body area and type any body text needed.

9 Tap **Attach** (📎).

The Attach menu opens.

10 Tap **Attach file**.

The Open From panel appears.

11 Tap the source for the file, such as **Gallery** (🖼️).

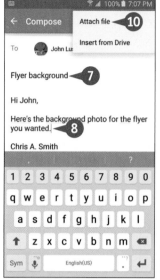

The source opens.

12 Tap the file you want to attach.

A A button for the file appears in the message.

13 Tap **Send** (➤).

Gmail sends the message and the attached file.

TIP

How large a file can I send via Gmail?

If you are sending the file from one Gmail account to another Gmail account, the maximum file size is 25MB per message — but because encoding an attachment for sending via e-mail adds some overhead, the actual file size must be smaller.

If you are sending the file from or to a non-Gmail account, you can determine the maximum file size only by trial and error. Generally speaking, it is unwise to send a file larger than 5MB — including the encoding overhead — via e-mail.

Label and Archive Your Messages with Gmail

To keep your Inbox under control, you should archive each message you no longer need in the Inbox and delete any message you do not need to keep. Before archiving a message, you can apply one or more labels to it.

Labels enable you to categorize messages so that you can find them later. You can label, archive, or delete a single message at a time, or you can select multiple messages in your Inbox and label, archive, or delete them all at once.

Label and Archive Your Messages with Gmail

Open Gmail

1 Press **Home**.

The Home screen appears.

2 Tap **Google** (▦).

The Google folder opens.

3 Tap **Gmail** (M).

Gmail opens, and your Inbox appears.

Select Messages, Label Them, and Archive Them

1 Tap the sender image, the icon to the left of a message.

A check mark (✓) appears on the message's icon.

The selection bar appears.

2 Tap the sender image for each message you want to label or archive.

A The readout shows how many messages you have selected.

3 Tap **Menu** (▤).

The menu opens.

4 Tap **Change labels**.

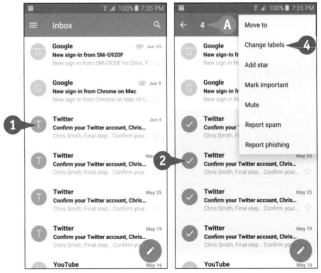

The Label As dialog box opens.

5 Tap each label you want to apply (☐ changes to ☑).

6 Tap **OK**.

Ⓑ The label or labels you selected appear on the messages.

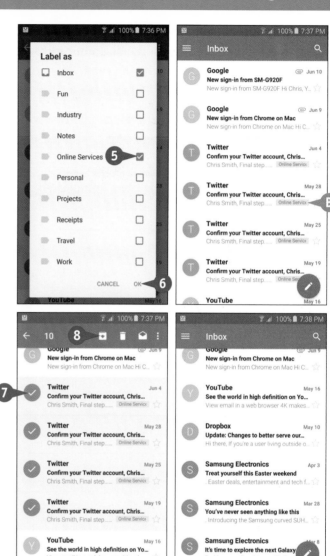

7 Tap the sender image to the left of each message you want to archive.

A check mark (✓) appears on the icon of each message you tap.

8 Tap **Archive** (⬇).

Gmail archives the messages and removes them from the Inbox.

Ⓒ You can tap **Undo** to undo the archiving.

How do I file my messages in folders?

Gmail uses labels instead of folders. So instead of moving a message to a folder, you apply one or more labels to it and then archive it. To retrieve the message, you use the label or labels rather than opening the folder as you would in most other e-mail apps.

How can I create new labels for marking my messages?

As of this writing, you cannot create new labels directly in the Gmail app. Instead, open the Internet app or another browser, log in to your Gmail account, and create the new labels in the browser.

Browse by Label and Search with Gmail

After you apply labels to your e-mail messages, as explained in the preceding section, "Label and Archive Your Messages with Gmail," you can use the labels to browse through your messages and find the ones you need. Browsing is useful when you need to look at a selection of messages to find the right one.

Another way to find a particular message is to search for it. Searching is the fastest approach when you can identify one or more keywords contained in the message.

Browse by Label and Search with Gmail

1 Press **Home**.

The Home screen appears.

2 Tap **Google** (📁).

The Google folder opens.

3 Tap **Gmail** (M).

Gmail opens, and your Inbox appears.

4 Tap **Menu** (☰).

The navigation panel opens.

Note: You may need to scroll down to reach the Recent Labels section or the All Labels section.

5 Tap the label by which you want to browse.

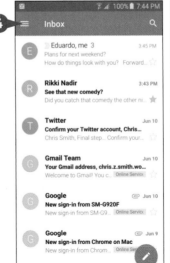

The messages marked with that label appear.

Ⓐ You can tap a message to open it.

❻ To search, tap **Search** (🔍).

Ⓑ The Search Mail box appears.

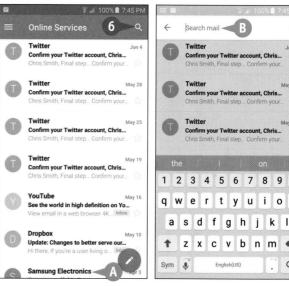

❼ Type your search terms.

Note: Gmail displays a pop-up menu containing your recent searches below the Search Mail box. You can tap a search to perform it.

❽ Tap **Search** (🔍).

Gmail searches and displays a list of matching messages, if any.

Ⓒ You can tap a message to open it.

TIP

How can I delete messages instead of archiving them?

❶ In Gmail, tap **Menu** (≡) to display the menu panel.

❷ Tap **Settings** (⚙) to display the Settings screen.

❸ Tap **General settings** to display the General Settings screen.

❹ Tap **Gmail default action** to open the Default Action dialog box.

❺ Tap **Delete** (◯ changes to ◉).

❻ Tap **Swipe actions** (☐ changes to ☑).

Now you can swipe a message in a conversation list left or right to delete it.

CHAPTER 9

Taking and Using Photos and Videos

Your Galaxy S6 includes two cameras, a high-resolution rear one and a lower-resolution front one, that you can use to take photos or videos with the Camera app.

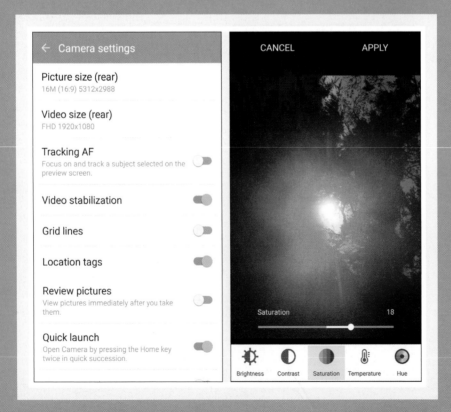

Take Photos with the Camera App. 200

Using Zoom, Manual Focus, and Tracking Auto-Focus. . . 202

Using Selective Focus 204

Using the Flash and HDR Mode 206

Using Pro Mode 208

Take Panoramic Photos. 210

Choose Settings for Taking Photos 212

Edit Your Photos 214

Capture Video 218

View Your Photos and Videos 220

Share Your Photos and Videos. 222

Take Photos with the Camera App

Your Galaxy S6 includes a high-resolution rear camera you can use to take photos, and a lower-resolution front camera that enables you to take photos and videos of yourself or to enjoy video calls.

To take photos with the cameras, you use the Camera app. This app includes capabilities for zooming in and out, using the flash to light your photos and a video clips, plus a rich tone or HDR — High Dynamic Range — feature for improving the exposure, lighting, and color balance in your photos.

Take Photos with the Camera App

1 Press **Home**.

The Home screen appears.

2 Tap **Camera** (●).

Ⓐ If Camera (●) does not appear on the Home screen, tap **Apps** (▦) and then tap **Camera** (●).

The Camera app opens, and the screen shows where the camera lens is pointing.

3 Aim your Galaxy S6 so that your subject appears in the middle of the photo area.

Note: If you need to take tightly composed photos, get a tripod and a mount that fits your Galaxy S6. You can find various models on Amazon, eBay, and photography sites.

4 Tap **Camera** (◉).

The Camera app takes the photo.

5 Tap the thumbnail.

The photo you just took appears.

Ⓑ The controls at the top and bottom of the screen appear at first. Both sets of controls disappear if you do not use them for a few seconds.

⑥ Swipe left to display other photos on the camera roll.

⑦ Tap the screen.

The controls reappear, and you can use them to navigate, manipulate, edit, and share the photos. See the other sections in this chapter for details.

⑧ Tap **Back** (⬅) or **Back** (↩).

The Camera app appears again.

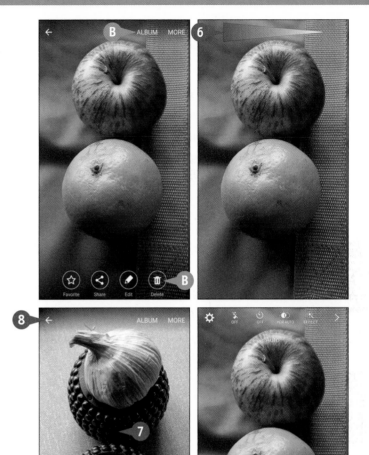

TIP

How do I switch to the camera on the screen side?
Tap **Switch Cameras** (▣) to switch from the main camera on the back of the Galaxy S6 to the camera on the screen side. The screen-side camera has more limited capabilities than the main camera and is designed for video chat and for taking self-portraits. Tap **Switch Cameras** (▣) again when you want to switch back to the main camera.

Using Zoom, Manual Focus, and Tracking Auto-Focus

Your Galaxy S6's Camera app enables you to zoom in so that your subject appears larger. The Camera app focuses automatically on the middle of the picture. When your subject is elsewhere in the picture, you can focus on it manually.

The Camera app also includes a Tracking Auto-Focus feature. After turning Tracking Auto-Focus on, you tap your subject. You can then move the camera, or the subject can move, and the Camera app maintains the focus on it.

Using Zoom, Manual Focus, and Tracking Auto-Focus

Use Zoom and Manual Focus

1 Press **Home**.

The Home screen appears.

2 Tap **Camera** (⦿).

A If Camera (⦿) does not appear on the Home screen, tap **Apps** (▦) and then tap **Camera** (⦿).

The Camera app opens.

3 Aim the camera at your subject.

4 To zoom in, place two fingers together on the screen and pinch outward.

B The zoom indicator appears, showing the zoom level — for example, ×2.0.

5 Tap where you want to place the focus.

C A white split focus circle appears as the Camera app focuses where you tapped.

6 Tap **Camera** (⦿).

The Camera app takes the photo.

Note: To lock the focus and exposure, tap the appropriate point on-screen and hold until a blue circle showing AF/AE appears. You can tap again to release the focus and exposure.

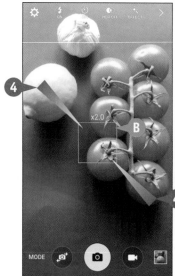

Use Tracking Auto-Focus

1. In the Camera app, tap **Settings** (⚙️).

   The Camera Settings screen appears.

2. Set the **Tracking AF** switch to On
   (⬜ changes to 🔵).

3. Tap **Back** (⬅️) or **Back** (↩️).

The Camera's view appears again.

4. Tap the subject on which you want to focus.

   Ⓓ A focus frame with yellow corners appears.

5. Move the camera or zoom to compose the photo.

   Ⓔ The Camera app keeps the subject in focus.

6. Tap **Camera** (📷).

   The Camera app takes the photo.

Note: To turn Tracking Auto-Focus off, tap
Settings (⚙️), and then set the **Tracking AF**
switch to Off (🔵 changes to ⬜).

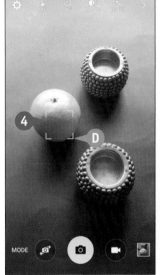

TIPS

Why do my pictures become grainy when I zoom in?
Your Galaxy S6's camera uses digital zoom, not optical
zoom. Digital zoom zooms in by enlarging the pixels that
make up the picture, so when you zoom in a long way, the
pictures can become grainy as the pixels become larger.
By contrast, optical zoom uses moving lenses to zoom in,
thus retaining full quality even at extreme zoom.

How can I add optical zoom to my Galaxy S6?
You can add optical zoom by using an external
lens. Some lenses come built into a case,
whereas others stick or clip onto the Galaxy S6.
You might also consider a Galaxy K Zoom, a
version of the Galaxy S5 that has a built-in
full-size lens with 10× optical zoom.

Using Selective Focus

The Galaxy S6 includes a feature called *Selective Focus* that enables you to manipulate the focus after taking a photo. First turn on Selective Focus and then take a photo of a subject that is close to the lens — preferably between 4 inches and 20 inches away — but more than twice that distance from the background. You then open the photo and choose whether to apply near focus, far focus, or pan focus, which makes both the subject and its background as sharp as possible.

Using Selective Focus

1 Press **Home**.

The Home screen appears.

2 Tap **Camera** (◉).

Ⓐ If Camera (◉) does not appear on the Home screen, tap **Apps** (▦) and then tap **Camera** (◉).

The Camera app opens and shows where the camera lens is pointing.

3 Tap **Mode**.

The Mode screen appears.

4 Tap **Selective focus** (▣).

The Camera app switches to Selective Focus Mode.

Ⓑ The Selective Focus message appears briefly.

5 Compose your shot with your subject close to the lens and the background more than twice as far from the subject as the subject is from the lens.

6 Tap the subject to specify the focus.

7 Tap **Camera** (◉).

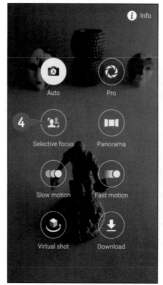

The Camera app captures the shot. The capture takes longer than usual, and the Camera app prompts you to hold the device steady.

8 Tap the photo's thumbnail.

The photo appears.

9 Tap **Selective focus** (⬚) in the middle of the photo.

The Selective Focus screen appears.

ⓒ The highlighted icon shows the current focus.

10 Tap **Near focus** (⬚), **Far focus** (⬚), or **Pan focus** (⬚), as needed. This example switches the focus from Near Focus, the default, to Far Focus (⬚).

The focus changes.

11 Tap **Save** to save your changes.

ⓓ You can tap **Save As** to save the file with a name you specify.

TIP

How do I work around the "Subject not detected" error when using Selective Focus?

If the Camera app displays the message *Picture saved, but unable to apply Focus contrast effect. Subject not detected*, try changing the distance between your Galaxy S6 and the subject and between the subject and the background. Even a small change in one or other distance — or both distances — can make the difference between Selective Focus failing and working. Keep trying the shot with small variations until it works.

Using the Flash and HDR Mode

Your Galaxy S6 includes a flash for lighting your photos. You can switch among three flash settings: On uses the flash for every photo, Auto lets the Camera app decide whether to use the flash, and Off disables the flash.

The Camera app includes a High Dynamic Range (HDR) Mode that takes several photos in immediate succession with varying exposure settings. It then combines the photos into a single composite photo that — in theory — has a better color balance and intensity than any of the individual photos.

Using the Flash and HDR Mode

Use the Flash

① Press **Home**.

The Home screen appears.

② Tap **Camera** (⬤).

Ⓐ If Camera (⬤) does not appear on the Home screen, tap **Apps** (▦) and then tap **Camera** (⬤).

The Camera app shows where the camera lens is pointing.

③ Aim the camera at your subject.

④ Tap **Flash Auto** (⚡AUTO), or tap **Flash Off** (⚡OFF) and then tap **Flash Auto** (⚡AUTO), depending on which icon appears.

Note: If Flash On (⚡) already appears, do not tap it.

Ⓑ Flash On (⚡) appears.

Note: The flash cycle is Flash Off, Flash Auto, Flash On.

⑤ Tap **Camera** (⬤).

The Camera app lights the subject with the flash and takes the photo.

Take a Photo Using High Dynamic Range

1 In the Camera app, tap **HDR Off** (🔲) and then tap **HDR Auto** (🔲); or tap **HDR Auto** (🔲), depending on which icon appears.

C HDR On (🔲) appears.

The HDR preview appears. You may notice that the color balance of the photo changes.

2 Compose your photo by aiming the lens and zooming as needed.

3 Optionally, tap to specify the point on which to focus.

4 Tap **Camera** (🔲).

The Camera app takes the photo.

D You can tap the thumbnail to view the photo.

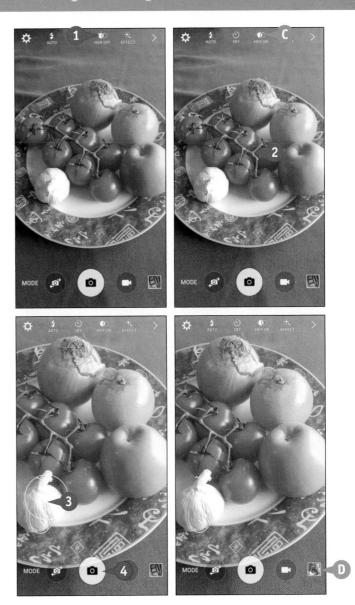

Is there any disadvantage to using High Dynamic Range, or should I use it all the time?
It is best to use High Dynamic Range only when you need it. Taking HDR photos takes longer than taking a regular photo, so you cannot normally capture motion successfully. When possible, use a tripod for your HDR photos to ensure that each photo has exactly the same alignment. If you move your Galaxy S6 while shooting HDR photos, the Camera app prompts you to hold the phone steady.

Using Pro Mode

The Camera app includes a Pro Mode that puts the controls for adjusting settings such as the sensitivity, the white balance, the exposure value, the focal length, and the color tone right at your fingertips. Switch to Pro Mode when you need to take full control of the Camera app.

Using Pro Mode

1 Press **Home**.

The Home screen appears.

2 Tap **Camera** (⦿).

Ⓐ If Camera (⦿) does not appear on the Home screen, tap **Apps** (▦) and then tap **Camera** (⦿).

The Camera app shows where the camera lens is pointing.

3 Tap **Mode**.

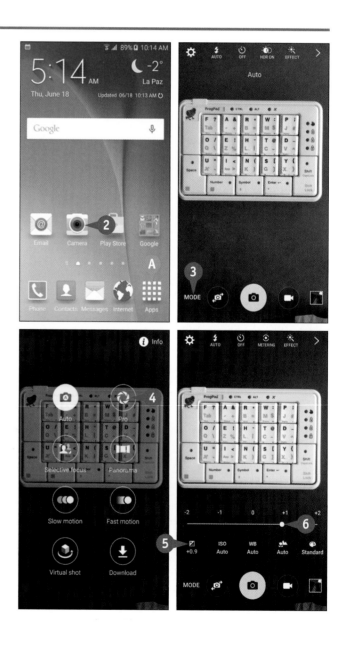

The Mode screen appears.

4 Tap **Pro** (⊙).

The Pro controls appear.

5 Tap **Exposure** (🖾).

The Exposure controls appear.

6 Adjust the exposure as needed by dragging the slider or tapping the numbers above it.

Note: Normally, you would increase the exposure if the picture is too dark, or decrease the exposure if the picture is too light.

7 Tap **ISO** (ISO).

The ISO controls appear.

8 Increase the ISO as needed by dragging the slider or tapping the numbers above it.

Note: Increase the ISO only if necessary. The more you increase the ISO, the more "noise" and incorrect colors you get.

9 Tap **White Balance** (WB).

The White Balance controls appear.

10 Tap **Auto** (Auto), **Daylight** (☼), **Cloudy** (☁), **Incandescent** (💡), or **Fluorescent** (🔆) to specify the prevailing lighting conditions.

11 Tap **Focus** (⛰).

The Focus controls appear.

12 Adjust the focus by dragging the slider between Near (🌷) and Far (⛰).

13 Tap **Color Tone** (🎨).

The Color Tone controls appear.

14 Tap the color tone you want to use.

15 Tap **Camera** (📷).

The Camera app takes the photo.

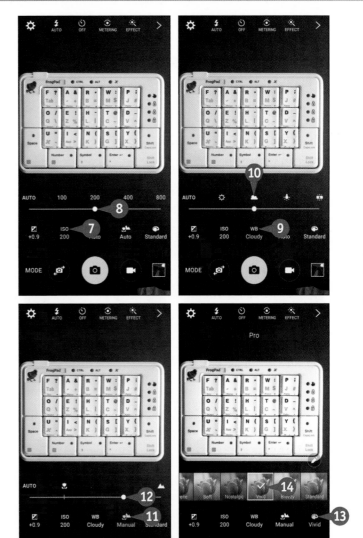

TIPS

What does the Custom button in Pro Mode do?
Use the Custom button to save the settings you have chosen. After configuring the settings you need, tap **Custom** (C), and then tap **Save current settings**. Tap the radio button you want to use (○ changes to ◉) — **Custom 1**, **Custom 2**, or **Custom 3** — and then tap **Save**.

What does the Metering button do?
Tap **Metering** (◎) to display the Metering Modes dialog box. You can then tap **Center-weighted**, **Matrix**, or **Spot** (○ changes to ◉) to specify the type of metering you need.

Take Panoramic Photos

One of the Camera app's most impressive modes is Panorama Mode, which enables you to take panoramic photos easily. You can take panoramic photos either horizontally or vertically. Taking a horizontal panorama produces a long, low photo looking around a single point; taking a vertical panorama produces a tall, narrow photo looking up and down.

To take a panoramic photo, you turn on Panorama Mode by using the Mode panel and then follow the prompts that appear.

Take Panoramic Photos

1 Press **Home**.

The Home screen appears.

2 Tap **Camera** (⦿).

A If Camera (⦿) does not appear on the Home screen, tap **Apps** (⊞) and then tap **Camera** (⦿).

The Camera app opens.

The screen shows where the camera lens is pointing.

3 Tap **Mode**.

The Mode screen appears.

4 Tap **Panorama** (▣).

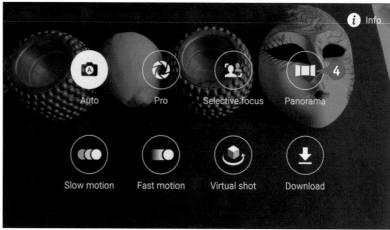

The Panorama controls appear.

5 Aim the camera at your subject.

6 Tap **Camera** (📷).

The Camera app starts capturing the panorama.

B The arrow shows you which way to turn the camera.

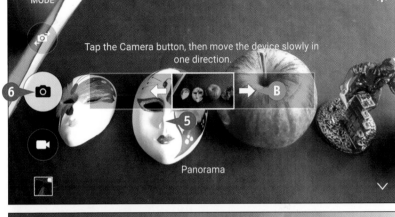

7 Turn the camera to follow the guide.

C The Panorama controls show what you have captured so far.

8 Either tap **Stop** (⏹) to stop capturing the panorama, or complete the circuit, which causes the Camera app to stop the capture automatically.

TIP

How can I take better panoramic photos?

The Panorama feature is designed for handheld use, so it takes a robust approach to minor imperfections in the interest of producing a workable photo. But you can take better panoramas by using a device to steady your Galaxy S6 as you shoot. Most standard tripods tend to be better for taking vertical panoramas than horizontal panoramas, but a monopod can be good for taking horizontal panoramas. A Steadicam rig can also help, as can a powered panorama gizmo that turns the camera automatically on a platform. If you prefer to be unencumbered, try a camera foot strap against which you apply tension to keep the camera steady.

Choose Settings for Taking Photos

The Camera app enables you to configure a wide range of settings for shooting correctly exposed photos that look the way you want. Beyond switching modes, as explained in the section "Using Pro Mode" earlier in this chapter, you can choose the resolution for photos and for videos, turn stabilization off for videos, and choose among three light-metering modes: Center-Weighted, Matrix, and Spot.

Choose Settings for Taking Photos

1 Press **Home**.

The Home screen appears.

2 Tap **Camera** (⬤).

A If Camera (⬤) does not appear on the Home screen, tap **Apps** (▦) and then tap **Camera** (⬤).

The Camera app opens.

3 Tap **Settings** (⚙).

Note: For photos, use the highest resolution available, 16M (16:9), unless you require a different aspect ratio, such as 4:3 or 1:1.

The Camera Settings screen appears.

B You can set the **Tracking AF** switch to On (◯ changes to ◉) to use the Tracking Auto-Focus feature, explained in the section "Using Zoom, Manual Focus, and Tracking Auto-Focus," earlier in this chapter.

4 Tap **Picture size (rear)**.

The Picture Size (Rear) screen appears.

5 Tap the picture size you want (◯ changes to ◉).

The Camera Settings screen appears again.

6 Tap **Video size (rear)**.

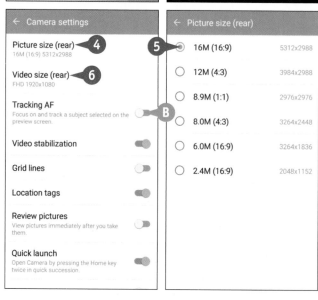

The Video Size (Rear) screen appears.

7 Tap the video resolution you want.

Note: For video, unless you actually need Ultra High Definition (UHD) resolution, shoot at FHD (Full HD) resolution, 1920 × 1080, which takes up only a quarter as much storage space as UHD video.

8 Set the **Video stabilization** switch to On (⬤ changes to ⬤) to use video stabilization.

9 Set the **Grid lines** switch to On (⬤ changes to ⬤) to display gridlines for composition.

10 Set the **Location tags** switch to On (⬤ changes to ⬤) to tag items with location information.

11 Set the **Review pictures** switch to On (⬤ changes to ⬤) only when you need to review each photo immediately after you take it.

12 Set the **Quick launch** switch to On (⬤ changes to ⬤) to be able to open the Camera app by double-pressing **Home**.

13 Tap **Volume keys function**.

The pop-up menu opens.

14 Tap **Take pictures**, **Record video**, or **Zoom**, as needed.

15 Tap **Back** (⬅) or **Back** (↰).

The Camera screen appears.

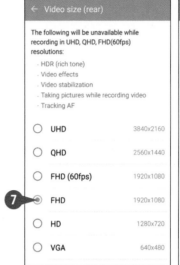

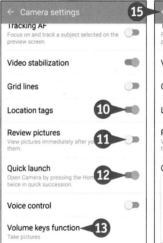

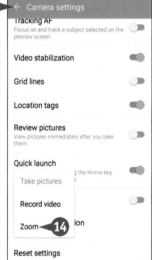

TIPS

How do I set picture size and video resolution for the front camera?

In the Camera app, tap **Switch Cameras** (▣) to switch to the rear camera. Then tap **Settings** (⚙) to display the Camera Settings screen. Tap **Picture size (front)** or **Video size (front)**, as needed, and choose settings on the resulting screen.

Should I use video stabilization and voice control?

Use video stabilization unless you have mounted your Galaxy S6 on a tripod or you need another feature that enabling stabilization makes unavailable.

Set the **Voice control** switch to On (⬤ changes to ⬤) if you want to be able to take pictures by saying "Smile," "Shoot," "Cheese," or "Capture," and to record video by saying "Record video."

Edit Your Photos

Your Galaxy S6 enables you to edit your photos easily by using the Gallery app. You can apply artistic effects, such as sepia or fish-eye, to change the overall color balance or look of the photo. You can apply borders in various styles, and you can draw on a photo to annotate it.

You can straighten a photo, crop it, rotate it, or flip it horizontally or vertically. You can apply a wide range of adjustments, such as correcting the photo's exposure or modifying its color temperature.

Edit Your Photos

Open the Gallery App

1 Press **Home**.

The Home screen appears.

Note: You can also start from the Camera app. Tap the thumbnail of the last photo to open it for editing. You can then navigate to other photos.

2 Tap **Apps** (⊞).

The Apps screen appears.

3 Tap **Gallery** (▨).

The Gallery app opens.

Open the Photo You Want to Edit

1 Tap the album that contains the photo you want to edit.

The photos in the album appear.

2 Tap the photo.

The photo opens.

Display the Editing Controls

1 Tap the photo.

The controls for manipulating photos appear.

A You can tap **Favorite** (⊛) to mark the photo as a favorite.

B You can tap **Share** (◁) to share the photo.

C You can tap **Delete** (🗑) to delete the photo.

2 Tap **Edit** (✏).

The editing controls appear.

D You can tap **Auto adjust** (🪄) to enhance the colors in the photo.

E You can tap **Rotate** (↻) to rotate the photo 90° clockwise.

F You can tap **Crop** (⛶) to crop the photo.

3 Tap **Photo Editor** (🖼) for other edits.

Straighten, Rotate, Flip, or Crop a Photo

1 With the photo open for editing, tap **Adjustment** (⊡).

The controls for straightening, rotating, flipping, and cropping appear.

G You can tap **Rotate** (🔄) to rotate the photo 90° clockwise.

H You can tap **Flip Vertical** (⬍) to flip the picture vertically.

2 Tap **Flip Horizontal** (⬌).

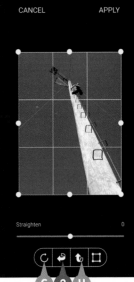

TIP

What does the Effect button do?

The Effect button enables you to apply any of a range of special effects to the photo you have opened for editing. For example, you can apply the Vintage effect for an old-style look, the Dawn Cast effect for a look with early-morning shadows, or the Negative effect for a reversed-color look. After applying the effect, drag the slider to adjust its intensity as needed.

continued ▶

The Gallery app enables you to crop a photo either to a specific aspect ratio, such as the square 1:1 aspect ratio or the widescreen 16:9 aspect ratio that many computer screens and TVs use, or to a freehand area you draw on the screen. You can also adjust many aspects of a photo's tone, including the red, blue, and green balance; the brightness and contrast; and the color temperature, the hue, and the saturation.

Edit Your Photos (continued)

The photo flips horizontally.

③ Drag the **Straighten** slider.

Ⓘ You can use the grid that appears to help judge the vertical and horizontal lines.

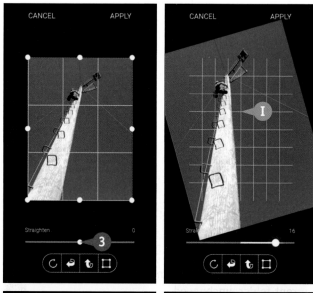

The photo appears in its straightened form.

④ Tap **Constrain** (▣).

The Constrain tools appear.

⑤ Tap the shape you want: **Free** (⋮⋮), **Rectangle** (▢), **1:1** (▣), **4:3** (▣), or **16:9** (▣).

⑥ Drag the cropping handles to select the area you want.

⑦ Tap **Apply**.

The Adjustment tools appear again, and you can edit the photo further if needed.

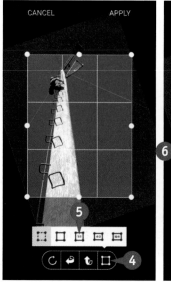

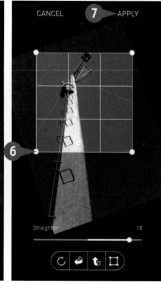

Adjust the Tone of a Photo

1 With the photo open for editing, tap **Tone** (⬤).

Note: In Portrait orientation, scroll the Tone controls bar left to display further controls.

2 Tap **Brightness** (☀), **Contrast** (◐), **Saturation** (⬤), **Temperature** (🌡), or **Hue** (⊙), as needed. This example uses **Hue** (⊙).

3 Drag the slider left or right to adjust the tone setting.

4 Tap **Apply**.

Save Your Edits to a Photo

1 After editing a photo and tapping **Apply**, tap **Save**.

J A message appears briefly, telling you the image has been saved in the DCIM/Photo Editor folder.

Note: The original photo remains in its current folder, unchanged.

2 Tap **Back** (⬅) or **Back** (↩).

The original photo appears.

3 Tap **Back** (⬅) or **Back** (↩).

The photo album appears.

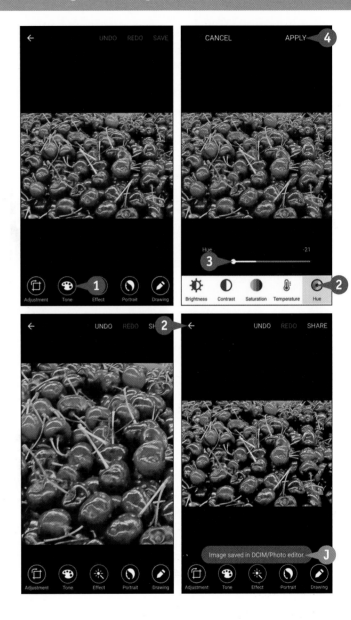

TIP

Can I undo my edits to a photo after I have saved them?

No — after you save the edits, you cannot undo them in the photo. But because Gallery saves the edited photo in the Photo Editor folder, you can return to the original photo by opening it from the folder in which it is stored. You can then edit the original photo as needed.

Capture Video

Your Galaxy S6 can capture video as well as take photos. The rear camera can capture high-definition video, whereas the screen-side camera can capture lower-resolution video suitable for online chat and similar uses. To capture video, you use the Camera app in Video Mode. After taking the video, you can review it on your Galaxy S6. You can also share the video with other people or play it back on your TV, as described in the next section, "View Your Photos and Videos."

Capture Video

① Press **Home**.

The Home screen appears.

② Tap **Camera** (⦿).

Ⓐ If Camera (⦿) does not appear on the Home screen, tap **Apps** (▦) and then tap **Camera** (⦿).

The Camera app opens.

③ Aim the lens at your subject.

④ Tap **Video** (▣).

The Camera app starts recording video.

Ⓑ You can tap **Capture** (▣) to take a still photo while the video is recording.

Ⓒ The readout shows the time elapsed.

Note: You can zoom in by placing a thumb and finger on the screen and pinching apart. You can zoom back out by pinching inward.

⑤ Tap **Pause** (▮▮).

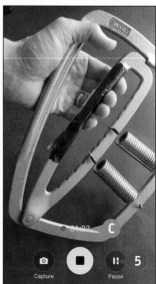

218

The recording pauses.

6 When you are ready to resume recording, tap **Resume** ().

The recording resumes.

7 Tap **Stop** (■).

The recording stops.

The video's thumbnail appears.

8 Tap the thumbnail.

The video appears, and you can play it back.

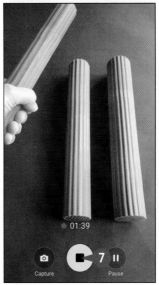

TIP

Can I record videos with the screen-side camera?

Yes. Tap **Camera** (●) on the Home screen to open the Camera app, and then tap **Switch Cameras** (⟳) to switch to the screen-side camera. You can then record video using the same techniques as for the rear camera, including pinching to zoom.

View Your Photos and Videos

You can view your photos and videos using the Gallery app. The Camera app saves your photos and videos into a folder called *Camera,* which you can access via the Album screen in the Gallery app. You can also access the Camera folder directly from the Camera app.

When you want to view your photos and videos at a larger size, you can connect your Galaxy S6 to a TV or monitor. This is great for enjoying your photos or videos with other people.

View Your Photos and Videos

1 Press **Home**.

The Home screen appears.

Note: You can also start from the Camera app. Tap the thumbnail of the last photo to view it. You can then navigate to other photos.

2 Tap **Apps** (▦).

The Apps screen appears.

3 Tap **Gallery** (🖼).

Gallery opens and displays its home screen.

Ⓐ You can tap the pop-up menu in the upper-right corner and then tap the item by which you want to browse: **Time**, **Albums**, **Events**, or **Categories**. This example uses **Albums**.

4 Tap the album you want to view.

Thumbnails of the photos in the album appear.

5 Tap the photo you want to view.

The photo opens.

B The controls at the top and bottom of the screen appear at first. They disappear if you do not use them for a few seconds.

6 Swipe left or right to display other photos.

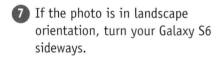

7 If the photo is in landscape orientation, turn your Galaxy S6 sideways.

The photo appears in landscape view, enabling you to view it better.

TIP

How do I view my photos and videos on my TV?
The easiest way to view your photos and videos on your TV is to connect your Galaxy S6 to your TV via a cable that has a micro-USB connector at one end and an HDMI connector at the other. Plug the micro-USB connector into the multipurpose jack on the Galaxy S6 and the HDMI connector into the HDMI port on the TV.

Share Your Photos and Videos

Your Galaxy S6 and its Camera app include a wide range of features for sharing the photos and videos you take. You can attach them to e-mail messages, include them in text messages, or post them to your accounts on social networks.

You can share photos and videos when you are browsing in the Gallery app, but you can also share them straight from the Camera app — even immediately after you take them.

Share Your Photos and Videos

1 Press **Home**.

The Home screen appears.

Note: You can also start from the Camera app. Tap the thumbnail of the last photo to open it. You can then navigate to other photos.

2 Tap **Apps** (▦).

The Apps screen appears.

3 Tap **Gallery** (▶).

Gallery opens and displays the last screen used, such as the Album screen.

4 Tap the album you want to open.

The photos in the album appear.

5 Tap the photo you want to share.

The photo opens.

6 Tap the photo.

The controls appear.

7 Tap **Share** ().

The Share panel opens.

Note: Swipe left to see other means of sharing.

8 Tap the app you want to use for sharing. This example uses **Gmail**.

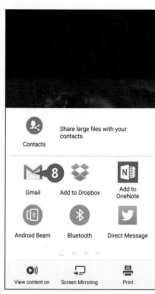

A new message opens with the photo attached.

9 Start typing the recipient's name.

The list of matches appears.

10 Tap the recipient's name.

11 Tap **Subject** and type the subject for the message.

12 Tap the body and type the body of the message.

13 Tap **Send** (➤).

Gmail sends the message and the photo.

TIP

How do I post a photo to Facebook?

1 With the photo open, tap **Share** () to display the Share panel.

2 Tap **Facebook** (📘) to start a new post containing the photo.

3 Type any text you want to post with the photo.

4 Tap **Location** (📍) if you want to add the location.

5 Tap **Post** to post the photo.

CHAPTER 10

Navigating, Working, and Productivity

Your Galaxy S6 includes the Maps app, the Clock app, and various other useful apps. For work, you can set up Private Mode on your Galaxy S6 and connect it to both work networks and Exchange Server systems.

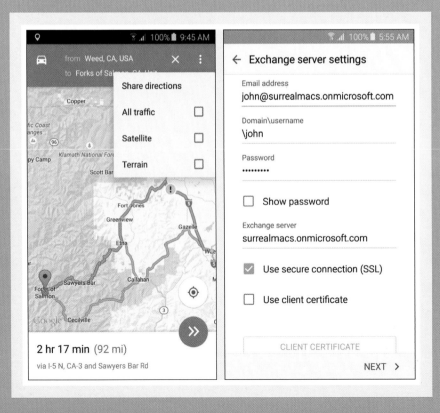

Find Your Location and Display Different Layers 226

Get Directions 228

Rotate, Zoom, and Tilt the Map 230

Make a Map Available Offline 232

Explore with Street View 234

Explore the Clock App 236

Explore Other Included Apps 238

Set Up Private Mode 240

Using Private Mode 242

Connect to a Work Network via VPN 246

Connect to Exchange Server 248

Install Credentials 252

Find Your Location and Display Different Layers

The Maps app on your Galaxy S6 enables you to pinpoint your location by using the Global Positioning System (GPS) or known wireless networks. You can choose to display different layers of map information, such as the Satellite layer, the Public Transit layer, or the Bicycling layer. To help you get your bearings, you can rotate the map to match the direction you are facing.

Find Your Location and Display Different Layers

1 Press **Home**.

The Home screen appears.

2 Tap **Apps** (⊞).

The Apps screen appears.

3 Tap **Maps** (📍).

The Maps screen appears.

Ⓐ The blue dot shows your current location.

Ⓑ The arrow next to the blue dot shows the direction your Galaxy S6 is facing.

4 Place your thumb and finger, or two fingers if you are dexterous, apart on the screen and pinch inward.

The map zooms out, showing a larger area.

5 Tap **Menu** (☰).

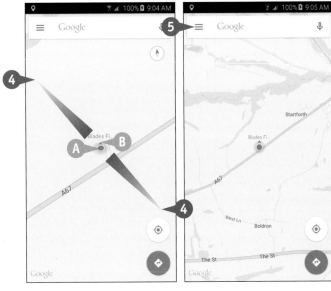

The menu panel opens.

6 Tap **Satellite**.

The map switches to the Satellite view, showing an overhead view of the area consisting of satellite photos with road names and place names overlaid.

7 Tap **Menu** (≡).

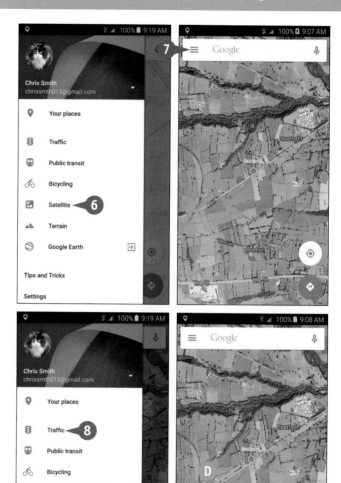

The menu panel opens.

C The shading and color change indicates Satellite is turned on.

8 Tap **Traffic**.

D Colored lines indicating traffic flow appear on the major roads.

Note: The Traffic layer, Public Transit layer, and Bicycling layer are mutually exclusive. Displaying one of these three layers hides any other of the three that is displayed.

TIP

How do I share my location with someone else?

In the Maps app, tap **Location** (◉) to display your current location. Tap and hold the location until Maps drops a pin (📍) on it and displays the location bar at the bottom of the screen with information about the location. Tap the location bar to display the info pane, then tap **Share** (➔). In the Sharing pane, tap the means of sharing, such as **Messages** (✉), and then follow the prompts to send the location.

Get Directions

The Maps app enables you to get step-by-step directions to exactly where you want to go. Maps can also show you current traffic information to help you identify the most viable route for a journey and avoid getting stuck in congestion.

Maps displays driving directions by default, but you can also display public transit directions and walking directions. It is wise to double-check that public transit directions and schedules are up to date before you use them.

Get Directions

1. Press **Home**.

   The Home screen appears.

2. Tap **Apps** (▦).

   The Apps screen appears.

3. Tap **Maps** (⚐).

   The Maps app opens.

4. Tap **Route** (◉).

   The Route screen appears.

5. Tap the type of directions you want: **Driving** (🚗), **Public Transit** (🚌), **Walking** (🚶), or **Cycling** (🚴). This example uses **Driving** (🚗).

Ⓐ The upper box shows **Your location** as the suggested starting point.

6. To use another starting point, tap the upper box.

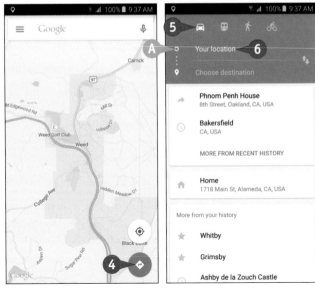

7 Begin typing the starting point.

A list of suggestions appears.

8 If a suggestion is correct, tap it. Otherwise, type the entire address.

9 Tap **Choose destination** and enter the destination.

The Route screen shows available routes.

B The Warning icon (!) indicates any problems.

C You can tap **Options** (🔧) to display the Options dialog box and then tap **Avoid highways** (☐ changes to ✓), **Avoid tolls** (☐ changes to ✓), or **Avoid ferries** (☐ changes to ✓), as needed. Tap **Done** to close the Options dialog box.

10 Tap the route you want to view.

The route appears on the map.

D A button showing the starting point, destination, and direction type appears.

E You can tap **Menu** (⋮) to share the directions or tap **All traffic** (☐ changes to ✓), **Satellite** (☐ changes to ✓), or **Terrain** (☐ changes to ✓), as needed.

F You can tap another gray route to view it.

11 Tap **Preview** (»).

The first direction in the route appears.

12 Tap **Next** (>) to display the next direction.

G You can tap **Back** (⬅) or **Back** (↰) to return to the map showing the entire route.

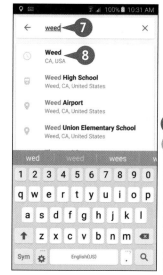

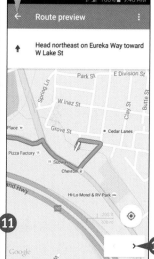

TIP

How can I get directions back to where I started?
After getting directions for a route, tap the button containing the starting point, destination, and direction type. The Directions screen appears. Tap **Reverse Start and End** (⬍) to switch the starting point and destination. The Maps app gets directions for the return trip. If the Directions screen shows a choice of routes, tap the route you want to view.

Rotate, Zoom, and Tilt the Map

The Maps app enables you to rotate, zoom, and tilt the map. Rotating the map aligns it with the direction in which you are looking, which helps you to get your bearings. Zooming enables you to move from viewing a large area at a small scale to viewing a small area at a large scale. Tilting the map can show you the lay of the land. You can combine the three movements to explore the map in great detail.

Rotate, Zoom, and Tilt the Map

Open the Maps App

1 Press **Home**.

The Home screen appears.

2 Tap **Apps** (⬛).

The Apps screen appears.

3 Tap **Maps** (🗺).

The Maps app opens, and you can navigate to the place you want to explore.

Rotate the Map

1 Place your thumb and index finger apart on the map and then rotate them in the direction you want to turn the map.

The map rotates.

A The compass arrow (🧭) appears. The red end points north, and the white end points south.

2 Tap the **compass arrow** (🧭) when you want to make the map point north again.

The compass arrow disappears when the map is pointing north again.

Zoom the Map

1 Place your thumb and index finger together on the screen and pinch outward.

The map zooms in, showing the area at a larger size.

2 Place your thumb and index finger apart and pinch together.

The map zooms out, showing a larger area.

Note: You can zoom in by increments by double-tapping the area. Double-tap with two fingers to zoom out in increments.

Tilt the Map

1 Place two fingers near the bottom of the screen and draw them up.

The map tilts away from you, giving a flatter perspective instead of a straight-down perspective.

2 When you finish using the tilted map, place two fingers near the top of the screen and draw them down.

Maps restores the straight-down perspective.

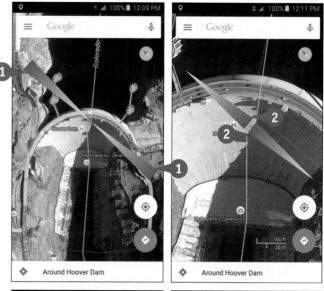

How can I see the scale of the map I am viewing?
Place your thumb and index finger on the screen and start to pinch them outward or inward. Maps displays a scale at the bottom of the screen. The scale disappears a few seconds after you stop pinching.

How do I change the measurement units Maps uses?
Tap **Menu** (≡) and then tap **Settings**. Tap **Distance Units** to display the Distance Units dialog box and then tap **Miles**, **Kilometers**, or **Automatic** (○ changes to ◉), as needed.

Make a Map Available Offline

The Maps app enables you to make a map available offline so you can use the map even when your Galaxy S6 has no Internet connection.

After saving a map to your device, you access it by going to the My Places screen and touching the **Offline** tab. You can keep offline maps for as long as needed and delete those you no longer need.

Make a Map Available Offline

① Press **Home**.

The Home screen appears.

② Tap **Apps** (▦).

The Apps screen appears.

③ Tap **Maps** (▨).

The Maps app opens, and you can navigate to the place you want to explore.

The Maps screen appears.

④ Navigate to the area you want to make available offline.

⑤ Tap **Menu** (≡).

The menu panel opens.

⑥ Tap **Your places**.

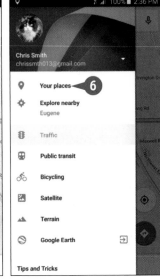

The Your Places screen appears.

7 In the Offline Maps section at the bottom of the screen, tap **View All and Manage**.

Note: If you have not yet saved an offline map, tap **Save a New Offline Map** in the Offline Maps section of the Your Places screen instead of tapping **View All and Manage**. Skip step **8**.

The Offline Maps screen appears.

8 Tap **Save a New Offline Map**.

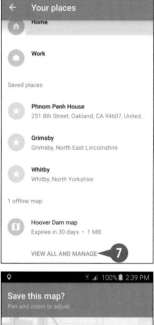

The map appears, showing the *Save this map?* prompt at the top.

Note: You can adjust the map by panning and zooming, if necessary.

9 Tap **Save**.

The Name Offline Map dialog box opens.

10 Type the name you want to give the map.

11 Tap **Save**.

The Maps app downloads the map and saves it to your Galaxy S6.

TIP

How do I use and manage my offline maps?
Tap **Menu** (≡) and then touch **Your places** to display the Your Places screen. In the Offline Maps section at the bottom of the screen, you can tap a map to display it, or tap **View all and manage** to display the Offline Maps screen. Here, you can tap **Menu** (⋮) for an offline map and then use the three commands on the menu: Tap **Rename** to rename the map, tap **Update** to update the map with the latest information, or tap **Delete** to delete the map.

Explore with Street View

Google's Street View feature, which you can access through the Maps app, enables you to get the view from ground level of places on the map. Street view displays images from Google's vast database of city streets and rural areas. You can pan around the area at which you enter Street view; you can move along some streets almost as if you were walking along them; and you can look upward or downward to see more.

Explore with Street View

1 Press **Home**.

The Home screen appears.

2 Tap **Apps** (⊞).

The Apps screen appears.

3 Tap **Maps** (🗺).

The Maps app opens.

4 Navigate to the place you want to explore.

5 Tap and hold the place where you want to enter Street view.

Ⓐ A dropped pin (📍) appears.

Ⓑ The location bar shows the location of the dropped pin.

6 Tap the location bar.

The info page for the dropped pin appears.

The Street view picture shows a preview of Street view for the location.

7 Tap **Street View**.

Street view appears.

Note: The images in Street view may be several years old, so what you see may be significantly different from reality.

8 Tap a white arrow to move in the direction indicated.

9 Drag left to look right or drag right to look left.

10 Drag up to look downward or drag down to look upward.

11 When you are ready to return to the map, tap the screen.

The controls appear.

12 Tap **Back** (⬅) or **Back** (↪).

Maps exits Street view and displays the info page.

13 Tap **Back** (⬅) or **Back** (↪) again.

Maps displays the map in the view you were using before.

TIP

What does the button with curving arrows do?

This button (⟳) is the Look Around button. Tap **Look around** (⟳ changes to ⟳) to turn on Look Around Mode, enabling you to control what Street view displays by panning and tilting your Galaxy S6. Look Around Mode is especially useful when you are using Street view to explore your current location, as it helps you to orient yourself to your surroundings. When you finish using Look Around Mode, tap **Look around** (⟳ changes to ⟳) to turn it off.

Explore the Clock App

Your Galaxy S6 includes a powerful Clock app with many features. The Alarm feature enables you to set as many alarms as you need, and the World Clock feature enables you to track the time in multiple locations simultaneously. The Stopwatch feature makes it easy to time events to within hundredths of a second, and the Timer feature provides a countdown of the duration you set with a warning when the time elapses.

Launch the Clock App

You can launch the Clock app by pressing **Home**, tapping **Apps** (), and then tapping **Clock** () on the Apps screen.

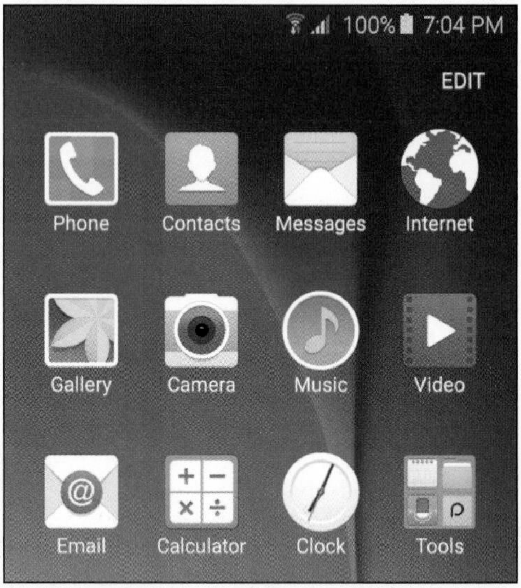

Set Alarms

To work with alarms, tap **Alarm** () on the tab bar. On the Alarm screen, tap **Create alarm** to start creating a new alarm. You can then set the time for the alarm, choose the days on which to use it, and control whether it repeats weekly. You can set the alarm type, which can be Sound, Vibrate, or Sound & Vibrate; select the alarm tone, such as Beep-Beep or A Rustling in the Trees; and set other options, such as choosing whether to allow snoozing the alarm. Tap **Save** when you have made your choices.

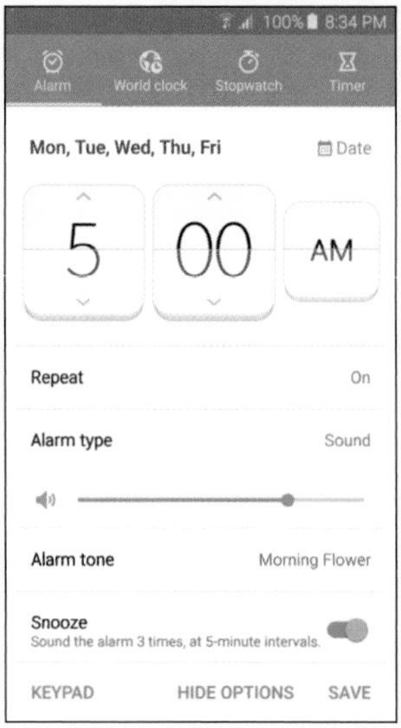

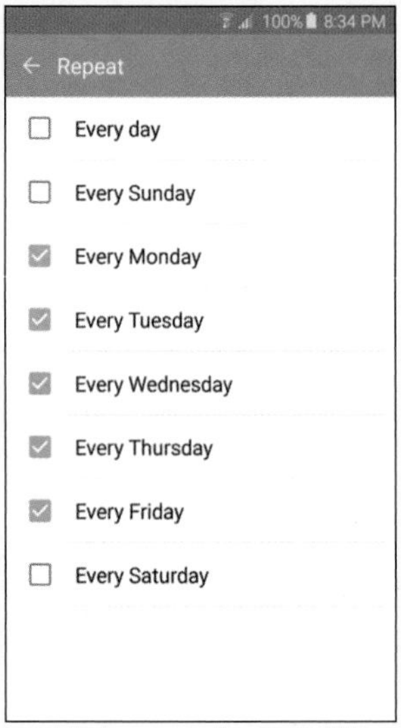

Use the World Clock

To use the World Clock, tap **World Clock** (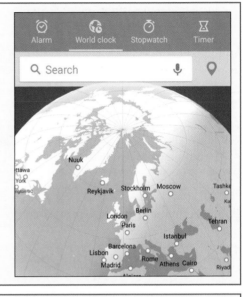) on the tab bar. Tap **Search** (Q) to display the Search screen, and then either browse the list of cities and tap the one you want, or search by typing or dictating the name, and then tap the city. You can tap a city on the map to display its current time.

Use the Stopwatch

To use the Stopwatch, tap **Stopwatch** (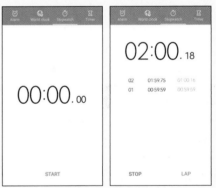) on the tab bar. You can then tap **Start** to start the stopwatch running, tap **Lap** to mark a lap time, or tap **Stop** to stop timing. After stopping the stopwatch, you can tap **Resume** to restart it from the current time total or tap **Reset** to reset it to zero.

Use the Timer

To use the Timer, tap **Timer** (⊠) on the tab bar. Tap **Hours** and then tap the buttons to set the number of hours; then tap **Minutes** and **Seconds** in turn and set the number of each. You can also tap **Keypad** to display the keypad if you prefer to type in the numbers.

Tap **Start** to set the timer running. You can then tap **Pause** to pause the timer or **Cancel** to cancel it.

Explore Other Included Apps

Your Galaxy S6 comes with a host of specialized apps you likely will want to try in order to get the most out of your phone. These apps include Calculator, S Health, Voice Recorder, Peel Smart Remote, and Galaxy Apps. You can run each of these apps by tapping its icon on the Apps screen.

Calculator

Calculator works in both portrait and landscape orientations. In portrait orientation, Calculator displays a set of buttons that enable you to do simple calculations, such as addition, subtraction, multiplication, and division. In landscape orientation, Calculator displays its full set of buttons, enabling you to perform more complex calculations. You can tap

$1+\log(45)\div 2.3$

1.7187880495

HISTORY							⊗
Rad	x!	√	C	( )	%	÷
sin	cos	tan	7	8	9	×
ln	log	¹⁄ₓ	4	5	6	−
e^x	x^2	y^x	1	2	3	+
|x|	π	e	.	0	+/−	=

History to display the History pane, which enables you to review your recent calculations. Tap **Clear History** at the bottom of the History pane if you want to erase the details of your calculations.

S Health

S Health aims to help you manage your health by defining fitness goals and measuring your progress. After accepting the extensive terms, conditions, and disclaimers, you set up a profile of your condition and your aims. You can then use tools such as Exercise Mate, Food Tracker, and Walking Mate to help achieve your goals. You can use the heartbeat sensor on the back of the Galaxy S6 to measure your heart rate, compare it to normal ranges of heart rates, and assign a status to it, such as Resting or After Exercise.

S Health can sync your data to your Samsung account for safekeeping and for sharing with other devices.

Voice Recorder

Voice Recorder gives you an easy and effective way to record voice memos or other informal audio. After launching the app, tap the pop-up menu (▼) in the upper-left corner of the screen and then tap the recording type: **Standard**, **Interview**, or **Voice Memo**. You can then start a recording quickly by tapping **Record** (●), place a bookmark by tapping **Bookmark** (★), and stop the recording by tapping **Stop Recording** (■).

Tap **Recordings** (▤) to display the Recordings screen, where you can tap a recording to play it back. Tap **More** on the Recordings screen to open the menu, which enables you to edit your recordings, share them with others, and search for recordings by name.

Peel Smart Remote

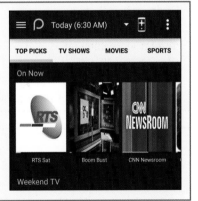

The Peel Smart Remote app enables you to use your Galaxy S6 as a remote control for your TV and other electronic devices. To use Peel Smart Remote, launch it from the Tools folder on the Apps screen, and then follow the steps for selecting your country or region, finding your service, and selecting the content you want to view.

Galaxy Apps

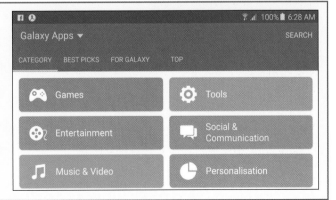

The Galaxy Apps app enables you to purchase, download, and install apps from Samsung's online store. The store offers a wide variety of apps designed for Samsung devices, so if you cannot find the apps you want on Google Play, try looking in the Galaxy Apps app. You can browse the store's offerings in various ways, such as by displaying the Category screen and then tapping the category of apps you want to browse.

Set Up Private Mode

If you plan to use your Galaxy S6 for work, it is a good idea to use Private Mode to keep your sensitive files safe from intrusion. Private Mode provides a secure storage area in which you can keep any file you do not want other people who can access your Galaxy S6 to be able to find or open. In Private Mode, you can use a limited selection of apps securely, such as Gallery, Video, Music, Voice Recorder, and My Files.

Set Up Private Mode

1 Press **Home**.

The Home screen appears.

2 Tap **Apps** (▦).

The Apps screen appears.

3 Tap **Settings** (○).

The Settings screen appears.

4 In the Personal section, tap **Privacy and safety** (●).

The Privacy and Safety screen appears.

5 Tap **Private mode**.

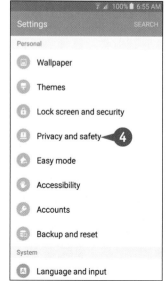
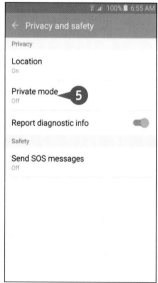

The Private Mode screen appears, with the Disclaimer dialog box open in front of it.

6 Read the disclaimer and tap **Confirm** if you want to proceed.

The Private Mode Access Type screen appears.

7 Tap the security method you want to use: **Pattern**, **PIN**, **Password**, or **Fingerprints**. This example uses PIN.

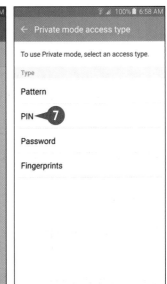

8 Follow the prompts to set the security method. For example, type your PIN on the Set PIN screen and then tap **Continue**.

The Private Mode screen appears, with the Private Mode switch at the top set to On (⬤).

Private Mode is now enabled.

9 Set the **Auto off** switch to On (⬤ changes to ⬤) if you want your Galaxy S6 to disable Private Mode when the screen turns off.

10 Tap **Back** (⬅) or **Back** (⟲).

The Privacy and Safety screen appears.

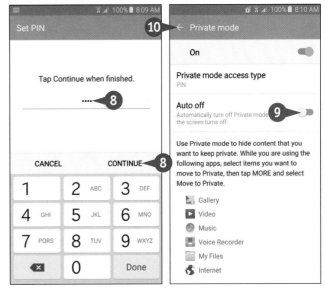

TIPS

How can I tell whether Private Mode is enabled?
Look at the status bar. If Private Mode (🔒) appears, Private Mode is enabled.

How can I enable and disable Private Mode quickly?
Add the Private Mode icon to the Quick Settings buttons. To do this, pull down from the top of the screen to open the Notification panel, then tap **Edit** at the top. On the screen that appears, drag an icon you do not need from the top section to the bottom section, and then drag **Private mode** (🔒) onto the first row. Tap **Done**.

Using Private Mode

After setting up Private Mode for the first time, as explained in the previous section, you can use it to keep your sensitive files secure.

After enabling Private Mode, you can move files to the Private storage area, making them accessible only when Private Mode is turned on. After using Private Mode and working with the files you have stored in the Private area, you turn Private Mode off again, making those files inaccessible to others.

Using Private Mode

Turn On Private Mode

1 Pull down from the top of the screen.

The Notification panel opens.

2 Tap **Private mode** (📷).

Note: If you have not put Private Mode (📷) on the Quick Settings bar, tap **Settings** (⚙) in the Notification panel, tap **Privacy and safety** (🔒) on the Settings screen, tap **Private mode**, and then set the **Private mode** switch to On (changes to).

Your Galaxy S6 prompts you to provide your unlock method. For example, the Enter Your PIN for Private Mode screen appears if you use a PIN.

3 Provide your unlock method. For example, type your PIN and then tap **Done**.

A Private Mode (📷) appears in the status bar.

B The *Private content available* message appears briefly toward the bottom of the screen.

Move Files to the Private Storage Area

1 Press **Home**.

The Home screen appears.

2 Tap **Apps** (⊞).

The Apps screen appears.

3 Tap **Tools** (🔧).

The Tools folder opens.

4 Tap **My Files** (◻).

The My Files app opens.

5 Navigate to the category or folder that contains the files you want to move to the Private storage area. This example uses the Documents category.

C When Private Mode is on, the Private storage area appears in My Files.

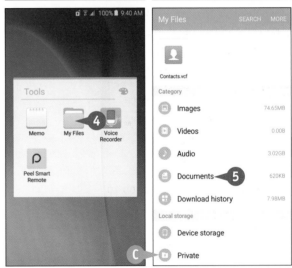

How do I move files to the Private storage area in the Music app?

In the Music app, tap the pop-up menu in the upper-left corner and then tap **Tracks** to display the list of tracks. Tap and hold the first track you want to move. A check box (☐) appears to the left of each track; the check box for the track you tapped and held is selected (☑). Tap each track you want to move (☐ changes to ☑). Tap **More** and then tap **Move to Private**.

How do I move photos and videos to the Private storage area?

In the Gallery app, tap and hold the first photo or video you want to move. A check box (☐) appears to the left of each item; the check box for the item you tapped and held is selected (☑). Tap each item you want to move (☐ changes to ☑). Tap **More** and then tap **Move to Private**.

continued ▶

When you finish using Private Mode, you turn it off to make sure nobody else can access your private files. The easiest way to turn Private Mode off is by tapping its icon in the Quick Settings panel, but you can also open the Notification panel and tap the Private Mode notification to go directly to the Private Mode screen in the Settings app, which includes a switch for turning Private Mode off.

Using Private Mode (continued)

The contents of the category or folder appear.

6 Tap and hold the first file you want to select.

The category or folder switches to Selection Mode.

A check box (☐) appears to the left of each file.

The check box for the file you tapped and held is selected (☑).

7 Tap each file you want to move to Private Mode (☐ changes to ☑).

8 Tap **More**.

The menu opens.

9 Tap **Move to Private**.

The Galaxy S6 moves the items to the Private storage area.

D The *Items moved to Private* readout appears briefly.

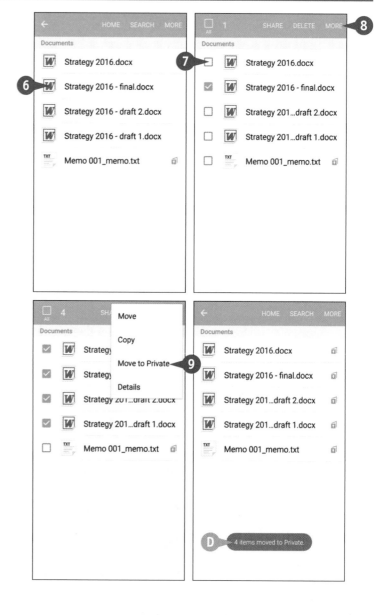

Access Your Private Files

1 In the My Files app, tap **Private** ().

The Private storage opens.

E You can tap a document to open it in the app associated with it.

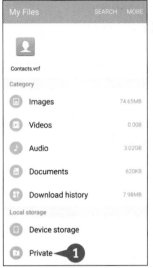

Turn Off Private Mode

1 Pull down from the top of the screen.

The Notification panel opens.

2 Tap **Private mode** ().

The Galaxy S6 turns off Private Mode.

The *Private content not available* message appears briefly.

TIP

How do I move files back from the Private storage area to regular storage?

To move files back from the Private storage area to regular storage, you use a similar method as when moving files to the Private storage area:

- In My Files, tap **Private** to display the Private storage. Select the files you want to remove. Tap **More** and then tap **Remove from Private**. On the Move screen, select the folder for the items, and then tap **Move Here**.

- In Music, select the tracks, tap **More**, and then tap **Remove from Private**. Tap the destination folder, and Music moves the tracks.

- In Gallery, open the Private album, select the photos and videos, tap **More**, and then tap **Remove from Private**. On the Remove from Private screen, tap the destination folder, and Gallery moves the items there.

Connect to a Work Network via VPN

Android includes the capability to connect to a remote network securely across the Internet. It uses a technology called *virtual private networking* (VPN) that encrypts data to create a secure connection between your Galaxy S6 and the VPN server on the remote network.

By using VPN, you can connect securely to your work network from anywhere you can establish an Internet connection. Before you set up a VPN connection, you must apply a lock screen PIN or password to your Galaxy S6.

Connect to a Work Network via VPN

1 Pull down from the top of the screen.

The Notification panel opens.

2 Tap **Settings** (⚙).

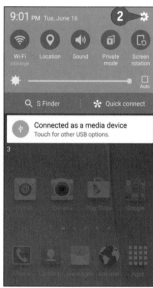

The Settings app opens.

3 In the Connections section, tap **More connection settings** (📶).

The More Connection Settings screen appears.

4 Tap **VPN**.

Note: If you have not yet set a lock screen PIN or password, the Enable Screen Lock dialog box opens. Tap **OK** to display the Screen Lock Type screen; tap **PIN**, **Password**, or **Fingerprints**; and then follow the prompts.

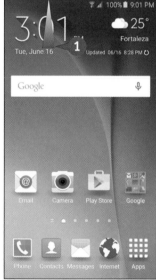

The VPN screen appears.

5 Tap **Add VPN**.

The Add VPN dialog box opens.

6 Type a descriptive name for the connection.

7 Tap the **Type** pop-up menu and then tap the VPN type.

8 Type the server address.

9 Type the security information.

10 Tap **Save**.

The VPN screen appears.

11 Tap the VPN's name.

The Connect To dialog box opens. The dialog box's title bar shows the VPN's name, such as Connect to Work VPN for a VPN called "Work VPN."

12 Tap **Username** and type your username.

13 Tap **Password** and type your password.

14 Tap **Save account information** (☐ changes to ☑) if you want to save your credentials.

15 Tap **Connect**.

Ⓐ The *Connected* readout appears. You can now work with network resources such as e-mail and network folders.

16 When you are ready to disconnect, tap the VPN's name.

17 Tap **Disconnect**.

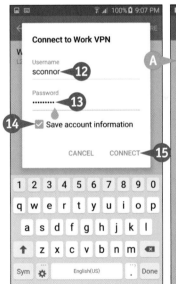

TIPS

What VPN type should I choose?

Ask your VPN's administrator what VPN type to use. PPTP, the Point-to-Point Tunneling Protocol, and L2TP, the Layer 2 Tunneling Protocol, are the most widely used VPN types, but it is hard to guess what type you need.

What is the pre-shared key?

The *pre-shared key*, or PSK, is a group password for the VPN. The pre-shared key is shared among a group of users instead of being specific to a single user. The pre-shared key is also called a *shared secret*.

Connect to Exchange Server

Microsoft Exchange Server is widely used server software that provides e-mail, contact management, and scheduling. If your company or organization uses Exchange Server, you can connect your Galaxy S6 to it and work with your e-mail messages, contacts, and calendars.

To connect to Exchange Server, you set up an account in the Email app. Depending on the Exchange Server setup, Email may be able set up the account automatically. If not, or if you use a digital certificate for authentication, you can configure the account manually.

Connect to Exchange Server

1 Press **Home**.

The Home screen appears.

2 Tap **Email** (⊚).

The Email app opens.

Note: If you have not yet set up an account in the Email app, the app automatically displays the Email screen on launch. Go to step **6**.

3 Tap **More** in the upper-right corner.

The menu opens.

4 Tap **Settings**.

The Email Settings screen appears.

5 Tap **Add account** (+).

The Email Accounts screen appears.

6 Type your e-mail address.

7 Type your password.

A You can tap **Show password** (☐ changes to ☑) to display the password characters.

8 Tap **Set this account as the default for sending emails** (☐ changes to ☑) to make this your default account.

9 Tap **Manual Setup**.

B You can tap **Next** to try automatic setup. If it works, go to step **19**.

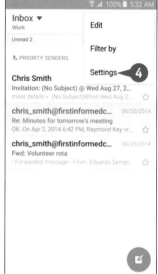

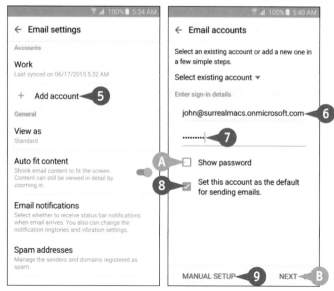

The Select Account Type screen appears.

10 Tap **Microsoft Exchange ActiveSync**.

The Exchange Server Settings screen appears.

11 Edit the contents of the **Domain\ username** field if necessary.

12 Edit the server name if necessary.

13 If your account requires a secure connection, tap **Use secure connection (SSL)** (☐ changes to ☑).

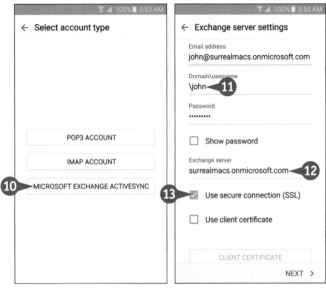

14 If your Galaxy S6 must use a certificate to authenticate to the server, tap **Use client certificate** (☐ changes to ☑). If not, go to step **18**.

15 Tap **Client Certificate**.

The Choose Certificate dialog box opens.

16 Tap the certificate you want to use (◯ changes to ◉).

C If the certificate does not appear, you can tap **Install** and follow the prompts to add it from your Download folder.

17 Tap **Allow**.

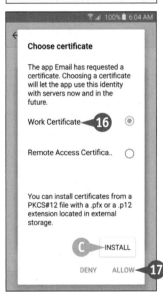

TIPS

How do I know whether to enter a domain for my Exchange account?

Ask your Exchange Server administrator whether to enter a domain and, if so, which one. Exchange Server systems tend to be complex, and you stand little chance of guessing the correct information.

Is my Exchange username the same as my e-mail address?

Your Exchange username may be the same as your e-mail address, or it may be different — for example, just the part of your e-mail address before the @ sign. Ask your Exchange Server administrator what your username is.

continued ▶

When setting up your Exchange account, you need to know your e-mail address and password. You may also need to know the Exchange domain name and the name of the Exchange Server to use. Some Exchange Server connections require your phone to use a *digital certificate,* a unit of encrypted computer code used to identify a device. You normally get this information, and a certificate if needed, from your Exchange administrator or systems administrator.

Connect to Exchange Server (continued)

The Exchange Server Settings screen appears again.

18 Tap **Next**.

The Activation dialog box opens.

19 Read the activation notice, and tap **OK** if you want to continue.

The Email app attempts to contact the appropriate Exchange Server. If so, it selects suitable settings automatically.

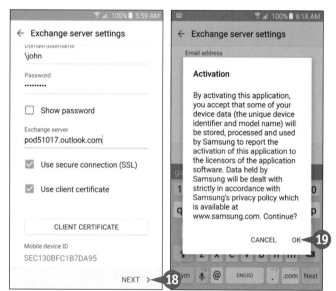

The Remote Security Administration dialog box opens.

20 Tap **OK**.

The Sync Settings screen appears.

21 Tap the **Period to sync Email** pop-up menu and tap the period, such as **3 days**.

22 Tap the **Sync schedule** pop-up menu and tap the schedule, such as **Auto (when received)**.

23 Tap **Emails retrieval size** and then tap the size limit, such as **No limit**.

24 Tap **Period to sync Calendar** and then tap the period, such as **2 weeks**.

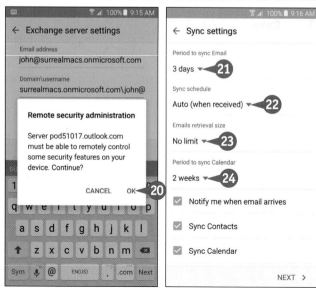

25 Tap **Notify me when e-mail arrives** (☐ changes to ✓) to receive notifications.

26 Tap **Sync Contacts** (☐ changes to ✓) to sync contacts.

27 Tap **Sync Calendar** (☐ changes to ✓) to sync calendar data.

28 Tap **Sync Task** (☐ changes to ✓) to sync tasks.

29 Tap **Sync Messages** (☐ changes to ✓) to sync messages.

30 Tap **Next**.

The Device Administrator screen appears.

Note: The Device Administrator screen explains the remote-control features that Exchange can exercise over your Galaxy S6. For example, an Exchange administrator can remotely erase all your data.

31 Tap **Activate** if you want to proceed.

The Email Accounts screen appears.

32 Type the name you want to assign to the account.

33 Tap **Done**.

Your Inbox appears, and you can start using your Exchange account.

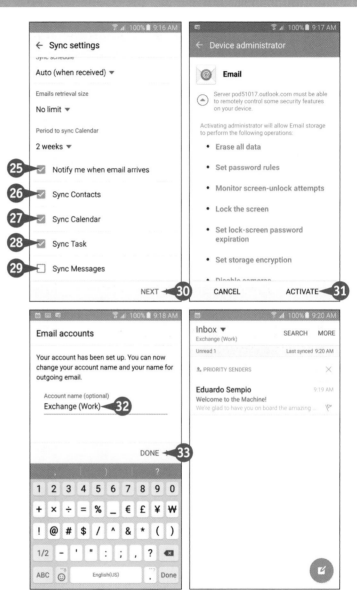

TIPS

Should I use the Auto (When Received) sync setting?
This sync setting makes the server notify your phone whenever new mail is available. Use this setting if you want to receive your messages as quickly as possible and do not mind sacrificing some battery power to get them.

Should I turn on the Use Secure Connection option?
You will probably need to select **Use secure connection (SSL)** (☐ changes to ✓) in order to log in to the Exchange Server. SSL is the abbreviation for *Secure Sockets Layer,* a communications technology for establishing a secure connection. In this case, the connection is between your Galaxy S6 and the Exchange Server.

Install Credentials

When connecting to Exchange Server systems or establishing a VPN connection, you may need to provide credentials to authenticate your Galaxy S6's identity and — by implication — your own identity. Android enables you to install digital certificates containing credentials on your Galaxy S6.

You can install a digital certificate either by opening a digital certificate attached to an e-mail message or by placing the digital certificate's file in your Google Drive storage and then using the Drive app to install it.

Install Credentials

Install a Digital Certificate from an E-Mail Message

1 In the Inbox of your e-mail app, tap the message that contains the digital certificate.

Note: This example uses the Gmail app. You can also install a digital certificate from the Email app.

The message opens.

2 Tap **Attachment** (📄).

The Extract Certificate dialog box opens.

3 Type the digital certificate's password.

4 Tap **OK**.

The Certificate Name dialog box opens.

5 Edit the name for the certificate as needed.

Note: Give each certificate you install a descriptive name so that you can easily distinguish it from other certificates.

6 Tap the **Used for** pop-up menu and tap **VPN and apps** or **Wi-Fi** to specify the certificate's uses.

7 Tap **OK**.

Ⓐ A message says that the certificate has been installed.

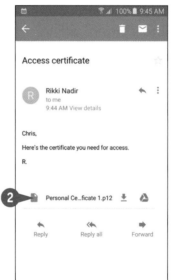

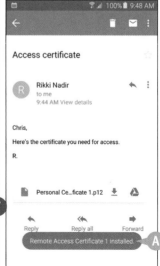

Install a Digital Certificate from Google Drive

1 Press **Home**.

The Home screen appears.

2 Tap **Google** (▦).

The Google folder opens.

The Apps screen appears.

3 Tap **Drive** (▲).

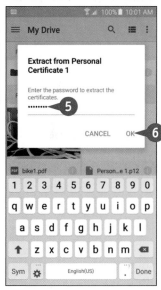

The My Drive screen appears.

4 Tap the certificate file.

The Extract From dialog box opens.

5 Type the password.

6 Tap **OK**.

The Certificate Name dialog box opens.

7 Follow steps **5** to **7** in the preceding subsection to complete the installation.

CHAPTER 11

Playing Music and Videos

You can pack a huge amount of music and many hours of video on your Galaxy S6, enabling you to enjoy music and videos wherever you go.

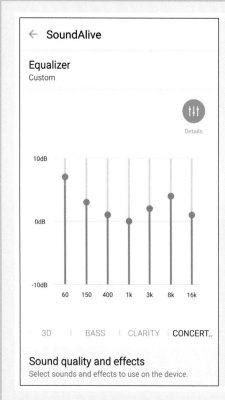

Play Music with the Music App 256

Adjust the Sound with the SoundAlive Equalizer 258

Create a Playlist 260

Customize the Audio Settings for Your Headset 262

Play Music Through Other Devices 264

Watch Videos 266

Using the Pop-Up Video Player 268

Play Music with the Music App

You can enjoy the music on your Galaxy S6 by using the Music app. You can browse your music by songs, artists, albums, playlists, or folders. You can browse the Recently Added playlist to find new music, the Recently Played playlist for songs you have enjoyed recently, or the Most Played playlist to find songs you listen to often. You can also mark any song as a favorite, which makes it appear in the Favorite playlist.

Play Music with the Music App

1 Press **Home**.

The Home screen appears.

2 Tap **Apps** (⊞).

The Apps screen appears.

3 Tap **Music** (●).

Note: The Music app can play various music formats including MP3, AAC without digital-rights management protection, FLAC, Ogg Vorbis, and WAV files. It cannot play Apple Lossless Encoding files, but you can use iTunes to create AAC versions of the music for the Galaxy S6.

The Music app opens.

4 Tap the pop-up menu in the upper-left corner. This menu shows the current category, such as Artists.

The pop-up menu opens.

5 Tap the category you want to use, such as **Tracks**.

Note: In addition to the Music app, your Galaxy S6 may have the Play Music app (◌), which can stream music via Google Play.

The category's screen appears.

6 Tap the song you want to play.

The song starts playing.

The background color changes to reflect that of the album art, if any.

Ⓐ You can tap **Pause** (❙❙) to pause playback.

Ⓑ You can tap **Next** (▶▶) to skip to the next song.

Ⓒ You can tap **Previous** (◀◀) once to return to the start of the song or tap again to go to the previous song.

7 Tap the album art or the song and artist name.

The song's screen appears.

Ⓓ You can drag the playhead to move through the song.

Ⓔ You can tap **Shuffle off** (⤨) to turn on shuffling.

Note: Tap **Shuffle on** (⤨) to turn off shuffling.

Ⓕ You can tap **Favorite** (☆ changes to ★) to mark the song as a favorite.

Ⓖ You can tap **Volume** (🔊) to change the volume.

8 Tap **Queue**.

The queue appears, showing the current list of songs with the playing song at the top.

9 Tap the song you want to play.

The song starts playing.

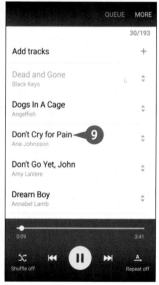

What does the A button do?

This is the Repeat button. Tap **Repeat off** (🄰 changes to 🄰) to turn on repeating for all songs. Tap **Repeat all** (🄰 changes to 🄰) to turn on repeating for the current song. Tap **Repeat 1** (🄰 changes to 🄰) to turn off repeating.

How can I prevent some songs from playing much more loudly than others?

In the Music app, tap **More** and then tap **Settings**. On the Settings screen, set the **Smart volume** switch to On (⚪ changes to 🔵). The Music app then "normalizes" the volume of songs, making the overall volume more consistent at the cost of some dynamic range.

Adjust the Sound with the SoundAlive Equalizer

The Music app includes the SoundAlive feature, an equalizer that enables you to adjust the sound balance to your liking. You can apply an equalization by adjusting the bass and treble, and the balance between instruments and vocals, or you can create a custom equalization that suits your ears and your speakers or headphones by adjusting the frequency bands. You can also add an effect such as Tube Amp, Small Room, or Concert Hall.

Adjust the Sound with the SoundAlive Equalizer

1 Press **Home**.

The Home screen appears.

2 Tap **Apps** (▦).

The Apps screen appears.

3 Tap **Music** (◉).

The Music app opens.

4 Start some music playing so that you can hear the effect of the changes that you make.

5 Tap **More**.

The menu opens.

6 Tap **SoundAlive**.

The SoundAlive screen appears, showing the Bass/Treble dial and the Instrument/Vocal dial.

Ⓐ You can drag the Bass/Treble dial to adjust the balance between bass and treble.

Ⓑ You can drag the Instrument/Vocal dial to adjust the balance between instruments and vocals.

⑦ Tap **Equalizer**.

The Equalizer panel opens.

⑧ Tap the equalization you want (○ changes to ◉).

The Equalizer panel closes.

⑨ Tap **Details** (⑴).

The equalizer controls appears.

Ⓒ You can drag the frequency sliders to set the equalization.

Ⓓ You can tap **3D**, **Bass**, **Clarity**, or **Concert Hall** to add an effect.

⑩ Tap **Sound quality and effects**.

The Sound Quality and Effects screen appears.

⑪ Set the **SoundAlive+** switch to On (changes to) to create surround sound.

⑫ Set the **Tube Amp** switch to On (changes to) if you want a tube-amp effect.

⑬ Tap **Back** ( ) or **Back** ( ) twice.

Your music appears.

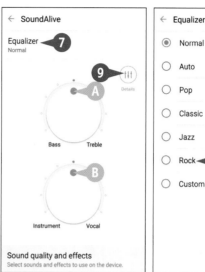
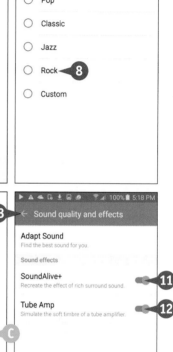
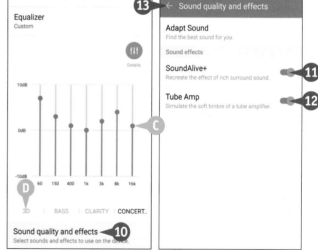

TIPS

What is the Adapt Sound feature in the Music app?
Adapt Sound applies a custom sound configuration. First, create your Adapt Sound configuration as discussed in the section "Customize the Audio Settings for Your Headset," later in this chapter. Then, in the Music app, tap **More**, tap **Settings**, tap **SoundAlive**, tap **Sound quality and effects**, tap **Adapt Sound**, and then set the **Adapt Sound** switch to On (changes to).

How do the frequency sliders in SoundAlive work?
The sliders are arranged from the lowest frequencies on the left to the highest frequencies on the right. Drag a slider up to increase the amount of that frequency or down to decrease it.

Create a Playlist

The Music app enables you to create playlists that contain the songs you want to hear in your preferred order. Playlists are a great way to enjoy music on your Galaxy S6. You can easily create playlists by working on the Playlists screen, or you can use the built-in playlists: Favorite Tracks, Most Played, Recently Played, and Recently Added.

After creating a playlist, you can add songs to it as needed, remove existing songs, and rearrange the remaining songs.

Create a Playlist

1 Press **Home**.

The Home screen appears.

2 Tap **Apps** (▦).

The Apps screen appears.

3 Tap **Music** (●).

The Music app opens.

4 Navigate to the first song you want to add to the new playlist.

5 Tap and hold the song.

A check box appears to the left of each song.

Ⓐ The check box for the song you chose is selected (☑).

6 Tap any other songs you want to add to the playlist (☐ changes to ☑).

7 Tap **More**.

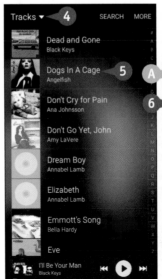

The menu opens.

8 Tap **Add to playlist**.

The Add to Playlist screen appears.

Note: Instead of tapping **Add to playlist**, you can tap an existing playlist to add the selected items to it.

9 Tap **Create playlist**.

The Create Playlist dialog box opens.

10 Type the name for the playlist.

11 Tap **Create**.

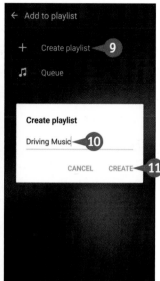

The playlist's screen appears.

12 Tap and hold a song.

A check box appears to the left of each song and a movement handle (⬍) appears to the right.

13 Tap and hold the movement handle (⬍) and drag the song up or down the list.

14 When you finish editing the playlist, tap **Back** (⟲).

The playlist's screen appears again.

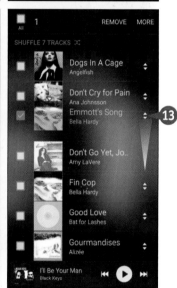

TIP

How do I rename a playlist?

Tap the pop-up menu in the upper-left corner of the screen and then tap **Playlists** to display the Playlists screen. Tap and hold the playlist you want to rename. A selected check box (☑) appears to the left of the playlist. Tap **Rename** at the top of the screen, type the new name in the Rename dialog box, and then tap **Rename**.

Customize the Audio Settings for Your Headset

The Adapt Sound feature on your Galaxy S6 enables you to create a custom audio configuration for listening to music or taking phone calls. First, you open the Settings app, go through the process of configuring Adapt Sound to suit your hearing, and choose which features may use your Adapt Sound configuration. Then you turn on Adapt Sound in the Music app when you want to use the configuration — for example, when you are listening through headphones.

Customize the Audio Settings for Your Headset

1 Connect the headset or headphones that you will use with the Adapt Sound feature.

2 Put on the headset or headphones.

3 Pull down from the top of the screen.

The Notification panel opens.

4 Tap and hold **Sound** (◀), **Mute** (◀), or **Vibrate** (◀) — whichever icon appears.

The Sounds and Notifications screen in the Settings app appears.

5 Tap **Sound quality and effects**.

The Sound Quality and Effects screen appears.

6 Tap **Adapt Sound**.

The Adapt Sound screen appears.

7 Tap **Start**.

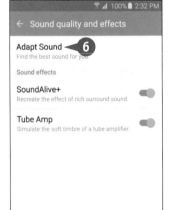

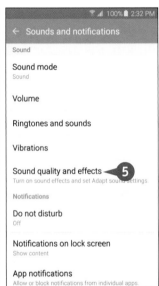

The Set Up Adapt Sound screen appears.

Adapt Sound plays a sequence of sounds at different pitches to test which pitches each ear can hear.

⑧ At each prompt, tap **Yes** if you can hear the sound or **No** if you cannot hear it.

When you finish the sequence, the Adapt Sound screen appears and the Frequently Used Side dialog box opens.

⑨ Tap **Left** (◯ changes to ◉) or **Right** (◯ changes to ◉) to indicate the ear to which you normally hold the phone.

The profile for your left ear appears.

Note: You can swipe left to display the profile for your right ear.

⑩ Tap **Preview**.

The Play Adapt Sound Sample screen appears.

⑪ Swipe left or right to move among the Left, Right, and Both screens. These screens show the profile of your left ear, right ear, or both ears, and play sounds in the appropriate channels.

⑫ Tap **Personalized** to hear your personalized sound.

⑬ Tap **Original** to hear your original sound.

⑭ Tap **Back** (⬅) or **Back** (↩) three times.

The Home screen appears.

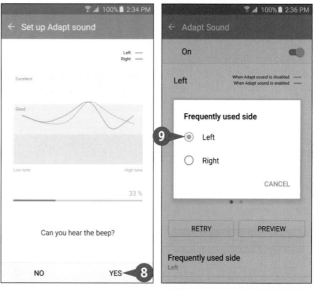

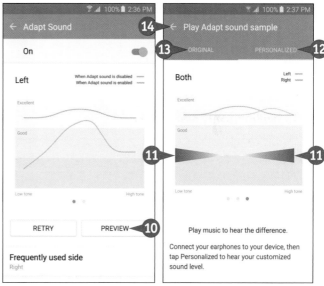

What is the frequently used side?
This is the side of your face to which you normally hold your phone when making calls. For example, if you hold the phone to your right ear, your frequently used side is right.

How do I customize my Adapt Sound profile?
As of this writing, Adapt Sound does not enable you to customize your profile, although earlier versions of Adapt Sound did offer this feature. Instead, tap **Retry** on the Adapt Sound screen to create a new profile in the hope that it will be better.

Play Music Through Other Devices

Your Galaxy S6 can play music through other devices that use the Digital Living Network Alliance (DLNA) standard. For example, you might turn on DLNA on your TV so you can play music through it from your Galaxy S6 using the Music app.

The Quick Connect feature enables you to easily connect your Galaxy S6 to other nearby devices. Once connected, you can play music, images, or videos.

Play Music Through Other Devices

1 Press **Home**.

The Home screen appears.

2 Pull down from the top of the screen.

The Notification panel opens.

3 Tap **Quick connect** (![icon]).

The Quick Connect screen appears.

The list of nearby devices appears.

4 Tap the device on which you want to play music.

Ⓐ If the device you want to use does not appear, tap **Refresh**.

The Play/View Content button appears.

5 Tap **Play/view content**.

The Play/View Content panel appears.

6 Tap **Image** (![icon]), **Video** (![icon]), or **Audio** (![icon]), as appropriate. This example uses **Audio** (![icon]).

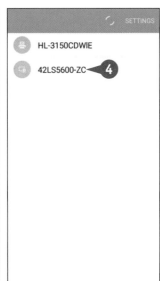

The Tracks screen appears, showing the music available in the Music app.

7 Tap each track you want to play (☐ changes to ☑).

8 Tap **Done**.

Your Galaxy S6 connects to the device and starts playing music through it.

You can control playback, as explained in the section "Play Music with the Music App," earlier in this chapter.

9 When you are ready to stop using the device, tap **More**.

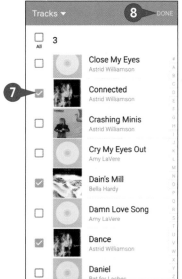

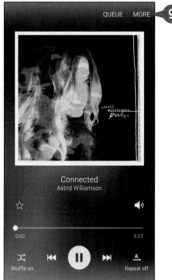

The menu opens.

10 Tap **Play on other device**.

The Select Device dialog box opens.

B The connection status appears.

11 Tap **Disconnect**.

Your Galaxy S6 disconnects from the device.

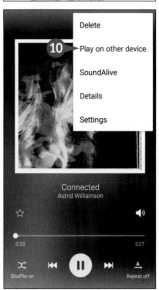

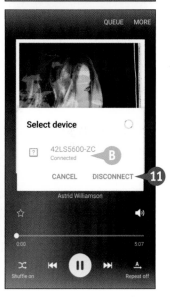

TIP

How can I troubleshoot the Quick Connect feature?

Make sure that each wireless device is connected to the same wireless network and to the same Wi-Fi access point. To determine which Wi-Fi access point your Galaxy S6 is using, pull down from the top of the screen to open the Notification panel, and then look at the network name under the Wi-Fi icon (🛜).

After opening Quick Connect, you may need to tap **Refresh** several times in order to show all nearby devices. If a nearby device still fails to appear, try restarting it.

Watch Videos

Your Galaxy S6 may include two or more apps for playing videos. Many Galaxy S6 models include both the Video app and the Photos app, both of which can play videos.

The Gallery app enables to browse your photos and videos together and to open a video in either the Photos app or the Video app. Alternatively, you can open the Photos app or the Video app from the Apps screen.

Watch Videos

1 Press **Home**.

The Home screen appears.

2 Tap **Apps** (▦).

The Apps screen appears.

3 Tap **Gallery** (▣).

Note: You can tap **Video** (▶) on the Apps screen and then open a video from within the app.

The Gallery app opens.

Ⓐ You can change the view by tapping the pop-up menu and then tapping the view you want: **Time**, **Albums**, **Events**, or **Categories**.

4 Tap the video you want to view.

The first frame of the video appears.

5 Tap **Play** (▶).

The Open With panel appears.

6 Tap **Photos** (🌀).

7 Tap **Just Once**.

Ⓑ Tap **Always** if you want to use Photos each time you open a video from the Gallery app.

Photos opens and starts playing the video.

Note: If the video is in landscape orientation, turn your Galaxy S6 to landscape orientation to view the video full-screen.

8 Tap anywhere on the screen when you need to display the controls.

The controls appear.

Ⓒ You can tap **Pause** (⏸) to pause playback and tap **Play** (▶) to resume playback.

Ⓓ You can drag the **playhead** (⬛) to move quickly through the video.

Ⓔ You can tap **Rewind** (⏪) to rewind the video.

Ⓕ You can tap **Fast-Forward** (⏩) to move forward.

Note: The controls disappear automatically a few seconds after you stop using them.

After the video ends, the Gallery app reappears.

TIP

How do I play a video from my Galaxy S6 on my TV?
If your TV has DLNA, use Quick Connect, as explained in the previous section. If your TV does not have DLNA, either connect a DLNA dongle to it or use an HDMI-to-micro-USB cable to connect the multipurpose jack on your Galaxy S6 to the HDMI port on the TV. Switch the TV's input to that port, and the contents of your Galaxy S6's screen appear on the TV screen.

Using the Pop-Up Video Player

Your Galaxy S6 includes a pop-up video player that enables you to keep watching a video in a small window that appears in front of whatever else is on the screen. You can adjust the size of the pop-up window and reposition it on-screen so you can continue watching the video while you work or play in other apps. You launch the pop-up video player from the Video app.

Using the Pop-Up Video Player

1 Press **Home**.

The Home screen appears.

2 Tap **Apps** (▦).

The Apps screen appears.

3 Tap **Video** (▶).

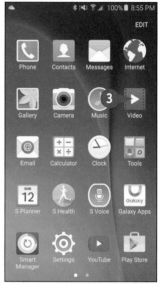

The Video app opens.

4 Tap the video you want to open.

The video starts playing.

5 Tap the screen.

The controls appear.

6 Tap **Pop-up** (▭).

The Video app displays the video in the pop-up player, still playing.

7 Press **Home**.

The Home screen appears.

Note: You can drag the pop-up player to where you want it to appear.

Note: You can pinch inward or outward with two fingers to resize the pop-up player to your preferred size.

8 Tap **Apps** (⊞).

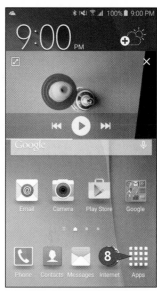

The Apps screen appears.

9 Tap the app you want to launch. This example uses **Keep** (⬤).

The app opens.

10 Work in the app, watching the video in the pop-up player.

11 Tap the video to display its controls. You can then tap **Pause** (❚❚) to pause playback, tap **Previous** (◀◀) to play the previous video, or tap **Next** (▶▶) to play the next video.

12 With the controls displayed, tap **Close** (✖) to exit the player.

The pop-up player window closes.

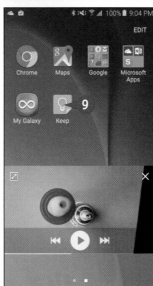

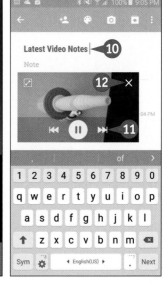

TIP

How do I return from the pop-up player to the Video app?
You can quickly return to the Video app from the pop-up player by double-tapping the pop-up player. Tap **Pop-up** (▣) if you want to go back to the pop-up player again from the Video app.

CHAPTER 12

Troubleshooting Your Galaxy S6

To keep your Galaxy S6 running well, you should update its software, keep backups in case of disaster, and learn essential troubleshooting steps, such as closing apps that have stopped responding and solving wireless connection problems.

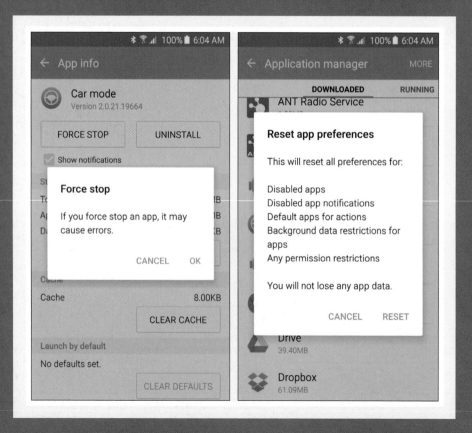

Close an App That Has Stopped Responding 272

Update Your Galaxy S6's Software. 274

Extend the Runtime on the Battery 276

Using Ultra Power Saving Mode 278

Reset Your App Preferences. 280

Check Free Space and Clear Extra Space 282

Back Up and Restore Online 284

Back Up Your Data with Smart Switch 286

Restore Your Data with Smart Switch 288

Reset Your Galaxy S6 to Factory Settings 290

Troubleshoot Wireless Network Connections. 292

Locate or Wipe Your Missing Galaxy S6 294

Close an App That Has Stopped Responding

If an app on your Galaxy S6 stops responding to your input, you need to close the app and then restart it before you can continue using it. To close the app, you force it to stop by using the Application Manager tool, which you access through the Settings app. After forcing an app to stop, you may need to restart your Galaxy S6 before you can use the app again.

Close an App That Has Stopped Responding

1 Pull down from the top of the screen.

The Notification panel opens.

2 Tap **Settings** (⚙).

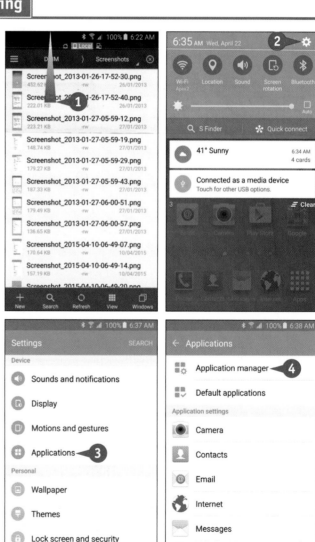

The Settings screen appears.

3 In the Device section, tap **Applications** (⊞).

The Applications screen appears.

4 Tap **Application manager** (📱).

The Application Manager screen appears.

The Downloaded tab appears at first.

5 Tap **Running**.

The Running tab appears.

Note: You can also swipe left on the Downloaded tab to display the Running tab.

6 Tap the app or service you want to stop.

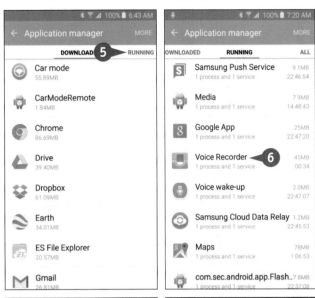

The Active App screen appears.

7 Tap **Stop**.

The Stop System Service? dialog box opens for a service. The Force Stop dialog box opens for an app.

8 Tap **OK**.

Android stops the app or service.

9 Tap **Back** (![back]) or **Back** (↰).

The Running tab appears again, where you can close other apps if necessary.

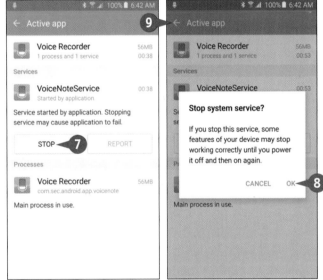

TIP

What else can I do in Application Manager?

On the Running tab, you can tap **More** and then tap **Show cached processes** to display the processes that your Galaxy S6 has cached. These processes are apps and services that you are not currently using, but that the operating system has stored so it can load them again quickly if you ask to use them. You can then tap a process to display the Active App screen, which shows information about the process. On the Active App screen, you can tap **Stop** to stop a process, but usually this is not necessary. Back on the Running tab, tap **More** and then tap **Show services in use** to display the list of running services again.

Update Your Galaxy S6's Software

Samsung periodically releases new versions of the Galaxy S6's operating system and TouchWiz skin to fix problems, improve performance, and add new features. To keep your phone running quickly and smoothly, you should update its software when a new version is available.

The usual way to update your Galaxy S6's software is by downloading it wirelessly. If your phone goes wrong, you can use Emergency Software Recovery and Initialization in the Smart Switch app on your computer to recover.

Update Your Galaxy S6's Software

Ⓐ When a software update is available, the Software Update icon (⬛) appears in the status bar.

① Pull down from the top of the screen.

The Notification panel appears.

② Tap the **Software Update** notification.

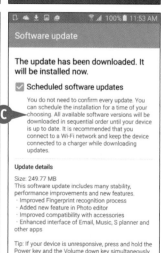

The Software Update screen appears.

③ Read the details of the update.

Ⓑ You can tap **Scheduled software updates** (☐ changes to ☑) if you want your Galaxy S6 to install some updates automatically.

Ⓒ If you select Scheduled Software Updates, information about the feature appears.

④ Tap **Install**.

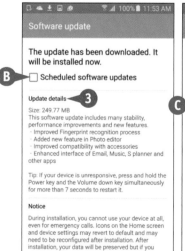

The Software Update dialog box opens.

5 Tap **OK**.

Your Galaxy S6 restarts and installs the updates.

D Android optimizes the apps on your phone.

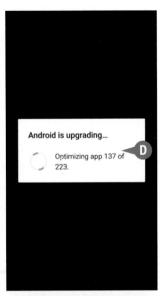

The lock screen appears.

6 Unlock your Galaxy S6 as usual. For example, place a registered finger on the fingerprint scanner in the Home button.

The Home screen appears.

The Software Update dialog box appears, telling you the device has been updated.

7 Tap **OK**.

The Software Update dialog box closes.

You can resume using your Galaxy S6 as normal.

TIP

How do I control when and how my Galaxy S6 checks for software updates?

Press **Home**, tap **Apps** (▦), and then tap **Settings**. Tap **About device** in the System section to display the About Device screen. Tap **Software update** to display the Software Update screen. Here, you can set the **Auto update** switch to On (⬭ changes to ⬬) to make your phone check automatically for updates, set the **Wi-Fi only** switch to On (⬭ changes to ⬬) to limit downloads of updates to when your phone is connected to Wi-Fi, or tap **Update now** to check for updates at this moment.

Extend the Runtime on the Battery

To keep your Galaxy S6 running all day long, you can turn on Power Saving Mode. Power Saving Mode can throttle back the processor, dim the screen and turn it off sooner, and shut off haptic feedback to save power.

For greater power saving, you can turn off Wi-Fi and Bluetooth and set a short screen timeout. When the battery runs dangerously low on power, you can use Ultra Power Saving Mode, discussed in the next section.

Extend the Runtime on the Battery

Turn On and Configure Power Saving Mode

1 Press **Home**.

The Home screen appears.

2 Tap **Apps** (▦).

The Apps screen appears.

3 Tap **Settings** (○).

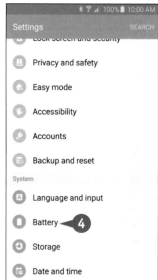

The Settings screen appears.

4 In the System section, tap **Battery** (○).

The Battery screen appears.

A You can tap **More** and then tap **Show battery percentage** or **Hide battery percentage** to show or hide the battery percentage readout in the status bar.

B You can tap **Detail** to see details on any apps that have used unusually large amounts of battery power.

5 Tap **Power saving mode**.

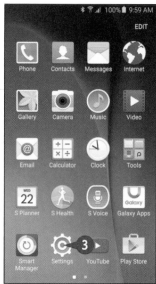

The Power Saving Mode screen appears.

6 Set the **Power saving mode** switch to On (⬭ changes to ⬭) to turn on Power Saving Mode.

7 Tap **Start power saving**.

The Start Power Saving screen appears.

8 Tap the point at which you want to start saving power, such as **Immediately** (○ changes to ◉).

The Power Saving screen appears.

9 Tap **Back** (⬅) or **Back** (⤺) twice.

The Settings screen appears.

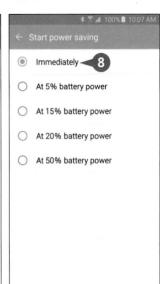

Turn Power Saving Mode, Wi-Fi, and Bluetooth On or Off

1 Pull down from the top of the screen.

2 To turn Power Saving on or off, tap **Power Saving** (⬚ changes to ⬚ or ⬚ changes to ⬚).

3 To turn Wi-Fi on or off, tap **Wi-Fi** (⬚ changes to ⬚ or ⬚ changes to ⬚).

4 To turn Bluetooth on or off, tap **Bluetooth** (⬚ changes to ⬚ or ⬚ changes to ⬚).

C You can tap **Turn Off** on the *Power saving mode on* notification to turn off Power Saving Mode.

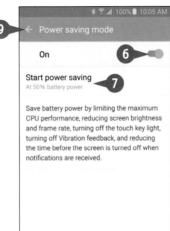

TIP

What else can I do to increase the runtime of my Galaxy S6?

You can reduce your usage of the phone. For example, you can avoid playing music, refrain from watching videos, or simply not make phone calls. But given that utility and enjoyment are largely the point of having a smartphone, you will usually do better to tackle the power problem from the other end and find ways to recharge the battery frequently. For example, get a second regular charger and keep it at work, get a car charger so that you can recharge your phone in the car, or get a portable battery pack from which you can recharge the phone anywhere.

Using Ultra Power Saving Mode

As well as Power Saving Mode, discussed in the preceding section, "Extend the Runtime on the Battery," your Galaxy S6 offers Ultra Power Saving Mode. This mode enables you to eke out the remaining battery life by switching to a spartan black-and-white interface, limiting the apps that you can run, and preventing you from using power-hungry features.

You can use Ultra Power Saving Mode at any time, but it is normally best saved for emergencies.

Using Ultra Power Saving Mode

1 Press **Home**.

The Home screen appears.

2 Tap **Apps** (▦).

The Apps screen appears.

3 Tap **Settings** (⚙).

The Settings screen appears.

4 In the System section, tap **Battery** (🔋).

The Battery screen appears.

5 Tap **Ultra power saving mode**.

Note: The first time you turn on Ultra Power Saving Mode, the Terms and Conditions screen appears. Tap **I have read and agree to all the terms and conditions above** (☐ changes to ☑) and then tap **Agree** to proceed.

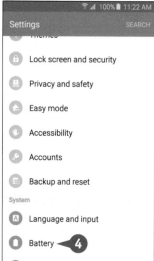

The Ultra Power Saving Mode screen appears.

6 Set the **Ultra power saving mode** switch to On (changes to).

The Ultra Power Saving Mode Home screen appears.

A The *Estimated usage time remaining* readout shows the maximum standby time that Ultra Power Saving Mode may be able to deliver.

B You can tap an app to launch it.

7 Tap **Add** ( ).

The Add Application screen appears.

8 Tap the app you want to add.

C The app appears on the Home screen.

9 When you finish using Ultra Power Saving Mode, tap **More**.

The menu opens.

10 Tap **Turn off Ultra power saving mode**.

Your Galaxy S6 turns off Ultra Power Saving Mode and becomes its colorful, vibrant self again.

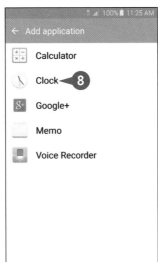

TIPS

What settings can I choose in Ultra Power Saving Mode?
In Ultra Power Saving Mode, the Settings screen contains only the Connections section and the Device section. The Connections section contains the Wi-Fi, Bluetooth, Airplane Mode, Mobile Networks, and Location settings. The Device section contains only the Sound and Brightness settings.

How do I remove an app from the Home screen in Ultra Power Saving Mode?
Press **Home**, tap **More**, and then tap **Remove**. On the screen that appears, tap **Remove** ( ) for the app you want to remove. You cannot remove the Phone app, the Messages app, or the Internet app.

Reset Your App Preferences

If the software on your Galaxy S6 becomes unstable, you may be able to sort out the problem by resetting all your app preferences to their default settings.

After resetting all the preferences, you can set the preferences for any individual app how you want them. You may also find resetting your app preferences useful when you have been experimenting with the settings for different apps but cannot find the settings needed to undo the changes that you have made.

Reset Your App Preferences

1 Pull down from the top of the screen.

The Notification panel opens.

2 Tap **Settings** (⚙).

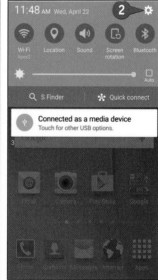

The Settings screen appears.

3 In the Device section, tap **Applications** (⊞).

The Applications screen appears.

4 Tap **Application manager** (🔧).

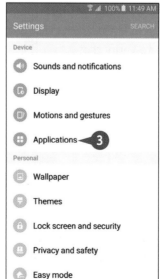
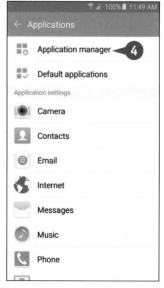

The Application Manager screen appears.

5 Tap **More**.

The More menu opens.

6 Tap **Reset app preferences**.

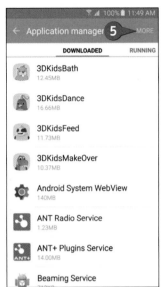

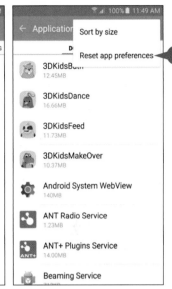

The Reset App Preferences dialog box opens.

7 Tap **Reset**.

Android resets the app preferences.

8 Press **Home**.

The Select Launcher panel opens.

9 Tap **TouchWiz home**.

10 Tap **Always**.

The Home screen appears.

You can now launch an app from the Home screen or the Apps screen to verify that resetting the app preferences resolved the problem.

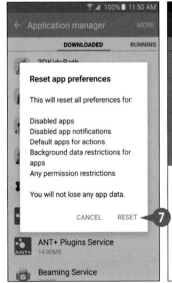

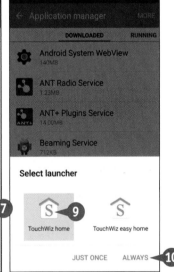

TIP

What other effects does resetting app preferences have?

Along with resolving instabilities, resetting app preferences also removes the associations you have made between particular file types and apps. So if you had associated a given file type with an app by tapping the **Always** button in the Select App panel, making Android always use that app for that file type, you will need to make that choice again after resetting app preferences. This is why the Choose Launcher panel opens when you press **Home** after resetting app preferences, giving you the choice between TouchWiz Easy Home and TouchWiz Home, the regular version of the TouchWiz user interface.

Check Free Space and Clear Extra Space

If you take your Galaxy S6 everywhere, you probably want to put as many data and media files on it as possible so that you can carry them with you. When you do this, your phone may become low on free space, which can cause it to run slowly or unstably. To avoid problems, you can check how much space is left. When free space runs low, you can clear extra space to help avoid problems.

Check Free Space and Clear Extra Space

1 Pull down from the top of the screen.

The Notification panel opens.

2 Tap **Settings** (⚙).

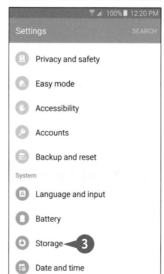

The Settings app opens.

3 In the System section, tap **Storage** (🔄).

The Storage screen appears.

Ⓐ Device Memory shows how much memory is in use.

Ⓑ Total Space shows the total storage space, minus the space taken up by the operating system and included apps.

Ⓒ Available Space shows how much space is free.

4 Tap **Used space**.

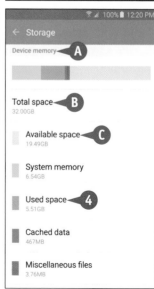
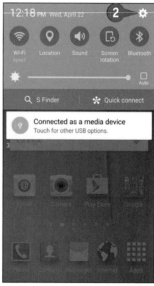

The Used Space screen appears.

5 Tap **Applications**.

The Application Manager screen appears, showing the apps listed in descending order of size.

6 To remove an app, tap its name.

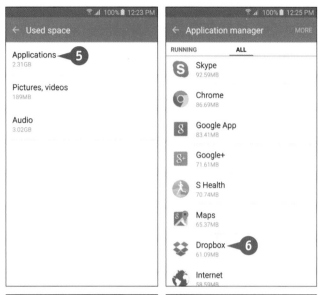

The App Info screen for the app appears.

7 Tap **Uninstall**.

The Uninstall App dialog box opens.

8 Tap **Uninstall**.

Android uninstalls the app.

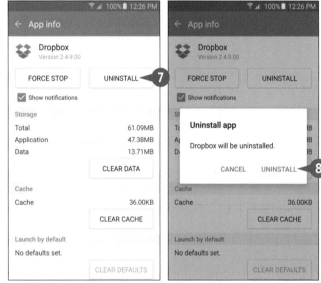

TIP

What other items can I delete to free up space on my Galaxy S6?
You can delete cached data, miscellaneous files, and media files. On the Storage screen, tap **Cached data** to display the Clear Cached Data dialog box and then tap **OK**. Next, tap **Miscellaneous files** to display the Miscellaneous Files screen. You can then tap each file you want to delete (☐ changes to ☑) and then tap **Delete**.

Although the Used Space screen contains a "Pictures, Video" button and an Audio button, it is easier to remove pictures, video, and audio files using your computer than directly using Android.

Back Up and Restore Online

You can back up your Galaxy S6 to your Google account to keep your data and settings safe. If your phone subsequently suffers problems, you can reset it to factory settings and then restore your data and settings to it from your Google account. You can also restore your data to a new phone.

Your Galaxy S6 can also automatically back up key content from apps such as Contacts, Email, Messages, and Phone to your Samsung account.

Back Up and Restore Online

1 Pull down from the top of the screen.

The Notification panel opens.

2 Tap **Settings** (⚙).

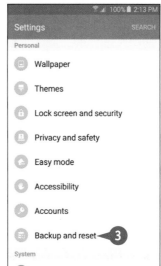

The Settings app opens.

3 In the Personal section, tap **Backup and reset** (🔄).

The Backup and Reset screen appears.

4 In the Samsung Account area, tap **Back up my data**.

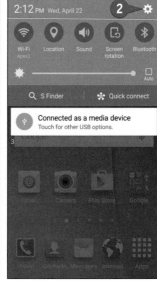

The Back Up My Data screen appears.

5 Set the **Auto back up** switch to On (changes to) to use automatic backup.

6 In the Content to Back Up area, tap each item (changes to ✓) you want to back up.

A You can tap **Details** to see details of which items the backup includes for each app.

B You can tap **Back Up Now** to run a backup now.

7 Tap **Back** ( ) or **Back** ( ).

The Backup and Reset screen appears.

8 Tap **Backup account**.

The Set Backup Account dialog box opens.

9 Tap the appropriate account.

C You can add an account by tapping **Add account**.

The Set Backup Account dialog box closes.

10 Set the **Back up my data** switch to On (changes to).

11 Set the **Automatic restore** switch to On (changes to) if you want to restore your settings and data when you reinstall an app.

12 Tap **Back** ( ) or **Back** ( ).

The Settings screen appears.

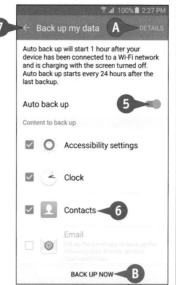

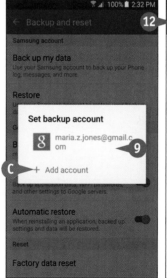

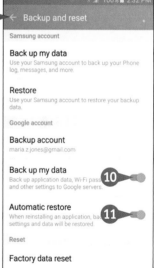

TIPS

What settings does Android back up to my Google account?

Android backs up your personal data, such as your contacts, web bookmarks, and Wi-Fi passwords. Android also stores the list of apps you have bought or downloaded from the Play Store and your customized settings — for example, your Display settings and Sound settings.

Should I use my Google account or my Samsung account for backup?

For security, it makes sense to use both accounts for backup unless you prefer not to entrust any more data to Google or to Samsung than you already do by having a Google account or a Samsung account.

Back Up Your Data with Smart Switch

S mart Switch, the companion app that Samsung provides with the Galaxy S6 and other devices, enables you to back up your phone to your PC or Mac for safety. You can choose between backing up all the contents of your Galaxy S6 and backing up only selected items.

This section shows Smart Switch running on Windows, but the app works in a similar way on OS X.

Back Up Your Data with Smart Switch

① Connect your Galaxy S6 to your PC via USB.

Note: If your Galaxy S6's screen is locked, unlock it.

The Smart Switch driver recognizes your Galaxy S6, and Smart Switch opens automatically.

Ⓐ Your Galaxy S6 appears in the Smart Switch window.

② Click **More**.

The pop-up menu opens.

③ Click **Preferences**.

The Preferences dialog box opens.

④ Click **Backup items**.

The Backup Items tab appears.

⑤ Click each item (☐ changes to ☑) you want to back up.

Ⓑ You can click **Select all** (☐ changes to ☑) to select all the check boxes.

⑥ Click **OK**.

The Preferences dialog box closes.

⑦ Click **Backup** (🖥).

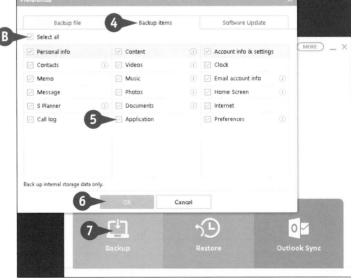

Smart Switch backs up the items you selected.

The *Galaxy S6 Backing up data finished* message appears.

8 Click **Check backup items**.

The Check Backup Items dialog box opens.

9 Verify that each item has a check mark (✓) next to it.

10 Click **Confirm**.

The Check Backup Items dialog box closes.

You have backed up your Galaxy S6 to your computer.

11 Disconnect your Galaxy S6 from your PC.

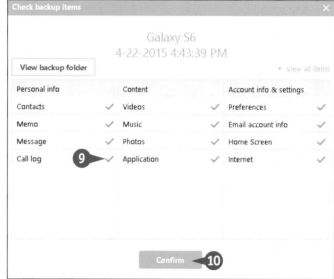

TIPS

What do I do if Smart Switch does not open automatically?
Click **Smart Switch** on the Start screen or Start menu to launch the app. Smart Switch may be in a folder called Samsung.

Should I back up all the contents of my Galaxy S6 to my computer?
Normally it is not worth backing up any files that already exist on your computer. For example, if you have synced music files from your computer to your Galaxy S6, you need not back up those same files from the phone to your computer. Similarly, you may choose not to back up any apps that you can easily reinstall by downloading them from the Play Store.

Restore Your Data with Smart Switch

If you have backed up some or all of the data from your Galaxy S6 to your computer using Samsung's Smart Switch app, you can restore data to your phone if it suffers a software or hardware failure. When restoring data, you can choose which backup to use and which items from the backup to copy to your Galaxy S6.

This section shows Smart Switch running on Windows, but the app works in a similar way on OS X.

Restore Your Data with Smart Switch

1 Connect your Galaxy S6 to your PC via USB.

Note: If your Galaxy S6's screen is locked, unlock it.

The Smart Switch driver recognizes your Galaxy S6, and Smart Switch opens automatically.

Note: If Smart Switch does not open automatically, click **Smart Switch** on the Start screen or Start menu to launch it.

Ⓐ Your Galaxy S6 appears in the Smart Switch window.

2 Click **Restore** (⟳).

The Restore pane appears.

3 Click **Change data to restore**.

The Change Data to Restore dialog box opens.

Note: You can click the **Select backup data to restore** pop-up menu and then click **Samsung device data**, **Non-Samsung device data**, or **Manually selected file.** Normally, you will want to restore Samsung Device Data, the default.

B You can click this pop-up menu and select a different backup file.

4 Click each item (☐ changes to ☑) you want to restore.

5 Click **OK**.

The Change Data to Restore dialog box closes.

6 Click **Restore Now.**

Smart Switch restores the data you selected.

The *Galaxy S6 Data restore completed* message appears.

7 Click **Check restored items**.

The Check Restored Items dialog box opens.

8 Verify that each item has a check mark (✓) next to it.

9 Click **Confirm**.

The Check Restored Items dialog box closes.

You have restored your data to the Galaxy S6.

10 Disconnect your Galaxy S6 from your PC.

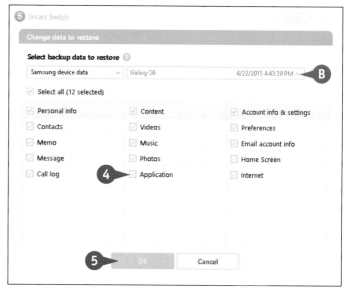

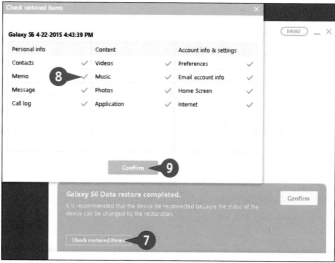

TIP

Which items should I restore to my Galaxy S6?

This depends on what problem your Galaxy S6 has suffered and how you are trying to resolve it. If only some of your data has become corrupted, try restoring only the affected data and see if that fixes the problem. If you need to replace a wide variety of data, you may choose to restore everything in the backup. But even when you do this, look quickly through the files involved and verify that you want to have them all on your Galaxy S6. For example, you may not need to restore many gigabytes of video files, especially if you have already watched them.

Reset Your Galaxy S6 to Factory Settings

Samsung makes your Galaxy S6 and the customized Android OS it runs as reliable as possible, but even so, the phone's software can become corrupted. If your Galaxy S6 cannot communicate with Smart Switch on a computer, or if you do not use Smart Switch, you may need to reset your phone to factory settings in order to resolve the problem. After resetting to factory settings, you can restore your data and settings from your Google account or Samsung account.

Reset Your Galaxy S6 to Factory Settings

1 Pull down from the top of the screen.

The Notification panel opens.

2 Tap **Settings** (⚙️).

Note: Restoring your Galaxy S6 to factory settings removes all your files and settings from the device. Back up your files and settings before performing a factory data reset so that you can restore them afterward.

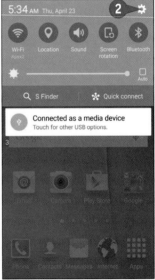

The Settings app opens.

3 In the Personal section, tap **Backup and reset** (🔄).

The Backup and Reset screen appears.

4 Tap **Factory data reset**.

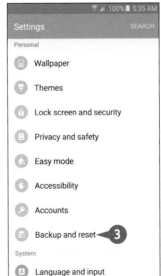

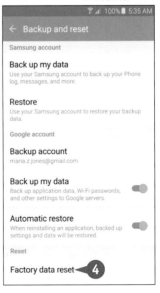

The Factory Data Reset screen appears.

5 Tap **Reset Device**.

Your Galaxy S6 prompts you to verify your identity by providing your fingerprint.

Note: If you use a different security method than a fingerprint, your Galaxy S6 displays the appropriate screen, such as the Confirm PIN screen.

6 Place your fingertip on the Home button.

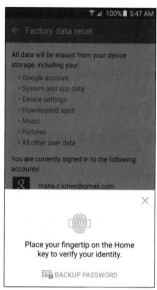

The final Factory Data Reset screen appears.

7 Tap **Delete All**.

Android resets your Galaxy S6 to factory settings.

Your Galaxy S6 restarts and goes into setup.

8 Follow through the setup steps, selecting your language and signing in to your Google account.

9 On the Google Services screen, tap **Back up your phone's apps, app data, settings, and Wi-Fi passwords** (☐ changes to ☑).

10 Tap **More**, tap **Next**, and allow setup to finish.

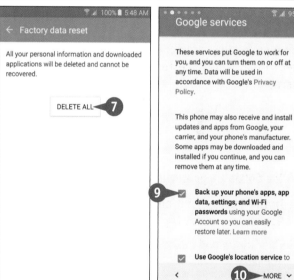

TIPS

Other than software problems, why might I reset my Galaxy S6 to factory settings?
First, if you have encrypted your Galaxy S6, you can reset it to remove the encryption. Second, if you plan to give or sell the phone to someone else, you can reset it to remove all your data and settings.

How do I restore data from my Samsung account?
Follow steps **1** to **4** in the main text to display the Backup and Reset screen. You can then tap **Restore** in the Samsung Account section to display the Restore screen, tap each item (☐ changes to ☑) you want to restore, and then tap **Restore Now**.

Troubleshoot Wireless Network Connections

Your Galaxy S6 can connect to many wireless networks, enabling you to use them instead of the cellular network. Using wireless networks is especially helpful if your phone has a meager data plan.

You may sometimes need to make your Galaxy S6 forget a network and then rejoin the network manually. You may also need to find your phone's IP address or its Media Access Control (MAC) address, the unique hardware address of its wireless network adapter.

Troubleshoot Wireless Network Connections

Reestablish a Faulty Wi-Fi Connection

1 Pull down from the top of the screen.

The Notification panel opens.

2 Tap **Wi-Fi** (🛜 changes to 🛜).

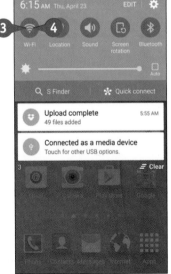

Android turns Wi-Fi off.

3 Tap **Wi-Fi** again (🛜 changes to 🛜).

Android turns Wi-Fi on and tries to reestablish the connection to the last wireless network used.

Note: If the Wi-Fi connection is now working satisfactorily, skip the remaining steps.

4 Tap and hold **Wi-Fi** (🛜).

The Wi-Fi screen appears.

5 Tap the network marked **Connected**.

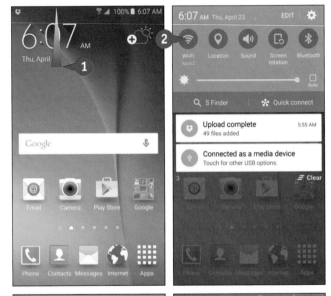

A dialog box opens showing the connection details, including the IP address.

6 Tap **Forget**.

Android forgets the network.

7 Tap the network's button again.

A dialog box opens for connecting to the network.

8 Type the password.

A You can tap **Show password** (☐ changes to ✓) to display the password.

9 Tap **Connect**.

Your Galaxy S6 connects to the wireless network.

Find Out the MAC Address for Your Galaxy S6

1 Pull down from the top of the screen.

The Notification panel opens.

2 Tap **Settings** (⚙).

The Settings screen appears.

3 In the System section, tap **About device** (ⓘ).

The About Device screen appears.

4 Tap **Status**.

The Status screen appears.

5 Look at the *Wi-Fi MAC address* readout.

B You can also see the IP address.

C You can also see the Bluetooth address.

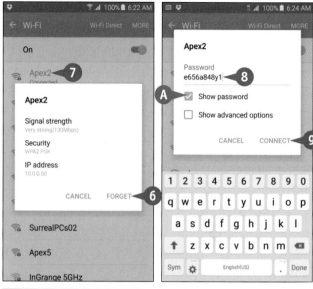

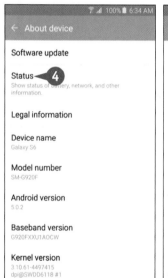

TIP

Why might I need to know my Galaxy S6's MAC address?

Many Wi-Fi networks use a whitelist of MAC addresses to control which computers and devices can connect to the network: Any device with a MAC address on the list can connect, whereas devices with other MAC addresses cannot. A MAC address whitelist is a useful security measure, but it is not foolproof. Although each network adapter has a unique MAC address burned into its hardware, an unapproved device can run software that *spoofs* — imitates — an approved MAC address.

Locate or Wipe Your Missing Galaxy S6

In case your Galaxy S6 goes missing, you should enable Samsung's Find My Mobile service in the Settings app so that you can locate the phone if necessary. Once Find My Mobile is on, you can log in to your Samsung account on any computer and use Find My Mobile to locate your phone. If you cannot reclaim it, you can remotely erase its contents to ensure that nobody else can access it.

Locate or Wipe Your Missing Galaxy S6

Set Up Find My Mobile

1. Pull down from the top of the screen.

   The Notification panel opens.

2. Tap **Settings** (⚙).

   The Settings screen appears.

3. In the Personal section, tap **Lock screen and security** (🔒).

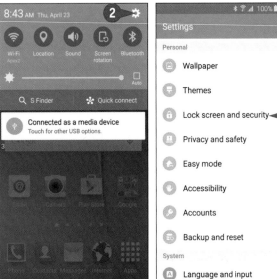

4. Tap **Find My Mobile**.

   The Samsung Account screen appears.

5. Type your password and tap **Confirm**.

   The Find My Mobile screen appears.

6. Set the **Remote controls** switch to On (⚪ changes to ⚫).

7. Set the **Google location service** switch to On (⚪ changes to ⚫).

8. Set the **Reactivation lock** switch to On (⚪ changes to ⚫) and then tap **OK** in the Reactivation Lock dialog box that opens.

Ⓐ You can tap **SIM change alert** to set up alerts if anyone changes the SIM.

Locate and Lock or Wipe Your Galaxy S6

1 Open a web browser on a computer and go to **findmymobile.samsung.com**.

2 Type your e-mail address.

3 Type your password.

4 Click **Sign In**.

The Locate My Device screen appears.

B The map shows your device's location.

C The Device Status list shows whether there is a connection to the device and whether Remote Controls and Reactivation Lock are on or off.

D The Find My Device section enables you to ring your phone, enable Emergency Mode, or turn on Ultra Power Saving Mode.

E The Protect My Device section enables you to lock the screen, apply reactivation lock, or wipe your phone.

TIP

What other action should I take if I lose my Galaxy S6?
It is a good idea to tell your carrier that you have lost the phone so that the carrier can block the SIM card from being used. Otherwise, even if your phone is locked, whoever has it can remove the SIM card and use it to make calls with another phone. Calls to premium services, overseas numbers, or both can run up massive charges distressingly quickly.

Index

A

Accept cookies switch, 185
accessibility features
    overview, 80–83
    transferring settings to another device, 83
Adapt Sound feature, 259, 262, 263
Add Fingerprint screen, 11–13
Add icon to Home screen, 167
Add Network dialog box, 15, 129
Add to Allowed Devices dialog box, 125, 127
Adjustment tools, 215, 216
Airplane Mode, 114–115
alarms, setting, 236
alerts, Notification panel, 24–25
Allow exceptions switch, 42–43
Android Beam feature, 132–133
Answering and ending calls, settings for, 83
App Info screen
    customizing your Galaxy S6, 39
    removing apps by using, 165
App notifications screen, 40, 41, 43
App Permissions dialog box, 161, 163, 171
Application Manager
    choosing which notifications to receive, 38–39
    closing an app that has stopped responding, 272
    displaying cached processes, 273
    resetting app preferences, 280–281
apps. *See also specific apps*
    choosing settings within, 35
    closing apps that have stopped responding, 272–273
    finding and downloading, from Google Play, 160–161
    Galaxy, 170–171
    on Home screen, 58
    installing manually (sideloading), 168–169
    location access requests, 49
    in Multi Window, 20–21
    permissions, 161, 163, 169, 171
    previously bought on Google Play, 161
    reinstalling removed apps, 165
    removing, 164–165
    resetting app preferences, 280–281
    switching quickly among, 156–157
    uninstalling, 39, 283
    updating, 162–163
        automatically, 166–167
Apps screen, 16, 17
    removing apps by using, 164
archiving, messages with Gmail, 194–195
aspect ratio, 216
Auto adjust photos, 215
Auto Backup feature, 149
Auto capitalize, 71
Auto check spelling, 57
Auto Fill feature, 182–183
Auto punctuate, 71
Auto replace, 57
Auto spacing, 71
Auto (When Received) sync setting, 251
Auto-fit messages, Gmail app, 95
Automatic restore switch, 285
Auto-update apps, 166, 167
Available Devices list, 117

B

background data, 119
backing up
    and restoring online, 284–285
    with Smart Switch, 286–287
    to your computer, 287
Back/Recents key feedback switch, 85
battery
    Power Saving Mode, 276–279
    turning Bluetooth off to save power, 115
    Ultra Power Saving Mode, 278–279
battery charger, 277
battery pack, portable, 277
Bcc (blind carbon-copy) recipients, 190, 191
Bicycling layer, 227
Block notifications switch, 41
Bluetooth
    Airplane Mode, 114, 115
    avoiding unintentional connections, 115

connecting devices, 116–117

files received via, 117

turning on or off, 115, 277

Bluetooth Pairing Request dialog box, 117

bookmarks

deleting, 177

opening bookmarked web pages, 178

for web pages, 176–177

bottom of the Galaxy S6, 5

brightness, screen, 46

browsing

messages with Gmail, 196–197

the web

overview, 174–175

privacy settings, 184–185

without the history recording pages visited, 179

buttons

physical, 4

Quick Settings, 34, 36 37

soft, 4

volume, 5, 44

C

Calculator, 238

Call back, in Notification panel, 25

call logs, 142–143

Camera app. *See also* photos

flash, 206

focus

manual, 202

Pro Mode, 209

Selective, 204–205

Tracking Auto-Focus (AF), 203, 212

High Dynamic Range (HDR) Mode, 206–207

Pro Mode, 208–209

settings for taking photos, 212–213

sharing photos and videos, 222–223

switching to the camera on the screen side, 201

taking photos with, 200–201

Video Mode, 218–219

viewing your photos and videos, 220–221

zooming, 202

Camera folder, 220

capitalize, Auto, 71

capturing video, 218–219

Car Mode, 171

Cc (carbon-copy) recipients, 190, 191

cellular access, 114–115

cellular data, 119

cellular usage, 118–119, 149

Center-weighted metering, 209

certificates, 250, 252, 253

Character preview, 57

Clear cache, 39

Clear data, 39

Clear History, 238

clearing extra space, 282–283

clipboard, 73–75

Clock app, 236–237

closing apps

in Multi Window, 20

that have stopped responding, 272–273

closing windows, from the Tabs screen, 175

Color Tone controls, 209

colors, negative, 81

compass arrow, 230

Complete Action Using dialog box, 145

computer

Bluetooth connection to, 117

copying files from your, 28–29

transferring contents of the clipboard to, 75

Concert Hall, 259

conference calls, 140–141

Configure Mobile Hotspot dialog box, 126

Confirm before archiving, Gmail app, 96

Confirm before deleting, Gmail app, 96

Confirm before sending, Gmail app, 96

Consent to Provide Diagnostic and Usage Data, 7

Conserve data usage, 149

Constrain tools, 216

contacts

choosing which contacts to display, 104–105

dialing a call to, 139

displaying all, 105

contacts *(continued)*

distinctive ringtone for, 45

favorites, 143

Frequently Contacted list, 142–143

importing into Contacts App, 106–107

Content filtering, 167

continuous input, 69–71

Conversation view, Gmail app, 95

conversations

forwarding or deleting messages, 146–147

Gmail settings, 95

cookies, 185

copying

files from your computer, 28–29

with Multi Window, 21

Create Shortcut on Desktop, 26

credentials, installing, 252–253

cropping photos, 215, 216

Custom button, Pro Mode, 209

D

data, background, 119

data roaming, 118

data usage, 118–119, 149

Dawn Cast effect, 215

Daydream feature, 64–65

Default Action, Gmail app, 95

Default Inbox, Gmail app, 96

default search engine, 180, 181

Delete Conversation dialog box, 147

deleting. *See also* removing

bookmarks, 177

to free up space, 283

instant messages, 146–147

messages, 197

Desktop view, 175

Device Administrator screen, 251

Dialing keypad tone, 45

digital certificates, 250, 252, 253

Direct Access settings, 83

directions, getting, 228–229

Disclaimer dialog box, 12, 241

disconnecting, from Wi-Fi Direct, 121

dismissing alerts, 25

DLNA (Digital Living Network Alliance) standard, 264–265, 267

Do Not Disturb feature, 42–43

domain, Exchange account and, 249

double-tapping, 22–23

double-touch, 22

downloading

apps from Google Play, 160–161

attachments when connected to Wi-File, automatically, 93

Galaxy Apps, 171

Smart Switch, 26

dragging, 23

Notification panel, 25

Dual Clock widget, 59

E

Easy Mode, 13

Edge lighting, 31

Edge Screen, 30–31

editing, photos, 214–217

Effect button, 215

e-mail accounts

POP3 or IMAP for, 91

removing, 98–99

setting up, in Gmail app, 88–93

e-mail address, Exchange username and, 249

e-mail messages. *See also* Gmail app

deleting, 197

Exchange Server and, 248–252

importing contacts attached to, 106

installing a digital certificate from, 252

labeling and archiving, 194–195

reading with Gmail, 186–187

Respond Inline feature, 189

writing and sending with Gmail, 190–191

Emergency Software Recovery and Initialization, 274

emoticons, 72, 73

Enable Fingerprint Lock dialog box, 13

encrypting Galaxy S6

procedure for, 54–55

removing encryption, 291

equalizer, SoundAlive, 258–259

Exchange Server, connecting to, 248–252

Exposure controls, Camera app, 208

F

Facebook, 152–153

factory settings, resetting Galaxy S6 to, 290

Fast encryption, 55

favorites, contacts, 143

Favorites tray, customizing, 59, 60

files

copying from your computer, 28–29

largest for sending via Gmail, 193

moving from Private storage area to regular storage, 245

moving to Private storage area, 243–244

received via Bluetooth, 117

sending and receiving with Gmail, 192–193

Filter By dialog box, 142

Find My Mobile service, 294–295

fingerprints

adding other, 13

recognition, 11–13

unlocking the screen, 51

flash, 206

Flash notification, 82

Flip Horizontal photos, 215

Flip Vertical photos, 215

focus

manual, 202

Pro Mode, 209

Selective, 204–205

Tracking Auto-Focus (AF), 203, 212

Focus on speech audio switch, 85

folder, Camera, 220

folders

filing messages in, with Gmail app, 195

moving e-mail messages to, 187

removing apps from, 61

for widgets, 60–61

Font size, 81

Force stop, 39, 274

forgetting a wireless network, 129

forms, Auto Fill, 182–183

forwarding

instant messages, 146

messages with Gmail, 188–189

free space, checking and clearing, 282–283

frequency sliders, in SoundAlive, 259

frequently used side, 263

G

Galaxy Apps app, 170–171, 239

Galaxy K Zoom, 203

Galaxy S6 Active, 30

Galaxy S6 Edge, 30–31

Galaxy TalkBack feature, 84–85

Gallery app

editing photos, 214–215

moving photos and videos to Private storage area, 243

playing videos, 266, 267

removing photos and videos from Private storage area, 245

using photos as wallpaper, 47

viewing photos and videos, 220

gestures

magnification, 81, 82

navigating with, 22–23

Gmail accounts. *See also* e-mail accounts

largest files that can be sent between, 193

syncing with, 89

Gmail app

essential settings for, 94–97

General settings, 95

inbox types, 96

labeling and archiving messages with, 194–195

largest files that can be sent via, 193

multiple signatures for the same account in, 101

Priority Inbox, 102–103

reading e-mail messages with, 186–187

replying to or forwarding messages with, 188–189

sending and receiving files with, 192–193

setting up e-mail accounts in, 88–93

writing and sending e-mail messages with, 190–191

Gmail widget, 59
Google+
    navigating, 150–151
    setting up, 148–149
Google account
    adding a, 89
    backing up to, 9
    for backup, 285
    creating a, 7
Google circles, 148, 150, 151
Google Drive, installing a digital certificate from, 253
Google Hangouts, 148
Google Photos, 149
Google Play, finding and downloading apps from, 160–161
Google subtitles, 82
Google Wallet, installing and configuring, 134–135
grayscale, 81
grid lines, 213

H

HDR (High Dynamic Range) Mode, 206, 207
headphone port, 5
headset, customizing audio settings, 262–263
hearing accessibility features, 82
Hide content on lock screen switch, 41
Hide Declined Events option, 111
Hide My Device option, 126, 127
High Dynamic Range (HDR) Mode, 206, 207
History pane, 238
Home screen, Easy Mode, 13
Home screens
    customizing, 58–61
    Favorites tray, 59
    overview, 17
    removing apps or widgets from, 61
    widgets on, 60–61
HoRNDIS, installing, 123

I

IMAP accounts, 91
Import/Export dialog box, 83
importing, contacts attached to e-mail messages, 106

Improve Location Accuracy? dialog box, 49
Inbound Transfers screen, 117
Incoming Server Settings, 92
initial setup routine, 6–13
Input Languages dialog box, 57
input settings, 56–57
Installation Complete dialog box, 26
installing Galaxy Apps, 171
instant messages, 144–147
Internet app
    browsing the web, 174–175
    searching for information, 180–181
Interview Mode, 77
Invitation to Connect dialog box, 121
IP address, 14, 15, 292, 293
ISO controls, Camera app, 209

K

Keyboard feedback, TalkBack, 85
keyboard feedback, 85
Keyboard sound, 45
Keyboard swipe, 69
keyboards
    Auto punctuate switch, 71
    different, 72–73
    input settings, 56–57
    using, 68–71
    vibration and sounds, 45
Keypad, dialing a call using, 138
Kids Mode, 171

L

labeling, messages with Gmail, 194–195
labels, browsing messages by, 196–197
landscape orientation
    Calculator in, 238
    email in, 187
    Multi Window in, 19
    video in, 267
languages, choosing, 56–57
LED indicator, 40
left/right sound balance, 82
Limit Data Usage dialog box, 119

Locating Method screen, 49

locating your missing Galaxy S6, 294

location, finding your, 226

location access, 48–49

location service, 8, 10

Location tags, 213

lock screen, 16

    customizing, 62–63

lock settings, 51, 63

long press, 23

Look Around Mode, 235

M

Mac

    copying files to Galaxy S6 using a, 29

    Smart Switch on, 27

MAC address, 125, 127, 292–293

magnification gestures, 81, 82

Magnifier window, 81

Make Call To dialog box, 143

malware (malevolent software), 184

manual installation (sideloading), 168–169

Maps app, 226–235

    finding your location and displaying different layers,
      226–227

    getting directions, 228–229

    making a maps available offline, 232–233

    measurement units, 231

    rotating, zooming, and tilting maps, 230–231

    scale of maps, 231

    Street View feature, 234–235

Mark important (Gmail), 103

Matrix metering, 209

measurement units, Maps app, 231

media, volume of, 44

Media Access Control (MAC) address, 125, 127, 293

Message, in Notification panel, 25

Message Options dialog box, 146, 147

messages

    e-mail *See also* Gmail app

      deleting, 197

      Exchange Server and, 248–252

      importing contacts attached to, 106

      installing a digital certificate from, 252

      labeling and archiving, 194–195

      reading with Gmail, 186–187

      Respond Inline feature, 189

      writing and sending with Gmail, 190–191

    hiding pictures in, 97

    instant, 144–147

Metering Modes dialog box, 209

microphone

    at the bottom of the Galaxy S6, 5

    for speakerphone, 5

Microsoft Exchange Server, connecting to, 248–252

minimizing an app, 20

minimizing apps, in Multi Window, 20

MMS (Multimedia Messaging Service), 144

Mobile Data dialog box, 119

Mobile data switch, 119

Mobile Hotspot, 124–127

Mobile view, of web pages, 175

Mono audio, 82

monopod, 211

Multi Window

    Copy feature, 21

    in landscape mode, 19

    minimizing or closing an app in, 20

    resizing, 19

    using, 18–21

multipurpose jack, 5

music, recording, 77

Music app

    Adapt Sound feature, 259

    moving files to Private storage area in, 243

    playing music with, 256–257

    playing through other devices, 264–265

    playlists, 260–261

    removing files from Private storage area, 245

    SoundAlive feature, 258

My Apps screen, 162

My Files, 83, 243, 245

N

navigating
    with gestures, 22–23
    Google+, 150–151
    multiple web pages, 175
Near Field Communication (NFC) chips, 7
Near Field Communications (NFC)
    Android Beam and, 132–133
    Tap and Pay feature and, 134–135
negative colors, 81
Negative effect, 215
Notification panel, 24–25
notifications
    choosing which to receive, 38–41
    Galaxy S6 Edge, 31
    priority, 41
    S Planner, 108–109
    volume of, 44

O

on-screen keyboard. *See* keyboards
optical zoom, 203
Outgoing Server Settings, 92

P

package file, 168–169
Paired Devices list, 117
panoramic photos, 210–211
passwords
    backup, for fingerprint recognition, 12–13
    e-mail accounts, 90
    for encrypting, 55
    guidelines for creating, 12
    IMAP or POP accounts, 91
    initial setup routine, 6, 9, 10, 12, 13
    unlocking the screen, 51
Pattern, unlocking the screen, 51
Peel Smart Remote, 239
People Edge, 31
period, 71
permissions, apps, 161, 163, 169, 171
Personal (IMAP/POP) accounts, 91

Phone app, opening, 138
phone calls
    call logs, 142–143
    conference calls, 140–141
    ending, 139
    Frequently Contacted list, 142–143
    making, 138–139
    through the speaker, 139
Photo Editor, 215
Photo Frame theme, 65
Photo Table theme, 65
photos. *See also* Camera app
    Auto Backup feature, 149
    editing, 214–217
    moving to Private storage area, 243
    panoramic, 210–211
    removing from Private storage area, 245
    saving a photo received in a message, 147
    settings for taking, 212–213
    sharing, 222–223
    viewing, 220–221
    as wallpaper, 47
Photos app, playing videos through, 266
Picture size (front), 213
Picture size (rear), 212
PIN (Personal Identification Number), 50–51
pinning a window to the screen, 158–159
Pitch changes, 85
Play Store, 160, 166, 167
playlists
    creating, 260–261
    renaming, 261
POP3 accounts, 91
pop-up video player, 268–269
pop-up view, Multi Window, 18
pop-up windows, 21
Power Saving Mode, 276–279
Predictive text, 57
pre-shared key (PSK), 247
Priority Inbox, Gmail app, 96, 102–103
priority notifications, 41
Privacy and Safety screen, 48, 240, 241

Privacy Policy, 9
privacy settings, browsing, 184–185
Private Mode, 240–245
    moving files to Private storage area, 243–244
    quickly enabling and disabling, 241
    setting up, 240–241
    status of, 241
    turning off, 244, 245
    unlock method, 242
    using, 242–245
Pro Mode, Camera app, 208–209
proximity sensor, 85
proxy server information, 14, 15
Public Transit layer, 227
Push, Gmail app, 93

Q

Quick Connect, 267
Quick Connect feature, 121, 264–265
Quick launch switch, 213
Quick Settings, 34–37
Quick Settings buttons, 34, 36–37
Quick Settings panel, 34, 36–37

R

Recents screen
    accessing Multi Window from, 18–19
    pinning a window to the screen, 158–159
    switching among running apps, 157
reinstalling removed apps, 165
reminders, S Planner, 108–109
removing. *See also* deleting
    apps, 164–165
    e-mail accounts, 98–99
Rename dialog box (Bluetooth device), 117
Repeat button, 257
Reply All option, Gmail app, 95
replying, to messages with Gmail, 188–189
Require authentication for purchases, 167
resetting
    app preferences, 280–281
    Galaxy S6 to factory settings, 290–291

resizing
    pop-up player, 269
    widgets, 60
    windows, 19
resolution
    for photos, 212
    for video, 213
Respond Inline feature, 189
restoring data and settings
    data, 9, 11, 291
    to factory settings, 55
    online, 284–285
    Quick Settings, 37
    with Smart Switch, 288–289
Restrict background data switch, 119
Reverse Start and End, 229
Review pictures switch, 213
ringtones
    selecting, 45
    volume of, 44
Ringtones and Sounds screen, 40, 45
rotating
    maps, 230
    photos, 215
runtime, extending, 276–279

S

S Health, 238
S Planner notifications and reminders, 108–111
S Voice, 78–79
Samsung account
    for backup, 285
    locating your missing Galaxy S6, 294
    overview, 10, 11
    restoring data from, 291
Samsung Galaxy Apps, 170–171
Samsung Keyboard
    Auto punctuate switch, 71
    different, 72–73
    input settings, 56–57
    using, 68–71
    vibration and sounds, 45

Samsung subtitles, 82

Satellite view, 227

saving

    edits to a photo, 217

    maps offline, 233

scale of maps, 231

screen brightness, 46

screen lock, 50–52, 55

Screen lock sounds, 45

Screen Timeout dialog box, 64

search engines

    changing, 181

    default, 180, 181

searching for information

    with Gmail, 196–197

    with Internet app, 180–181

Secret Mode, 179

Secure Sockets Layer (SSL), 251

security, screen lock methods and, 63

Select Screen Lock screen, 51

Selective Focus, 204–205

selling your phone, resetting Galaxy S6 before, 291

Send SOS Messages feature, 48

Sender image, Gmail app, 95

Set as priority switch, 41

setting up your Galaxy S6. *See also* initial setup routine

    manually, 9

Settings app, using, 34, 36 37

7-Day Weather Forecast command, 109

shared secret, 247

sharing

    locations, 227

    photos and videos, 222–223

shortcuts, Smart Switch, 26

Show password, 14

sideloading, 168–169

signatures, setting up, 100–101

SIM card

    importing contacts from, 106

    installing, 4

sleep settings, 64

Smart Lock feature, 50–53

Smart Network Switch, 6, 7, 129

Smart Switch

    backing up with, 286–287

    downloading, 26

    installing, 26–27

    launching, 27, 287

    overview, 26–27

    restoring data with, 288–289

Smart Typing section, 57, 101

Smart volume, 257

smartphones, as trusted devices, 53

SMS (Short Message Service), 144

SMTP server, 92

software updates, 274–275

SOS Messages feature, 48

Sound detectors, 82

Sound feedback, Galaxy TalkBack, 85

Sound Mode button, 45

Sound quality and effects, 259

SoundAlive equalizer, 258–259

sounds

    Do Not Disturb feature, 42

    keyboard, 45

    Screen lock, 45

    system, 44

    Turn off all sounds, 82

    volume of, 44–45, 257

space, free, 282–283

speaker, phone calls through the, 139

Speech rate, Galaxy TalkBack, 85

Speech volume, Galaxy TalkBack, 85

split-screen view, Multi Window, 18

spoofing, 293

Spot metering, 209

SSL (Secure Sockets Layer), 251

starting the Galaxy S6, 4

Steadicam rig, 211

Stopwatch, 237

Straighten slider, 216

Street View feature, 234–235

"Subject not detected" error, 205

Swipe, unlocking the screen, 51

Swipe actions, Gmail app, 95
swiping, 23
    Notification panel, 25
Switch Cameras, 201, 213, 219
switching apps
    in Multi Window, 20
    quickly, 156–157
Sync Settings screen, 99, 250
system sounds, volume of, 44

T

tablets, as trusted devices, 53
Tabs screen, 175, 179
TalkBack feature, 84–85
Tap & Go dialog box, setting up Galaxy S6 using,
    6–9
Tap and Pay feature, 134–135
tap-and-hold gesture, 23
Terms and Conditions screen, 7, 9
tethering, USB, 122–123
Tethering or hotspot active message, 122
text shortcuts, 57
Text-to-Speech feature, 81–82
time zone settings, S Planner, 110–111
Timeout Settings dialog box, 126
Timer, 237
tone of photos, 217
Touch sounds, 45
TouchWiz user interface, 17, 22, 281
Tracking Auto-Focus (AF), 203, 212
Traffic layer, 227
tripods, 211
trusted devices, 52
trusted places, 53
trusted voice, 53
Tube Amp, 259
Turn off all sounds, 82
Turn on Pin Windows dialog box, 159
TV, viewing photos and videos on, 221, 267
Twitter, 152–153

U

Ultra Power Saving Mode, 278–279
uninstall updates, 39
uninstalling apps, 39, 283
unknown sources, installation of apps from, 169
unlocking the lock screen, by swiping, 16
unlocking your Galaxy S6, with Fingerprints, 13
updating
    apps, 162–163
        automatically, 166–167
    Galaxy S6's software, 274–275
USB tethering, 122–123
Use Secure Connection option, 251
User Account Control dialog box, 26
user interface, exploring, 16–17

V

vCard files, creating, 107
Vibration feedback
    intensity of, 44–45
    overview, 45, 57, 85
    S Planner, 109
Video app (pop-up video player), 266, 268, 269
Video size (front), 213
Video size (rear), 212, 213
video stabilization, 213
videos
    Auto Backup feature, 149
    capturing, 218–219
    moving to Private storage area, 243
    playing, 257
    pop-up video player, 268–269
    removing from Private storage area, 245
    sending via MMS, 145
    sharing, 222–223
    viewing, 220–221, 266–269
Vintage effect, 215
vision accessibility features, 80–81
voice, trusted, 53
voice control, Camera app, 213

voice input, 72–73

voice memos, 77, 239

Voice Recorder, 77, 239

Voice Wake-Up, 78

volume buttons, 5, 44

volume of sounds and music, 44–45, 257

VPN (virtual private networking), connecting to a work
  network via, 246–247

W

wake-up command, 10, 11

wallpapers, 46–47
    using photos as, 47

web pages
    bookmarks for, 176–177
    browsing without the history recording pages visited,
      179
    full version of, 175
    opening a saved page, 179
    opening and navigating multiple, 175
    opening bookmarked, 178
    saving for future reading, 179

week settings, S Planner, 110–111

Welcome screen, 6

White Balance controls, 209

widgets, 59–61

Wi-Fi
    Airplane Mode and, 114, 115
    automatically downloading attachments when connected
      to, 93

logging in to Wi-Fi hotspots, 130–131

managing wireless networks, 128–129

Smart Network Switch and, 7

troubleshooting network connections, 292–293

turning on or off, 277

Wi-Fi Direct devices, 120–121

Wi-Fi hotspots, logging in to, 130–131

Wi-Fi MAC Address, 125, 293

Wi-Fi Protected Setup (WPS), 15

Wi-Fi screen, 6

windows
    closing, from the Tabs screen, 175
    Multi Window, 18–21
    pinning a window to the screen, 158–159
    pop-up, 21
    resizing, 19

wireless networks. *See also* Wi-Fi
    connecting to, 14–15
    managing, 128–129

World Clock, 237

WPS (Wi-Fi Protected Setup), 15

WPS push button, 15

Z

zoom(ing)
    with Camera app, 202
    grainy pictures and, 203
    maps, 231
    optical, 203